Political Contexts of Educational Leadership

Co-published with UCEA, this exciting new textbook is the first to tackle the ISLLC Standard 6—the political context of education. This unique volume helps aspiring school leaders understand the dynamics of educational policy in multiple arenas at the local, state, and federal levels. Leaders are responsible for promoting the success of every student by understanding, responding to, and influencing the political, social, economic, legal, and cultural contexts in which education and learning reside. By presenting problem-posing cases, theoretical grounding, relevant research, and implications for practice, this book provides aspiring leaders with the background, learning experiences, and analytical tools to successfully promote student success in their contexts.

Special Features:

- Case Studies—provide an authentic illustration of the political dynamics that emanate from individual, social, economic, and cultural issues surrounding all schools.
- Suggested Activities—further aspiring school leaders' understanding of political issues through experiences.
- Companion Website—includes shared resources relevant to all ISLLC Standards, along with particular activities for ISLLC Standard 6.

Jane Clark Lindle is Eugene T. Moore Distinguished Professor of Educational Leadership at Clemson University, USA.

ISLLC LEADERSHIP PREPARATION SERIES

Series Editors: Michelle Young, Margaret Terry Orr

The New Instructional Leadership
ISLLC Standard Two
Edited by Rose M. Ylimaki

Political Contexts of Educational Leadership
ISLLC Standard Six
Edited by Jane Clark Lindle

Political Contexts of Educational Leadership

ISLLC Standard Six

Edited by
Jane Clark Lindle

Routledge
Taylor & Francis Group

NEW YORK AND LONDON

First published 2014
by Routledge
711 Third Avenue, New York, NY 10017

and by Routledge
2 Park Square, Milton Park, Abingdon, Oxon OX14 4RN

Routledge is an imprint of the Taylor & Francis Group, an informa business

Library of Congress Cataloging in Publication Data
Political contexts of educational leadership: ISLLC standard six / [edited]
    by Jane Lindle.
    pages cm. -- (ISLLC leadership preparation series)
    Includes bibliographical references and index.
    1. Educational leadership—Political aspects—United States. 2. School
    management and organization—Political aspects—United States.
    I. Lindle, Jane Clark, editor of compilation.
    LB2805.P66 2014
    371.2—dc23
    2013039828

ISBN: 978-0-415-82381-4 (hbk)
ISBN: 978-0-415-82382-1 (pbk)
ISBN: 978-0-203-54976-6 (ebk)

Typeset in Aldine 401 and Helvetice Neue
by Florence Production Ltd, Stoodleigh, Devon, UK

Printed and bound in the United States of America by Publishers Graphics,
LLC on sustainably sourced paper.

A co-publication of Routledge and the University Council for Educational Administration—UCEA

Contents

Series Foreword

As with the evolution of schooling in the U.S., the history of educational administration can be traced in a variety of ways. One of the most important of these avenues is the examination of major pieces of reflective scholarship and seminal professionally sponsored reports. Much of this work has left few fingerprints on the profession. But some has had robust influence on shaping choices made in school administration at critical junctions in its development. The best of this work has also provided action maps once those choices were selected.

We know some things about this work. It is always context sensitive. There is a time to galvanize action and times when proposed stakes in the ground and new architectural designs will be ignored. The cardinal reports in the history of educational leadership arrived when people were ready for them. We also know that except for historians few people are aware of these foundational analyses. Once new pathways are chosen, it is difficult to remember that there were alternative possibilities. By achieving the goal of becoming deeply embedded in the fabric of the profession, new ideas lose their uniqueness and singular position as markers. Finally, we know that pathways that seem illuminatory sometimes turn out to provide less than salutary designs and building materials. Only time can provide the scale to assess this point.

Historical analysis shows us that there are a small handful of these critical markers in educational administration. One is the development of the Interstate School Leadership Licensure Consortium (ISLLC) *Standards for School Leaders*, itself an outgrowth of an earlier historical marker, the National Commission on Excellence in Educational Administration (NCEEA). Founded in 1985 under the leadership of the University Council for Educational Administration (UCEA), the NCEEA laid out a broad framework of improvement for educational leadership writ large, with particular attention to the education of school administrators. One of its cornerstone recommendations was for the creation of the National Policy Board in Educational Administration (NPBEA), a new guiding body for the profession consisting of ten national associations with considerable interest in school leadership. Created in 1988, the NPBEA elected to make the development of national standards for the profession its signature work. Between 1994 and 1996, half of the states in the nation and the ten associations that comprised the NPBEA worked to forge an empirically and value-based vision for school administrators. That effort culminated in the publication of the ISLLC Standards in 1996. A dozen years later the NPBEA commissioned work that produced an update of those Standards, ISLLC 2008. It was my privilege to chair all this work.

It is safe to say that the ISLLC Standards have had a significant influence on the shape and texture of school administration in the U.S. As noted above, some of this had to do with context. The profession was unquestionably ready for a recentering of academic and practice work, away from an organizational foundation built up over the 20th century and toward one that would honor a steadfast focus on student success broadly defined—success achieved through an ethic of care, a commitment to community, and a strong sense of academic press.

The Standards by design operate at a high level of guidance. Based on best research and commitment to non-negotiable values they establish a distinct infrastructure for the profession. But most of the heavy lifting began after the Standards were crafted. They need to be yoked to essential leverage points for improvement, e.g., program accreditation, licensure, administrator evaluation, and so forth. Equally important they need to be fleshed out, deepened, and to be brought to life, made accessible. Much commendable work has been occurring over the last 15 years on these two intertwined needs in every domain of the profession—policy, research, development, and practice.

This UCEA-sponsored project to provide heft, meaning, and concreteness to the ISLLC Standards is a cardinal example of this heavy lifting work. Designed to support preparation programs by helping their students understand and use the Standards, this series of textbooks, one for each of the six Standards, provides a critically needed, unique, and powerful tool to rebuild educational leadership around what we know works and what we value as a profession.

Joseph Murphy
Leipers Fork, TN
May 2013

Preface

Inexorably, schools serve as the yoke between their local communities' issues and global social trends. The school is the link between current combined effects of global and local trends on students and families. More importantly, schools occupy a unique position to ameliorate what will affect them next. A wealth of contextual dynamics has affected U.S. schools from their inception as community-based agencies entrusted with the growth and development of youth.

This series of books about each of the ISLLC Standards supports the development of educational leaders across the multifaceted responsibilities of leadership in schools. The purpose of this book on ISLLC Standard 6, Political Contexts, is to provide an understanding of how the politics of schooling join both knowledge and practice in school leadership. Schools are linked inextricably to their political contexts, and perceptive school leaders must utilize an inseparable alloy of practical wisdom and knowledge about political contexts to lead schools successfully.

Over time, considerable criticism of school leaders arose from their own declared avoidance of politics in any form. Popular books and movies tended to depict school officials as remote or utterly foolish. Much of the criticism focused on the distance between practitioners' experiences and the seemingly disconnected theories of leadership described in coursework. As an interesting point, many mid-20th century texts on politics in schools only focused on party politics and voting in school board elections and failed to acknowledge politics in school buildings and neighborhoods. In the latter part of the 20th century, the standards movement focused on outcomes and seemingly split the work and skills of a profession from the knowledge and wisdom of that profession. Conversely, realities of politics in education, as well as the burgeoning knowledge from studies of politics surrounding educational policies, provide the strongest connection between what school leaders feel and do and their abilities to strategically think about how to handle it all. This book makes the connection between daily issues arising in schools, and how school leaders use community or global trends to anticipate and resolve conflicts in and around schools.

WHO SHOULD USE THIS BOOK?

This book is designed for use as a textbook for aspiring school leaders focused on ISLLC Standard 6:

> An education leader promotes the success of every student by understanding, responding to, and influencing the political, social, economic, legal, and cultural context.

In this volume, aspiring school leaders and their instructors will find school-based cases that depict the dynamics in schools where conflicts percolate daily. The chapter authors acknowledge that school leadership is a collective enterprise, and as such, requires that all involved recognize and engage in the give-and-take of daily moments in education. While none of these chapters promotes politics as a zero-sum game, all of them encourage understanding of, and appropriate responses to, what happens when some people get what they want, and others do not.

Because schools are continually lacking resources, and are overwhelmed in wants and needs, someone, students or other stakeholders, will lack something in even the most optimized decisions. All school decisions are fraught with constraints and likely to produce unintended consequences. The school leader needs to remain alert and aware of options to alleviate those unintended consequences.

This level of alert and strategic decision making, we argue, is a form of political acumen. Additionally, we argue that school leaders must form alliances to address schools' constant state of resource scarcity, and that too, requires a proactive form of political adeptness and strategic thinking.

This book also balances the education profession's long-held, altruistic stance that the benefits of education apply, not just to the individual, but society as well. To be an ethical school leader often requires finding a way of voicing the needs of marginalized and underserved students and their families. That proactive voice of advocacy on behalf of students—that too—requires a complex comprehension of when to speak to have the most impact, while simultaneously sustaining credibility to continue working and living in that community including protecting one's job. That level of strategically raising one's voice is not merely a matter of courage, but particularly tied to a well-informed understanding and analytic use of proactive civic advocacy, that is, political savviness.

Taken in sum, critical moments of practicing school leadership require a constant calculation of why? who? how? and what the next steps involve (Lasswell, 1965). Decision making about schooling involves a careful approach to involving those affected by the decision, and for understanding who ought to be invited into the process for their expertise. These decision issues also require skilled awareness and mediation of conflicting and legitimate interests in each decision and its consequences (Stout et al., 1995). This volume argues that politically adept school leaders can manage these moments as well as move their schools and communities steadily forward to the benefit of both students and society.

HOW TO USE THIS BOOK

The organization of this book moves readers from the daily conflicts that arise in the school leaders' offices and the school building to an expanding array of contexts surrounding schools, moving onward through ever-enlarging influences on school districts' leadership to the politics of regional, national, and international interests. The chapters move from the feelings and insights of daily conflicts at the most personal and professional level to the macro-levels of politics involved in educational policies. Chapter authors are among the researchers who have investigated the political dimensions of leadership in schools. The chapter authors introduce the political science and research-based insights for school leaders to draw on in addressing inherent conflicts and dilemmas of the roiling case issues. In this manner, readers can parse the ways in which politics are simultaneously both local and global.

Several terms unique to research about politics in education are used throughout the chapters so the book includes a glossary. Many of these terms may seem familiar, yet are used in theory and research with a different connotation than in common daily discussions. The vocabulary of political contexts shift connotations depending on contexts and specific cases. Careful readers will want to check the glossary as they move through the chapters to glean the nuances of these terms.

The chapters are organized in an inductive manner presenting an overview, an instructive case, and then a discussion and analysis of that case in the context of the knowledge and research on politics in education. Case-based learning has a long history in enhancing prospective leaders' awareness and understanding of how knowledge about leadership feels in practice (Ellet, 2007). University-based leadership preparation programs also have a long history of using multiple instructional methods to link knowledge and practice (Copland, 2000; Culbertson, 1988, 1995; Orr & Orphanos, 2011; Ylimaki & Jacobson, 2013). The focus for school leadership preparation must be on action-oriented, experiential learning (Hallinger & Lu, 2013).

Cases offer sample situations, enlivening readers' recognition of these omnipresent moments of politics in schooling. The design of the cases moves readers through the feelings attached to the political conflicts surrounding the daily practice of leadership. The idea behind each chapter is that aspiring school leaders vicariously explore school leaders' common dilemmas, and then are guided through expert and research-based analyses of these conflicts. By the end of the book, readers will have a variety of tools for thinking through their daily political contexts. The chapters are organized to move prospective school leaders from the moment-to-moment of meeting their job responsibilities to the larger political contexts affecting their students, communities and schools.

After the cases, an analysis section introduces relevant political theory. Each chapter provides an overview of how the embedded case addresses the overall standard and its sub-elements (also known as functions). For Standard 6, the sub-elements (numbered in some literature as 6.1, 6.2 and 6.3) include:

	ISLLC 2008 Standard 6 An education leader promotes the success of every student by understanding, responding to, and influencing the political, social, economic, legal, and cultural context		
Chapter	ELLC Standard Element 6.1: Candidates understand and can advocate for **district and school students**, families, and caregivers	ELCC Standard Element 6.2: Candidates understand and can act to influence local, district, state, and national decisions affecting student learning in a **district and school environment**	ELCC Standard Element 6.3: Candidates understand and can anticipate and assess emerging trends and initiatives in order to adapt **district and school-based leadership strategies**
1 Politics in Education and its Importance in School Leadership	✓	✓	✓
2 School Micropolitics for Improving Teaching and Learning		✓	✓
3 The Politics of School-level Community Engagement and Decision Making		✓	✓
4 The Politics of District-Level Decision Making	✓	✓	✓
5 Politics, Culture, Social Conditions: Jambalaya con sazón	✓		
6 The Politics of Community Collaboration	✓	✓	✓
7 The Politics of Interest Groups in Education		✓	✓
8 The School Leader's Professional and Civic Political Voice	✓	✓	✓
9 Forecasting Future Directions for Political Activism in School Leadership	✓	✓	✓

Figure 1 Matrix of ELCC 2011 Elements

A. Advocate for children, families, and caregivers.
B. Act to influence local, district, state, and national decisions affecting student learning.
C. Assess, analyze, and anticipate emerging trends and initiatives in order to adapt leadership strategies (NPBEA, 2007).

The individual chapters specify one or more of these sub-elements as germane to the case. For textbook use, a matrix of how the chapters encompass the sub-elements is included here.

Both instructors and aspiring school leaders can use the matrix in reading these chapters to ascertain associated knowledge about politics in education as they play out across the multidimensional work of theorists and researchers. The chapters also offer insights into the skills and practices associated with these sub-elements and dimensions of politics in schooling.

Learning Activity boxes are dispersed at intervals among the cases in the chapters. Given the different policy and political issues in each case, some of the Learning Activities punctuate specific points within a case. Other Learning Activities appear as reflective opportunities within or after the case discussion and among the various theories supporting the cases. Like the many complexities of politics in education, the authentic presentation of cases interspersed with Learning Activities replicates the non-linear experience of politics in education faced by school leaders.

The political contexts of education are messy. Finding solutions to the messy conflicts that these political contexts generate requires creativity and collaboration among multiple stakeholders. To practice creative thinking and collaboration, aspiring school leaders need opportunities to discuss the cases, make observations in their own contexts, and then practice working with others to resolve conflicts. One of the ways to obtain these opportunities inside and out of coursework is the companion website for this text. The website offers suggestions for extended learning based on Standard 6 and its sub-elements.

POLITICAL CONTEXTS

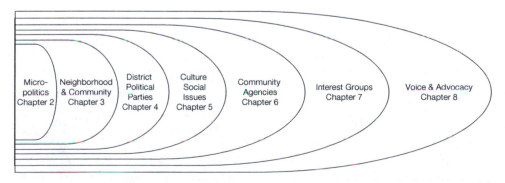

Figure 2 Political Contexts as Reflected in this Book's Design

OVERVIEW OF CHAPTERS

This book, focused as it is on political contexts, is designed around an ecological and environmental conceptualization. The figure depicts how the book's design reflects the political contexts faced by school leaders. This book's organization moves from the intimate, micropolitical interactions of schooling to the macro-contexts where policies are debated and designed. The following descriptions of each chapter explain each expanding level of the book's depicted design.

Chapter 1: Politics in Education and its Importance in School Leadership

Jane Clark Lindle and Kenyae L. Reese

Chapter 1 presents the general thesis of this book; politics in education is inevitable and aspiring school leaders need to develop their political strategies for ensuring that each and every student, not only has opportunities to learn, but is successful in learning. The chapter also explains why and how professional educators were discouraged from participating in politics since the early days of schooling in the U.S. The history of ISLLC Standard 6 also is reviewed as the Council of Chief State School Officers (CCSSO) 1996 version was focused primarily on awareness of political influences on schools, but did not necessarily require that school leaders take action. The 2008 version (CCSSO, 2008) more explicitly calls for school leaders' direct action. The Education Leadership Constituent Council (ELCC), an accrediting body involving licensing and certification of principals and superintendents in many states, has offered further evidence that school leadership requires political activism on behalf of students and their families (NPBEA, 2011a, 2011b).

Chapter 2: School Micropolitics for Improving Teaching and Learning

Brenda R. Beatty

In this chapter, readers will find, literally, the heart and heat of working with politics in schooling. Novice and experienced school leaders report a wealth of conflict that generates passion, emotions, and perplexing situations that make their way into the school's main office. It plunges readers into the emotions that arise when school leaders are caught between the power of their boss and the professional decision making of colleagues. Beatty describes the importance of emotional meaning making (Beatty, 2002) and communication to confront both conflict and passions attached to the micropolitical features of moment-to-moment school life. This chapter compellingly addresses the emerging awareness about the risks of not preparing school leaders for emotional work in schools (Bridges 2012). She expands on the literature on micropolitics to explain how emotional awareness and health is linked to conflicts in schools. The literature on micropolitics explains the essence of individual negotiating and bargaining. Teachers bargain with each other and students bargain with each other. Many days, students and teachers strike bargains, and some deal with school leaders in their negotiations. Parents bargain on behalf of their children with teachers, each other, and the principal. Often, school leaders are drawn into the aftermath of bargains that have gone wrong. The challenges for school leadership focus on more than bargaining and conflict, but on the necessary emotional development necessary for all involved to work toward solutions.

Chapter 3: The Politics of School-Level Community Engagement and Decision Making

Timothy A. Drake and Ellen B. Goldring

The third chapter in this book opens up the ways that power is used politically inside and out of schools. Power plays occur not just in bargaining and conflict, but also arise over choices facing school personnel, students, and their families on a daily basis. As with Chapter 2, this chapter is about intimate power issues rather than the kind of power dynamics found in larger arenas, such as state legislatures or voter issues at the district levels. Instead, the authors offer an ecological perspective on how leadership involves collaboration among stakeholders to ensure that students learn. They confront one of the key political questions in daily school decision making: Who decides? Their answer sustains a consistent finding in research and principles of politics and democratic, participatory decision making: the people affected by decision consequences have a say in making decisions. For school leaders, that answer predicates their role in negotiating the prerogatives of professional judgment and the individual rights of each student and family.

Chapter 4: The Politics of District-Level Decision Making

Lance D. Fusarelli and George J. Petersen

In this chapter, politics in education encounters political party affiliation in a city school district. The case highlights the interplay of political platforms and the management of enrollments through drawing geo-physical lines on the city map for school attendance areas. At this level of political interactions, the influence of traditional and new media in defining the conflict is inserted into the mix. This chapter also reviews research on the effects of school board elections on the longevity of the top school leader, the superintendent. The authors raise issues about the internal and external political ramifications of hiring and firing superintendents and the resultant turmoil that shapes the politics of learning in a churning school district. The case exposes another view of how professional judgments that lack political insight implode.

Chapter 5: Politics, Culture, Social Conditions

Gerardo R. López

Chapter 5 uncovers aspects of common human conditions that lead to political turmoil across a region, throughout a school district, into communities and neighborhoods, into a school building, and affecting students' relationships, school safety, and ultimately, an individual student's ability to learn successfully. This chapter reveals some common issues in U.S. communities arising from the nation's historic migration and immigration patterns. This mix of transience in regions and neighborhoods is further complicated by socially and culturally historic events that add to a community's identity and reputation. Then the case presented in this chapter also illustrates how natural history events, such as weather, add to the socio-cultural stew, or jambalaya, to affect students in schools. The case illustrates how one student's chances at graduating from high school also are affected by policies that have unintended consequences because these policies may be overly simplistic and applied without incorporating consideration of multiple individual and social dynamics. This case challenges aspiring school leaders to consider how they may face advocates with important points who use a single student's plight as a rallying point. From the political perspective, this case reveals how changing social conditions affect the conditions of schooling and require cultural responsiveness; in fact, a level of responsiveness that is nimble in its adaptation to change.

Chapter 6: The Politics of Community Collaboration

Bonnie C. Fusarelli and Cathy Chada Williams

This chapter illustrates the territorial, and thus political, pressures on agencies and organizations that serve students and their families. The case in Chapter 6 illustrates how community agency coordination is affected by both community politics and inter-professional conflicts. In this ecological picture of politics surrounding learning, the authors explain the ways that social services require collaborative leadership. They review the literature on how scarce resources for students and families at-risk or in crises create political moments that can be bridged with cooperation and by pooling resources. On the other hand, a failure to coordinate among community agencies erodes the safety net for students and their families. As with Chapter 5, readers are confronted with questions about how aspiring school leaders can address each and every student need by linking with other community groups and organizations to ensure successful learning.

Chapter 7: The Politics of Interest Groups in Education

Sue Winton and Deborah Gonzalez

For many communities, schools are the focus of the region's social life. That is, schools are not solely where youth are educated, they also serve as a public space for various groups and societies in the community. In this chapter, the scarcity of resources affects how the school relates to specific groups in the community. Scarcity sets up the conditions of political action because not everyone has or will get what they need or desire. This chapter offers insights into how school leaders must calculate strategically from among the following considerations (a) who will get what they want; (b) who might not get all that they want; and (c) whether or not the students and school can live with the consequences. These authors' case illustrates the strategies that school leaders can use to remain aware of what triggers these groups' concerns and then how to negotiate for what is in the best interests of students.

Chapter 8: School Leaders' Professional and Civic Political Voice

Bradley W. Carpenter and Sarah Diem

School leaders often occupy a position between the wisdom of professional practice and educational policies with poor and unintended consequences. In this chapter, the primary question facing readers concerns when and how school leaders speak publicly to ensure students' learning. School leaders face risks in raising their concerns about poorly designed policies, and this chapter helps illustrate some of these frustrating dilemmas. When can school leaders engage in political activism in a way that optimizes outcomes for students? When must they take care to not lose their jobs in the process of their activism? When is it necessary to risk even their jobs and engage in the politics surrounding educational policy? This chapter illustrates an issue raised in Chapter 2; advocacy requires courage and with that requirement, an emotional awareness is generated about confronting risk and consequences.

Chapter 9: Forecasting Future Directions for Political Activism in School Leadership

Kenyae L. Reese and Jane Clark Lindle

In the final chapter, multiple political trends raised across all chapters are summarized. This chapter also points to the ongoing contextual issues surrounding schools. As explained throughout the book, the political environment of schooling in the U.S. features influences that span the history of public schooling over more than a century. Many of these influences reflect the socio-cultural and political history of the nation. Migration and immigration continue to derive from economic events as well as natural disasters. Other issues such as the phenomenon of educational policy transfer ricochet globally. International testing regimes affect U.S. educational policies. All of these conditions exist alongside the scarcity of resources available to schools. All of these conditions, along with scarcities, ensure that school leaders must think and act strategically in forming alliances, sharing power, and raising their voices to advocate on behalf of students and families.

REFERENCES

Beatty, B. (2002). *Emotion matters in educational leadership: Examining the unexamined*. Unpublished doctoral dissertation, Ontario Institute for Studies in Education, University of Toronto.

Bridges, E. (2012). Administrator preparation: Looking backwards and forwards. *Journal of Educational Administration, 50*(4), 402–419.

Copland, M. A. (2000). Problem-based learning and prospective principals' problem-framing ability. *Educational Administration Quarterly, 36*(4), 585–607.

Council of Chief State School Officers (1996). *Interstate School Leaders Licensure Consortium's standards for school leaders*. Washington, DC: Author.

Council of Chief State School Officers (2008). *Educational leadership policy standards: ISLLC 2008*. Washington, DC: Author. Retrieved from: www.ccsso.org/Documents/2008/Educational_Leadership_Policy_Standards_2008.pdf

Culbertson, J. A. (1988). A century's quest for a knowledge base. In N. Boyan (Ed.), *Handbook of research on educational administration* (pp. 3–26.) New York: Longman.

Culbertson, J. A. (1995). *Building bridges: UCEA's first two decades*. University Park, PA: University Council for Educational Administration (UCEA).

Ellet, W. (2007). *The case study handbook: How to read, discuss, and write persuasively about cases*. Cambridge, MA: Harvard Business School Press.

Hallinger, P. & Lu, J. (2013). Preparing principals: What can we learn from MBA and MPA programmes? *Educational Management Administration & Leadership, 41*(4) 435–452.

Lasswell, H. D. (1965). *Politics: Who gets what, when, and how* (9th ed.). Cleveland, OH: Meridian Books, The World Publishing Company.

National Policy Board for Educational Administration (2007, December). *Educational leadership policy standards: ISLLC 2008*. Washington, DC: Author. Retrieved from: www.principals.org/s_nassp/sec_inside.asp?CID=1298&DID=56055

National Policy Board for Educational Administration (2011a). *Educational leadership program standards: 2011 ELCC building level*. Washington, DC: Author. Retrieved from: www.ncate.org/LinkClick.aspx?fileticket=zRZI73R0nOQ%3d&tabid=676

National Policy Board for Educational Administration (2011b). *Educational leadership program standards: 2011 ELCC district level*. Washington, DC: Author. Retrieved from: www.ncate.org/LinkClick.aspx?fileticket=tFmaPVlwMMo%3d&tabid=676

Orr, M. T. & Orphanos, S. (2011). How graduate-level preparation influences the effectiveness of school leaders: A comparison of the outcomes of exemplary and conventional leadership preparation programs for principals. *Educational Administration Quarterly, 47*(1), 18–70.

Stout, R. T., Tallerico, M., & Scribner, K. P. (1995). Values: the "what?" of the politics of education. In J. D. Scribner & D. Layton (Eds.), *The study of educational politics: The 1994 commemorative yearbook of the Politics of Education Association (1969–1994)* (pp. 5–20). Washington, DC: Falmer.

Ylimaki, R. & Jacobson, S. (2013). School leadership practice and preparation: Comparative perspectives on organizational learning (OL), instructional leadership (IL) and culturally responsive practices (CRP). *Journal of Educational Administration, 51*(1), 6–23.

Acknowledgments

As with politics in education, success comes with the cooperation, generosity, and collaboration of many others. First, much appreciation goes to Ms. Kenyae L. Reese's intense and unfailingly cheerful attention to all aspects of this book. She has enthusiastically embraced the behind-the-scenes nature of many tasks assigned to doctoral students and turned every moment into a learning experience for all of us. Dr. Amanda B. Werts, as a graduate assistant, also spent many hours laying the foundation for the prospectus of this book. Her patience and attention to tracking down fugitive case studies is greatly appreciated.

Since its inception, many members of the Politics of Education Association also welcomed the notion of this book. They encouraged the strengthening of connections between scholarship and practice through this opportunity. Not surprisingly, given their orientation to all things political, they continually seek to improve leadership in schools through understanding politics in education. For their encouragement, understanding, and support, words of appreciation seem small payment.

Another group of stalwart supporters should be named. The following individuals commented on the chapter manuscripts. Many also made a point of joining a discussion of the book's many concepts, and then gave their considerable insights to authors in small group and individual conversations. All the editors and contributors to this volume appreciate the efforts of the following individuals:

Dorothea Anagnostopoulos, Michigan State University
Lora Cohen-Vogel, University of North Carolina—Chapel Hill
W. Kyle Ingle, Bowling Green State University
Karen Seashore Louis, University of Minnesota
Hanne Mawhinney, University of Maryland—College Park
Stacey Rutledge, Florida State University
Dana Thompson-Dorsey, University of North Carolina—Chapel Hill
Susan Perkins Weston, Kentucky education consultant
Shaneka Williams, University of Georgia.

CHAPTER 1

Politics in Education and its Importance in School Leadership

Jane Clark Lindle and
Kenyae L. Reese

Schools reverberate to the fortunes and misadventures of their students, their families, and their neighborhoods and communities. These daily, even moment-to-moment, interactions mirror the social conditions in a local milieu. Schools also function as the nexus for educational policies developed outside their walls from school district boards, state legislatures, and the U.S. Congress with regulatory guidance generated by the federal Department of Education. In many ways schools expose a phenomenon known as *policy transfer*; that is, the remarkable adoption and adaption of policy features found in many other democratic nations worldwide (Ball, 2001, 2003; Levi-Faur & Vigoda-Gadot, 2006). Schools experience global politics in a microcosm. Schools exist locally, and simultaneously absorb global impacts of social and economic conditions, politics, and culture.

Since the genesis of the Interstate School Leaders Licensure Consortium's (ISLLC) Standards for school leaders in the mid-1990s, Standard 6 emphasized educational leaders' awareness of strategies promoting student success through recognition of the contexts in which education and student learning reside (Council of Chief State School Officers, CCSSO, 1996; National Policy Board for Educational Administration, NPBEA, 2011a, 2011b). The ensuing version of ISLLC (CCSSO, 2008) re-articulated Standard 6 requiring educational leaders more directly engage in the certitudes of politics in education. Such an emphasis combines political activity with cultural responsiveness across multiple arenas from the school to worldwide issues and trends (Riehl, 2000; Skrla et al., 2004). ISLLC Standard 6 states:

> An education leader promotes the success of every student by understanding, responding to, and influencing the political, social, economic, legal, and cultural context.

ISLLC provides three more guiding aspects to Standard 6, which call for school leaders to proactively engage and shape the political contexts of student success. For preparation programs, the Educational Leadership Constituent Council (ELCC) provides even more detail about the knowledge and skills associated with each of the guidelines (NPBEA 2011a, 2011b). These three guidelines include the following:

6.1   Advocate for children, families, and caregivers.

6.2   Act to influence local, district, state, and national decisions affecting student learning.

6.3   Assess, analyze, and anticipate emerging trends and initiatives in order to adapt leadership strategies.

(NPBEA, 2007)

The Standard and its guidelines are grounded in "research informing craft knowledge that is derived from a foundation of 'doing' school [and district] adminis-tration" (NPBEA, 2011a, pp. 32–33; NPBEA, 2011b, p. 34). The action verbs in these guidelines reflect decades of school leaders' descriptions of their work on behalf of students. Additionally, these guidelines include demands for school leaders' actions backed by more than a half century of research about leadership in schools, in the U.S. and internationally, where students, despite their social, economic, and political situations, are successful (Edmonds & Frederickson, 1978; Leithwood et al., 2006; Lezotte, 1992; Louis et al., 2010). Schools need these kinds of leaders.

Schools require leaders who are empowered to speak for their students and schools. Standards-based preparation, supported by decades of research, demands that school leaders find their civic and professional voices as active participants in their political contexts. All of the chapters address ISLLC Standard 6 holistically as each provides multidimensional insight into the political and politicized social, economic, and cultural issues that surround and impact schools and schooling.

While each of the chapters in this book offers a particular insight into one or more of the guiding elements associated with ELCC, Chapter 1 sets the background for the variety of case-based learning in the remaining chapters. Chapter 1's primary purpose is to provide an orientation to the field of politics in education's concepts—or as referenced by NPBEA's documents (NPBEA, 2011a, 2011b)—knowledge and skills. Chapter 1 sets the stage for instructors' and their students' use and application of case-based learning about politics in education and school leaders' legitimate role in the politics of schooling.

MAPPING CONCEPTS IN THE POLITICS OF SCHOOL LEADERSHIP

Politics in education remains firmly embedded in every school's environment whether professional morés permit admitting its existence or not. From the beginning to well into the latter half of the 20th century, those morés held a firm recommendation that school leaders avoid politics in education (Layton & Scribner, 1989; McCarty & Ramsey, 1971). Today's 21st century requirements for educational leadership recognize the necessity of adopting professional and civic agendas for ensuring every student's success.

Historically, the avoidance of politics in schooling was a matter of professional survival for teachers and other educators (Clifford, 1987; McCarty & Ramsey, 1971). In the early history of U.S. schools, school boards often required teachers to register with a certain political party, vote to elect, or re-elect, certain board members, and in a related intrusion into citizen's rights, attend certain churches (Cuban, 1985; Eliot, 1959; Tyack & Cuban, 1995). Some of these constraints were related to then-current paternalistic social concerns about protecting predominantly female teachers, and by extension, their impressionable charges, from making incorrect choices (Blount, 1999; Clifford, 1987). By the beginning of the 20th century, the progressive public school movement sought to sanitize education from the taint of party politics and to promote a more professional standing for teachers and school leaders by placing them apart from party machines (Dewey, 1903; Tyack & Cuban, 1995.) The result of this attempt to purify schooling added to its complexity in the U.S. system.

Even today, the vast majority of the more than 13,000 school systems in the U.S. are *special districts* deliberately differentiated from, and independent of, local municipalities such as counties, cities, towns, or townships (Bowman & Kearney, 1986; U.S. Department of Education, 2012). Typically, but not in all cases, these special districts remain independent financially from local municipal oversight. Typically, but not in all cases, most school districts operate as empowered local agents of state legislatures, while simultaneously holding a quasi-independent relationship with state education agencies. Like these special districts, state education agencies vary in the degree of authority delegated to them by state constitutions and laws. Thus, the essence of U.S. public schooling is a jumble of at least 13,000 systems with all their accompanying jurisdictional diversity encompassing the human diversity of hundreds of thousands of people, students, and communities.

This jurisdictional complexity derives from the 10th Amendment of the U.S. Constitution, which reserved specified powers to the states (Spring, 1993; Wirt & Kirst, 1992). In short, the 10th Amendment removed the federal government from direct authority over education and asserted sovereignty for each state in determining its approach to schooling its citizens. This arrangement is peculiar to the U.S. Moreover, the consequence of the 10th Amendment has relegated federal intervention in the states' schools to a variety of influential, thus political, policy strategies (Goertz, 2005; Wirt & Kirst, 1992). These policy strategies include the blunt instrument of funding contingencies as well as slightly more finessed requirements for testing and quality indicators (Goertz, 2005; McDonnell, 1994).

As a result, considerable court case law has been generated to adjudicate the powers of the federal government in addressing matters of schooling in each state (Alexander & Alexander, 2012; Tyack & James, 1986; Zirkel, 1997). Litigation is one signal of conflict over how schools should operate as well as stimulating competition over which person, groups, or entities have a say in that operation (Stout et al., 1995; Zirkel, 1997).

The enduring questions in political struggles in education include questions about who decides what curriculum to teach, which people are permitted to teach that curriculum, and which students are allowed to attend classes (Stout et al., 1995). From the civil rights era to the inclusion of students with disabilities to the issues of practicing [which?] religion in public schools, political questions about schooling frequently rise to litigation surrounding schools. The involvement of courts further diffuses power and authority over decision making in U.S. schools (Sergiovanni et al., 2004; Spring, 1993; Wirt & Kirst, 1992).

Because the authority over U.S. public schools has dispersed over many jurisdictions, the means of enacting educational policy hinges on influence, a basic political ploy (Ball, 1987). The ploys of both macro- and micropolitics arrive at the schoolhouse door on a daily, if not hourly or moment-to-moment, basis (Fowler, 2004; Sergiovanni et al., 2004; Spring, 1993). School leaders must be prepared to engage in schoolhouse politics with particular attention to the best interests of students and their families (NPBEA, 2011a, 2011b; Stefkovich, 2006).

The image of the stalwart school administrator as pillar of the community also is an image as old as the position of school manager (Tyack & Hansot, 1982). The difference between yesteryear's community role model and today's politically savvy school leader is a level of proactive engagement with both schools' and surrounding communities' cultures and social conditions (Begley & Johansson, 2003; Cubberley, 1916; Stefkovich, 2006).

Multiple studies over decades depict the degree of necessary leadership and responsiveness to the contextual conditions of schools and the people in them. Today's school leaders negotiate scarce resources for their students and families, expressly championing the cause of the underserved and marginalized (Bustamante et al., 2009; Cooper, 2009; Jacobson et al., 2007; Johnson & Fauske, 2000; Johnson, 2003, 2006; Mawhinney, 2010; Murphy, 2005; Murtadha & Watts, 2005; NPBEA, 2011a, 2011b; Owen, 2006; Riehl, 2000; Schoen & Fusarelli, 2008; Shields, 2010; Shields et al., 2002; Theoharis, 2008, 2010; Ylimaki & Jacobson, 2013). The research on the proactive political engagement of successful school principals is extensive (NPBEA, 2011a) and expands beyond the decades of debates about the political role of school superintendents (Buchanan, 2006; Iannaccone & Lutz, 1970; Kirst & Wirt, 2009; Kowalski, 1995; McCarty & Ramsey, 1971; NPBEA, 2011b).

Instructors' and students' access to extensive literature on politics in schools and especially the roles of school leaders are included in both publications of the National Policy Board for Educational Administration: (a) one focused on preparation programs at the building level, the principalship, (2011a, pp. 50–55) and (b) the other, on the district level, the superintendency (2011b, pp. 52–57). Further information about these publications and their access are included on the website for this book. These research studies and the accompanying literature about the political concepts necessary for school leaders also support the instructional design for each of this book's chapters. This textbook joins the political concepts obtained from research with the associated experiences of politics in the practice of school leadership.

APPLICATION OF POLITICS IN SCHOOLING: A SCHOOL LEADER'S PLIGHT

School leaders have long expressed their concern that the ups-and-downs of any school day encompass politics, with a lowercase p (Lindle, 1999). School leaders write few memoirs, but those that exist depict a rollercoaster ride of influence and emotions in a school day (Beatty, 2002; Bridges, 2012; Malen, 1995). Not surprisingly, these mountains and valleys of emotional and political work come from teachers' and students' struggles in implementing external teaching policies and trying to learn in conscripted ways (Ball, 2003; Hargreaves, 2000). The implementation of standards-based professional preparation adds more impetus for the use of case methods in school leadership preparation (Bass et al., 2011). This book is organized specifically to immerse students and their instructors in the complexity of the cases drawn from current issues in schools. Those issues range from individual to group concerns, from the lack of necessary resources to address a plethora of student needs, and at all times, multiple adults, agencies, and policies applying pressures and intruding into the teaching and learning process. Throw in external issues ranging from natural disasters to crime to global economic conditions, and on some days, school leaders might wonder what educational achievements are possible at all.

From the perspective of the school leader, the issues among any individual or group of students require a balancing of competing needs, demands, and benefits. Furthermore, the wisdom of practice alongside the research on politics in schools underlines the limits of any single leader's ability to achieve this equilibrium alone (Goldring & Sullivan, 1996; Spillane et al., 2003; Ylimaki & Jacobson, 2013). Politics is only a zero-sum game if the focus is on accruing power, rather than combining collaborative forces, or distributing or sharing power (Auerbach, 2012; Bacharach & Lawler, 1980; Griffin & Moorhead, 1998; Spillane, 2006).

Today's and tomorrow's schools require leadership, a collective effort, rather than heroic, or power-obsessed, individual leaders. Leaders who operate from a base of their positional authority clearly do not comprehend the nature of the political contexts in education. The political contexts of schooling require leaders who have the political understanding of how to get people to work together for students to be successful. These kinds of leaders empower others to offer leadership to schools and to negotiate education's political contexts toward a common goal of success for all students.

REFERENCES

Alexander, K. & Alexander, M. D. (2012). *American public school law* (8th ed.). Belmont, CA: Wadsworth.

Auerbach, S. (Ed.). (2012). *School leadership for authentic family and community partnerships: Research perspectives for transforming practice.* New York: Routledge.

Bacharach, S. B. & Lawler, E. J. (1980). *Power and politics in organizations*. San Francisco, CA: Jossey-Bass.

Ball, S. J. (1987). *The micro-politics of the school: Towards a theory of school organization*. London: Methuen.

Ball, S. J. (2001, December). Global policies and vernacular politics in education. *Curriculo sem Fronteiras*, *1*(2), xxvii–xliii. Retrieved from: www.curriculosemfronteiras.org/vol1iss2 articles/balleng.pdf

Ball, S. J. (2003). The teacher's soul and the terrors of performativity. *Journal of Education Policy*, 18(2), 215–228. Doi: 10.1080/0268093022000043065

Bass, L., Garn, G., & Monroe, L. (2011). Using JCEL case studies to meet ELCC Standards. *Journal of Cases in Educational Leadership*, *14*(1), 1–12.

Beatty, B. (2002). *Emotion matters in educational leadership: Examining the unexamined*. Unpublished doctoral dissertation, Ontario Institute for Studies in Education, University of Toronto.

Begley, P. T. & Johansson, O. (2003). *The ethical dimensions of school leadership*. Norwell, MA: Kluwer Academic.

Blount, J. M. (1999). Manliness and the gendered construction of school administration in the USA. *International Journal of Leadership in Education*, *2*(2), 55–68.

Bowman, A. O. & Kearney, R. C. (1986). *The resurgence of the states*. Upper Saddle River, NJ: Prentice Hall.

Bridges, E. (2012). Administrator preparation: Looking backwards and forwards. *Journal of Educational Administration*, *50*(4), 402–419.

Buchanan, B. (2006). *Turnover at the top: Superintendent vacancies and the urban school*. Blue Ridge Summit, PA: Rowman & Littlefield Education.

Bustamante, R. M., Nelson, J. A., & Onwuegbuzie, A. J. (2009). Assessing school wide cultural competence: Implications for school leadership preparation. *Educational Administration Quarterly*, *45*(5), 793–827.

Clifford, G. J. (1987). "Lady teachers" and politics in the United States, 1850–1930. In M. Lawn & G. Grace (Eds.), *Teachers: The culture and politics of work* (pp. 3–30). New York: Routledge.

Cooper, C. W. (2009). Performing cultural work in demographically changing schools: Implications for expanding transformative leadership frameworks. *Educational Administration Quarterly*, *45*(5), 694–724.

Council of Chief State School Officers (1996). *Interstate School Leaders Licensure Consortium's standards for school leaders*. Washington, DC: Author.

Council of Chief State School Officers (2008). *Educational leadership policy standards: ISLLC 2008*. Washington, DC: Author. Retrieved from: www.ccsso.org/Documents/2008/ Educational_Leadership_Policy_Standards_2008.pdf

Cuban, L. (1985). Conflict and leadership in the superintendency. *Phi Delta Kappan*, *67*(1), 28–30.

Cubberley, E. P. (1916). *Public school administration: A statement of the fundamental principles underlying the organization and administration of public education*. Cambridge, MA: Riverside/ Houghton Mifflin.

Dewey, J. (1903). Democracy in education. *The Elementary School Teacher*, *4*(4), 193–204.

Edmonds, R. R. & Frederiksen, J. R. (1978). *Search for effective schools: The identification and analysis of city schools that are instructionally effective for poor children*. (ERIC Document Reproduction Service No. ED170396).

Eliot, T. H. (1959). Toward an understanding of public school politics. *The American Political Science Review*, *53*(4), 1032–1051.

Fowler, F. (2004). *Policy studies for educational leaders: An introduction* (2nd ed.). Upper Saddle River, NJ: Pearson Merrill Prentice Hall.

Goertz, M. E. (2005). Implementing the No Child Left Behind Act: Challenges for the states. *Peabody Journal of Education*, *80*(2), 73–89.

Goldring, E. & Sullivan, A. (1996). Beyond the boundaries: Principals, parents and communities shaping the school environment. In K. Leithwood, J. Chapman, D. Corson, P. Hallinger, & A. Hart (Eds.), *International handbook of educational leadership and administration*, Volume 1 (pp. 195–222). Norwell, MA: Kluwer Academic.

Griffin, R. W. & Moorhead, G. (1998). *Organizational behavior: Managing people and organizations*. Boston: Houghton Mifflin Company.

Hargreaves, A. (2000, April). *Emotional geographies: Teaching in a box*. Paper presented at the annual meeting of the American Educational Research Association, New Orleans, Louisiana.

Iannaccone, L. & Lutz, F. W. (1970). *Politics, power and policy: The governing of local school districts*. Columbus, OH: Merrill.

Jacobson, S. L., Brooks, S., Giles, C., Johnson, L., & Ylimaki, R. (2007). Successful leadership in three high-poverty urban elementary schools. *Leadership and Policy in Schools*, *6*(4), 291–317.

Johnson, B. L. & Fauske, J. R. (2000). Principals and the political economy of environmental enactment. *Educational Administration Quarterly*, *36*(2), 159–185.

Johnson, L. (2003). Multicultural policy as social activism: Redefining who counts in multicultural edition. *Race, Ethnicity and Education*, *6*(2), 107–121.

Johnson, L. (2006). Making her community a better place to live: Culturally responsive urban school leadership in historical perspective. *Leadership and Policy in Schools*, *5*(1), 19–37.

Kirst, M. W. & Wirt, F. M. (2009). *The political dynamics of American education*. Richmond, CA: McCutchan Publishing Corporation.

Kowalski, T. J. (1995). *Keepers of the flame: Contemporary urban superintendents*. Thousand Oaks, CA: Corwin.

Layton, D. & Scribner, J. D. (Eds.), (1989). *Teaching educational politics and policy*. Tempe, AZ: University Council for Educational Administration.

Leithwood, K., Day, C., Sammons, P., Harris, A. & Hopkins, D. (2006). *Seven strong claims about successful school leadership*. Nottingham, UK: NCSL/DfES. Retrieved from: http://scholr.ly/paper/1096202/wwwncslorguk-seven-strong-claims-about-successful-school-leadership

Levi-Faur, D. & Vigoda-Gadot, E. (2006). New public policy, new policy transfers: Some characteristics of a new order in the making. *International Journal of Public Administration*, 29, 247–262. Doi: 10.1080/01900690500437147.

Lezotte, L. W. (1992). "Principal" insights from effective schools. *Education Digest*, *58*(3), 14–16.

Lindle, J. C. (1999). What can the study of micropolitics contribute to the practice of leadership in reforming schools? *School Leadership & Management*, *19*(2), 171–178.

Louis, K. S., Leithwood, K., Wahlstrom, K. L., & Anderson, S. E. (2010). *Learning from leadership: Investigating the links to improved student learning*. Final report of research to the Wallace Foundation. Retrieved from: www.wallacefoundation.org

Malen, B. (1995). The micropolitics of education: Mapping the multiple dimensions of power relations in school politics. In J. D. Scribner & D. H. Layton (Eds.), *The 1994 commemorative yearbook of the Politics of Educational Association (1969–1994)* (pp. 147–167). Washington, DC: Falmer.

Mawhinney, H. B. (2010). Shifting scales of education politics in a vernacular of disruption and dislocation. *Educational Policy*, *24*(1), 245–263.

McCarty, D. J. & Ramsey, C. E. (1971). *The school managers: Power and conflict in American public education*. Westport, CT: Greenwood.

McDonnell, L. M. (1994). Assessment policy as persuasion and regulation. *American Journal of Education, 102*, 394–420.

Moorhead, G. & Griffin, R. W. (1998). *Organizational behavior: Managing people and organizations*. Boston: Houghton Mifflin Company.

Murphy, J. (2005). Unpacking the foundations of the ISLLC standards and addressing concerns in the academic community. *Educational Administration Quarterly, 41*(1), 154–191.

Murtadha, K. & Watts, D. M. (2005). Linking the struggle for education and social justice: Historical perspectives of African American leadership in schools. *Educational Administration Quarterly, 41*(4), 591–608.

National Policy Board for Educational Administration (2007, December). *Educational leadership policy standards: ISLLC 2008*. Washington, DC: Author. Retrieved from: www.principals. org/s_nassp/sec_inside.asp?CID=1298&DID=56055

National Policy Board for Educational Administration (2011a). *Educational leadership program standards: 2011 ELCC building level*. Washington, DC: Author. Retrieved from: www.ncate. org/LinkClick.aspx?fileticket=zRZI73R0nOQ%3d&tabid=676

National Policy Board for Educational Administration (2011b). *Educational leadership program standards: 2011 ELCC district level*. Washington, DC: Author. Retrieved from: www.ncate. org/LinkClick.aspx?fileticket=tFmaPVlwMMo%3d&tabid=676

Owen, J. C. (2006). *The impact of politics in local education: Navigating white water*. Blue Ridge Summit, PA: Rowman & Littlefield Education.

Riehl, C. J. (2000). The principal's role in creating inclusive schools for diverse students: A review of normative, empirical, and critical literature on the practice of educational administration. *Review of Educational Research, 70*(1), 55–81.

Schoen, L. & Fusarelli, L. D. (2008). Innovation, NCLB, and the fear factor—The challenge of leading 21st-century schools in an era of accountability. *Educational Policy, 22*(1), 181–203.

Sergiovanni, T. J., Kelleher, P., McCarthy, M. M. & Wirt, F. M. (2004). *Educational governance and administration 5/e*. Boston: Pearson Allen & Bacon.

Shields, C. M. (2010). Transformative leadership: Working for equity in diverse contexts. *Educational Administration Quarterly, 46*(4), 558–589.

Shields, C. M., Larocque, L. J., & Oberg, S. L. (2002). A dialogue about race and ethnicity in education: Struggling to understand issues in cross-cultural leadership. *Journal of School Leadership, 12*, 116–137.

Skrla, L., Scheurich, J. J., Garcia, J., & Nolly, G. (2004). Equity audits: A practical leadership tool for developing equitable and excellent schools. *Educational Administration Quarterly, 40*(1), 135–163.

Spillane, J. P. (2006). *Distributed leadership*. San Francisco, CA: Jossey-Bass.

Spillane, J. P., Hallett, T. & Diamond, J. B. (2003). Forms of capital and the construction of leadership: Instructional leadership in urban elementary schools. *Sociology of Education, 76*(1), pp. 1–17.

Spring, J. (1993). *Conflict of interests: The politics of American education* (2nd ed.). New York: Longman.

Stefkovich, J. A. (2006). *Best interests of the student: Applying ethical constructs to legal cases in education*. Mahwah, NJ: Lawrence Erlbaum Associates.

Stout, R. T., Tallerico, M. & Scribner, K. P. (1995). Values: the "what?" of the politics of education. In J. D. Scribner & D. Layton (Eds.), *The study of educational politics: The 1994 commemorative yearbook of the Politics of Education Association (1969–1994)* (pp. 5–20). Washington, DC: Falmer.

Theoharis, G. (2008). "At every turn": The resistance public school principals face in their pursuit of equity and justice. *Journal of School Leadership*, *18*, 303–343.

Theoharis, G. (2010). Disrupting injustice: Principals narrate the strategies they use to improve their schools and advance social justice. *Teachers College Record*, *112*(1), 331–373.

Tyack, D. B. & Cuban, L. (1995). *Tinkering toward utopia: A century of public school reform*. Cambridge, MA: Harvard University Press.

Tyack, D. B. & Hansot, E. (1982). *Managers of virtue: Public school leadership in America, 1820–1980*. New York: Basic.

Tyack, D. & James, T. (1986). State government and American public education: Exploring the "primeval forest". *History of Education Quarterly*, *26*(1), 39–69.

U.S. Department of Education, National Center for Education Statistics, Common Core of Data (CCD) (2012). *Local Education Agency Universe Survey, 2010–11, provisional version 2a*. Washington, DC: Author. Retrieved from: http://nces.ed.gov/pubs2012/pesagencies10/tables/table_01.asp

Wirt, F. M. & Kirst, M. W. (1992). *Schools in conflict*. Berkeley, CA; McCutchan.

Ylimaki, R. & Jacobson, S. (2013). School leadership practice and preparation: Comparative perspectives on organizational learning (OL), instructional leadership (IL) and culturally responsive practices (CRP). *Journal of Educational Administration*, *51*(1), 6–23.

Zirkel, P. (1997). The "explosion" in education litigation: An update. *West's Education Law Reporter*, *114*(2), 341–351.

CHAPTER 2

School Micropolitics for Improving Teaching and Learning

Brenda R. Beatty

CHAPTER OVERVIEW

Micropolitics and the inextricably related phenomenon of emotions have become important points to acknowledge and discuss openly in school leadership. The current conditions within which educational leaders must do their work, place them in an emotional vortex of perfunctory, and in many cases unreasonable, policy demands at the same time that the very nature of human development places high demands on their emotional awareness, competence, and ability to make wise judgments. A powerful area of research on school leadership has identified subjectivities within the micropolitics of educational leadership (Ellis & Flaherty, 1992; Greenfield, 1975) and their emotionally loaded complexities (Hargreaves, 1998; Leithwood & Beatty, 2008; Nias, 1996), and this research illustrates convincingly what goes on in schools. This chapter's case (Pollock & Winton, 2012) depicts decision-making processes that involve power dynamics, policy tensions, and emotional complexities. The likelihood of conflict within and between individuals and various factions across the school system is inherent in this case. The roles of school and district leaders in the teaching and learning relationship reside in contested professional arenas. Instructional leadership is an essential, though indirect, requirement for student success; the mix of appropriate individual leader versus collective professional contributions is sensitive to the micropolitical context of each school and school district (Hallinger, 2003; Leithwood et al., 2002; Leithwood et al., 2008; Louis et al., 2010; Silins, 1994; Silins & Mulford, 2004). Teachers, principals, and superintendents may engage in symbolic rituals and negotiated bargains that can support student learning, or fail to do so (Ball, 2003; Beatty, 2007a; Blase, 2006). A deeper understanding of the inner workings of micropolitics ". . . sometimes understood as the study of how things really work, not how an organizational chart or a principal's action plan would like them to work" (Flessa, 2009, p. 331) can be helpful to leaders. This is particularly true if, as a point of departure in problem solving, they appreciate the challenges complexities and opportunities that manifest individually, relationally, and collectively (Leithwood & Steinbach, 1995). These understandings and the skill to apply them can help leaders ensure that they advocate for and influence improvement in teaching and learning.

This chapter focuses on two elements of Standard 6 (National Policy Board for Educational Administration, 2007):

B. Act to influence local, district, state, and national decisions affecting student learning.

At both the building and district levels, this aspect of Standard 6 requires leaders to address power and decisions so that they can advocate to promote equitable learning opportunities and student success, and communicate policies and procedures to stakeholders:

C. Assess, analyze, and anticipate emerging trends and initiatives in order to adapt leadership strategies.

Beyond the bureaucratic status quo, advocacy and influence are skills that invite leaders to prepare for an adventure in courage and skill. For instance, proactive leadership is bound to be personally and professionally challenging. What methods can help leaders to engage in meaningful dialogue with teachers, parents, community members, interest groups, as well as policy makers and administrators? Methods that attend to rather than avoid dealing with overt and potential conflicts require an appreciation of micropolitics and the foundational role of emotions in all human endeavors. This chapter features the micro level within and between individuals and groups.

Micropolitics manifest in lived experiences, signaled through our emotions and understood through *emotional meaning making* (e.g., Beatty, 2000a, 2000b, 2002, 2006, 2007a, 2007b, 2009a, 2009b, 2011a). This process of emotional meaning making goes on with or without our conscious participation. By actively and explicitly participating in emotional meaning making leaders can learn to access their own inner processes and recognize with others the things about which they feel most strongly. With preparation for being fully present to others, leaders develop the core strength and serenity to offer increased openness to learning and the creation of new possibilities together. When left unrecognized or denied, emotions remain; they are powerful notwithstanding any degree of acknowledgment or avoidance. Emotions can become the greatest part of the problem or, by working respectfully from holistic acknowledgment of emotions' presence in any dilemma, leaders can forge new neural and relational pathways for solution finding and decision making.

Emotions form the substrate of all human experience. Leaders who foster emotional awareness in themselves and others offer opportunities for collaboration that are otherwise difficult to achieve. Individuals who work from a place of active emotional understanding (Denzin, 1984), can transcend potential complications associated with power and position to form, maintain, and repair relationships. Such emotionally grounded relationships have authentic vitality and powerful transformational potential. Whether sharing school-level decision making with parents and community organizations and agencies (Chapters 3 and 6 in this volume); dealing with tensions over district v. school-level authority (as exemplified in this chapter's case by Pollock and Winton (2012)); or creating coalitions with interest groups or political agency and proactive advocacy on a wider scale (Chapter 7 in this volume), collaborations are essential. Collaboration requires trust and mutual understanding to enable the transcendence of emotional barriers that can be associated with perceptions and realities of power. Perceptions of power evoke emotions associated with a sense of relative safety or danger. Acknowledgment of the omnipresent role of emotion enhances meaningful dialogue.

This chapter helps leaders recognize the emotionally loaded complexities associated with sharing authority and expertise about classroom practices and school policies with others. Such boundary crossings can be threateningly destructive or powerfully generative, depending on how they are undertaken. Successful leadership of teaching and learning requires a recognition that the relationships among people at different positions within the micropolitical hierarchy are emotionally complex. For principals, leading with their own and their teachers' emotions in mind (Leithwood & Beatty, 2008) can make all the difference. For superintendents, leadership that is mindful of their own and their principals' emotions can be just as important.

"All politics is local," proclaimed Tip O'Neill Jr., Speaker of the House for the U.S. Congress from 1977–1986. As all politics manifest locally, local educational issues manifest deep passions, emotionally expressed. As people think, feel, act, and/or refrain from acting based on their perceptions of their own and others' formal and informal power, they weave the micropolitical tapestry of their affiliations, a microsystem that is politically imbued. This has significant implications for leaders. Indeed foundational to success in all of the ISLLC Standards is a deep understanding and appreciation for the role of emotions.

LEARNING ACTIVITY 2.1

Mastery of the interplay between emotional meaning making and micropolitics can foster perceptive decision making, the preparation for which is the overarching learning goal for this chapter. From the ideas presented to this point and your own experience, reflect upon a conflict situation in which you were directly involved where positional power differences and associated emotions played a role.

CASE 2.1: COMPETING PRIORITIES

Wanda Miller, principal of Maple Leaf Elementary School is facing a dilemma: she, the vice principal, and the teachers in her school believe improving students' behavior should be the school's number one priority. Until behavior improves, they argue, substantial academic gains are unlikely. The school district and provincial government, however, demand that the school prioritize increasing students' academic achievement (as indicated by test scores). Which stakeholder group should have the final word? To whom is Wanda accountable? How can Wanda persuade her staff and district officials to accept the other group's position?

Maple Leaf Elementary.Maple Leaf Elementary School is an urban, public, English, Pre-K[1]–8 school with one classroom for developmentally challenged children within the Green Acres District School Board in Ontario, Canada. Green Acres District School Board is one of 72 publicly funded school districts in Ontario. Maple Leaf Elementary School serves approximately 650 students from the surrounding community. Ninety percent of the students are Canadian born. Approximately 10 percent of them are learning English as a second language, and roughly, 5 percent are identified as having special needs. Twenty percent of students live in low-income households. Twenty percent of parents have some university education. The school population is fairly stable: about 85 percent of the students have been enrolled in the school for at least one year.

Like all students in Ontario's public schools, students in Grades 3 and 6 at Maple Leaf write provincial standardized tests in reading, writing, and math. Test scores vary from year to year, but reading and writing scores for both grades are consistently lower than both the school district and provincial averages; the school has also not met the provincial target of 75 percent of all students meeting or exceeding the provincial standards (determined by test scores). To help schools meet this target, Ontario's Ministry of Education has invested substantial financial and human resources into improving student achievement in numeracy and literacy and developing school leaders. Other provincial mandates include character education and an equity and diversity strategy.

The former principal, Mr. Frank Bill, was well liked by teachers and parents, but school test scores remained below the board and provincial targets despite slight improvement during Frank's time as principal. Frank retired and subsequently Ms. Wanda Miller became principal. The school district hoped Wanda would do what was necessary to bring the school's test scores closer to meeting targets.

Wanda's Dilemmas. Wanda transferred to Maple Leaf School almost halfway through an academic school year. She was not totally new to the school; she had worked with school staff and students when she was the literacy coordinator for the district so she thought she understood the school's successes and challenges. However, upon her arrival, Wanda realized that low test scores were not the school's only problem: student behavior was out of control. She recalls that, "There were kids fighting, swearing, spitting, and running through the halls. Teachers and support staff were at their wits' end." Wanda spent the rest of that academic school year assessing the school situation. She spent much time "listening, talking, walking, talking, walking, and listening." Wanda personally felt that the students' behavior was not supporting student learning, and she wanted to change the school's atmosphere in the upcoming academic school year to be one that was orderly and supportive.

Wanda also spent her first six months developing positive relationships because she knew everyone missed Frank's warm, approachable style. She hoped using the new School Effectiveness Framework (SEF) would help bring her closer to the teachers and vice principal as they developed a shared vision for the school. The SEF is a research-based provincial initiative to support school improvement and student success. The SEF functions as an assessment tool to help schools identify areas of strength and areas requiring improvement. All school staff are expected to participate in this annual process, which includes, for example, reviewing recommendations from previous school self-assessment and district reviews; completing an annual school self-assessment for the current school year; reviewing and analyzing all assessment data (student achievement, demographic, and program); selecting, revising, and refining goals and setting targets for student achievement; identifying curriculum expectations and examining indicators for those curriculum expectations; and engaging in ongoing monitoring of the agreed school improvement plan. The framework is not meant to be used as a checklist but rather as support for thoughtful inquiry (Ontario Ministry of Education, 2010).

In June, Wanda held a retreat for teachers and, using the SEF as her starting point, she initiated a discussion with teachers about previous school improvement plans and the school's priorities for the upcoming year as required by the district. She facilitated a prioritizing activity in which areas identified in the SEF were posted on signs on the walls in one of the rooms used for the retreat. Teachers indicated, using stickers, the areas they thought were most in need of deliberate attention. Wanda recalls the moment when she realized others shared her concerns about student behavior: the bulk of teachers' stickers were on character education. The teaching staff also wanted to get the building under control. Further discussions after the activity led the teachers and Wanda to make character development their school goal. Wanda forwarded this information to the school district office and, for the first time since taking the position, looked ahead to the upcoming school year with excitement.

This good feeling did not last long. Within two weeks, Wanda received a call from the district office telling her that character education could not be the school's priority. The school's goal must be an academic goal. She recalls the phone conversation with her local superintendent: "We followed the School Effectiveness Framework! An indicator of student achievement is character education!" Indeed, as part of its focus on student achievement the framework states, "The collaboratively developed character attributes are clearly articulated, modeled, taught, and expected throughout the instructional day." Nevertheless, Wanda was told, the school had to adopt an academic goal.

At the next staff meeting, Wanda broke the news to teachers that they had to come up with a different goal and that it had to be academic. The teachers argued that without changing student behavior, little meaningful learning was going to occur and so it would not really matter what academic goal they chose. Of course, teachers recognized that academic achievement was important, but they felt strongly that improving student behavior should be the first priority. Agreeing with the staff, Wanda presented a compromise to the district office: the school would have two goals—character education and writing. However, character education was the main priority for Wanda and the teachers. Wanda successfully persuaded the central office that without character education and getting the school "under control" no academic goals would be achieved. Central office agreed to the compromise.

Over the summer, Wanda and her vice principal attended workshops to learn about different approaches to character education. They chose an approach to character education that they thought best fit their school environment, and in August, invited a speaker for the teaching staff to see whether they thought it could meet the school's needs. Wanda recognized that she needed group consensus for this initiative to work. Teachers agreed to give the program a try. In discussions with her superintendent, Wanda pointed out how the program aligned with the goals and expectations of the province's character development initiative and how, without improvement in student behavior, test scores would not improve.

To accomplish this, Wanda supported sweeping professional learning for not only teachers but also teaching assistants, administrative support staff, and custodians. To keep the message clear and consistent for the most important group in the school— the students—an assembly was held to introduce the program; the teachers then followed up within their classrooms. The school's code of conduct was revised to align with the character education program and was visible throughout the school.

During the first six weeks of the new school year, everyone within the school needed some time to become familiar and comfortable with the new initiative. But six months into the year, most teachers and parents felt the initiative was successfully improving student behavior. There were fewer suspensions, expulsions, and students visiting the principal's office compared with the previous year. Teachers also felt there were fewer in-class discipline issues so students were spending more time on-task and more learning was occurring.

Aware of the district's expectations of improved test scores, Wanda also made key changes in an effort to strengthen students' writing abilities. She scheduled classes in a way that enabled grade-level teachers to meet during the school day to plan writing lessons, assess students' work together, and visit one another's classrooms. Literacy blocks were created and protected for all grades.

Teachers took turns attending workshops focused on writing instruction and shared new information and ideas with their colleagues. The teachers of English language learners (ELL) worked closely with classroom teachers to ensure alignment between strategies and expectations in the children's home classrooms and the ELL classroom. A literacy night was organized for parents to come to the school to learn how their children were developing their reading and writing skills and how parents could support literacy development at home. Students showcased their writing by publishing books and putting them in the library. As the time neared for the provincial standardized tests, Wanda and the teachers were confident that students would perform well.

The test scores showed otherwise: students at Maple Leaf Elementary performed more poorly on the writing tests than they had in the previous two years. Furthermore, the district average was higher than ever so the gap between Maple Leaf Elementary and the district's scores had widened. Wanda met with her teachers to discuss and try to make sense of the test results. To her surprise, the teachers were not that upset. The Grades 3 and 6 teachers felt that their current students were not as capable as past groups but that overall the kids had made huge gains since the start of the year. "In fact," one sixth-grade teacher suggested, "I think as a whole this year's bunch learned and improved much more than last year's group because they started off so much further behind. The tests don't measure growth." Fifth-grade teachers who had taught these students the previous year concurred, and lower scores on this year's math and reading scores supported their assertions. "Don't worry," said a second-grade teacher, "our kids this year are really strong. The marks will be back up next year." Wanda was unsure how to respond to the teachers' comments. Could they be right? She chose to remain silent for the rest of the meeting until she sorted out her thoughts. She also had to prepare for a parent council meeting later that week.

That Thursday, an hour before the school council meeting, Wanda received a phone call from her superintendent. Wanda could tell by the way he said "We need to talk" that he was upset.

> Wanda, I've just left a meeting with the director, and I've been asked to explain why Maple Leaf Elementary grades slipped in all subjects in both Grades 3 and 6. Now, I think I was accommodating this year with your character ed. stuff, but now it's time to focus. I want to know—specifically—what changes you are going to make to get those scores up. We can discuss your plans next Monday when I come in to do your assessment.

He hung up. In all the excitement of the test scores, Wanda had forgotten she was being evaluated the following week. She put her head on her desk, counted to 100, and headed to the library to meet the school council.

Excerpted from Pollock & Winton, 2012, pp. 11–16. Permission granted

LEARNING ACTIVITY 2.2

Based on your reading of the case consider the following questions:

- What strategies in use are apparent for each of the leaders?
- What understanding and skills have these leaders demonstrated?
- Have these leaders exercised power and if so, in what ways?
- What evidence is there of advocacy to promote equitable learning opportunities and student success?
- How have these leaders communicated polices and procedures to their stakeholders?
- What emotions seem to be evident? For whom?

EXPLORING COMPLEXITIES IN THE CASE

Complexities about power (micropolitics) and relationships permeate this case. These complexities include the following: (a) *intrapersonal power*, (b) *interpersonal power*, (c) *positional power*, and (d) *professional perspectives*.

Intrapersonal power complexities are intense here and emotionally loaded. The principal must manage both the excitement and fears of being a building leader who is new to the school. Beginning principals are likely to worry about long-ranging career implications in conflicts of early years. Understandably, she needs to remain accountable to all stakeholders, including and especially the learners. Wanda, the principal, purposefully used collaborative decision making e.g., empowering and connecting with colleagues, strengthening relationships and fostering trust, providing a vision of self-determination that classically ensures engagement and uptake of new initiatives (Gideon & Erlandson, 2001). This strategy has powerful staff motivation and engagement benefits. The integrity of her commitment to her own leadership style choices is on the line as well. Her intrapersonal work to weigh the values she honors with the values of her superintendent could assist with resolving the tensions between their perspectives.

A gendered micropolitical factor may also be in play here. Blackmore's research (1993, 1996) suggested that the role of principal, with its intensity and complexity, may come to be one that predominantly only women will be prepared to occupy. The superintendent's decision to question and insist on change in the first year of the school's new priority could be among other possibilities, an assertion of his authority. This assertion might be a matter of principle and strategic importance, as well as an issue of ostensibly performing his duties in terms of what Ball (2000) calls performativity.[2] The superintendent determines degrees of conflict by the manner in which he manages the micropolitics of resistance, whether overt or covert. Both of these leaders need a critical pause to reflect (Schön, 1983) on how they have explored their inner power issues and in what way they attend to the interpersonal as well as school- and system-level issues. To address school improvement trends focused on standardized tests, both leaders need to adapt their perspectives to some extent. Consider the shift in perspective both leaders will need to achieve to *address the trends and emerging school issues* in this situation.

Interpersonal power complexities also abound. Given the principal's observations of problematic student behavioral and attitudinal exhibitions in the hallways, the establishment of interpersonally safe and respectful relationships throughout the school should promote all students' equitable learning opportunities. Such a goal might seem unassailable. Consider how these respective leaders have communicated the policies and procedures to their stakeholders. In Wanda's case, the decision to determine the school goals collaboratively has communicated both shared purpose and shared leadership with teachers. Proactive professional culture building builds trust. At the same time, the superintendent is a stakeholder too and the principal needs to build trust with all stakeholders. How might Wanda have communicated with the superintendent in a way that could have averted the present standoff?

Uppermost among all constituencies is the principal's interpersonal and professional responsibility to students and families. Not only does this case reveal potential interpersonal issues between the superintendent and the principal, the principal and staff, but also with the wider community. Hargreaves and Fullan (1998) suggest that building communication and understanding with parents, communities, corporate and other partners is the way to achieve powerful and successful teaching and learning. *Community involvement with the decision to feature character education creates an added complexity that is important to consider here.* Shared leadership is best served by attending to a strongly evidence-informed, decision-making protocol. Consider how a more robust database could have informed the collaborative goal-setting exercise, and assisted Wanda in communicating with the full range of stakeholders in this situation.

Positional power issues emerged immediately in this case and range among these possibilities: *Power Over, Power Through or Power With* (Blase & Anderson, 1995). The principal took a stand by modeling a use of power that favors Power With in contrast to traditionally authoritative styles, Power Over or Power Through. Most staff likely welcomed this approach. From one perspective, empowering teachers is nothing less than what successful principals do (Blase & Blase, 1994, 1997, 2001). While Ball (1987) acknowledged there may be school organizations with little or no conflict, as Townsend's (1990) review of Ball's work noted, such peace was not common: "Is the micropolitics of schools mostly shorthand for teachers living with the anguish of conflict?" (p. 212). Correspondingly, one might ask if expectations are that principals simply live with the anguish of conflict with their superintendents. Hargreaves and Fullan (1998) proposed that, until morale as well as the quality of teachers [and one might add morale and quality of leaders (Beatty, 2006, 2009b)] are considered together, efforts at reform are bound to fail. Staff participation with their principal in the school's decision making process is likely to have given a boost to their morale. Simultaneously it is likely to improve school climate (Dinham, 2000) and foster Wanda's enjoyment of her role. The optimism associated with teacher empowerment connects directly to teachers' trust in the principal (Marks & Printy, 2003; Tschannen-Moran, 2004a, 2004b). Conversely, if the pressure from the superintendent mounts sufficiently to override the collective decision, the principal must anticipate heightened conflict with teachers. Unless Wanda, the principal, finesses communication with teacher stake-holders, their blossoming relationship will falter. Such skilled communication can grow confidence and further commitment, even in the face of disappointment. If Wanda can manage this communication with openness about her own sense of vulnerability, respect for all parties and a genuine non-anxious presence, there is a win-win-win potential in the offing. The balance is delicate as the superintendent's power differential is apparent.

Professional perspectives may be at odds here, also. Roland Barth (2004) refers to matters that go unconsidered in the professional discourse as the undiscussables. Deeply held ideologies may seem too sensitive to explore, but they cast shadows over all interactions and decision processes. The elephant-in-the-room phenomenon is a good metaphor for the reason leaders need to learn how to apply lessons from micropolitics. With the undiscussables moved from subtext to text, people can get on with the task of truly collaborating.

Another form of undiscussables is found in a term coined by Marshall and Mitchell (1991), *assumptive worlds*. Was Wanda inculcated in a traditional initiation in roles of assistant principal or as a district staff member to keep her head down and make as few waves as possible (Marshall & Mitchell, 1991)? These researchers found that the common career path for school leaders moving through the positions of assistant principalships led to some un-leader-like behavior. Most assistant principals thought they were successful when they suppressed their professional perspectives, ideologies, along with their professional judgments and quietly followed the preferences of their supervising principal. They learned to "work within the assumptive worlds parameters. As a result, assumptive worlds function to constrain initiative and value choices" (Marshall & Mitchell, 1991, p. 410). Assumptive worlds may seem calm, but lose the benefits of conflict. Conflict can generate creative energy. The collaborative approach to conflict is likely to produce many positive results in contrast to aggressive conflict, or the assumptive world's norm of conflict avoidance. Educational leaders who take this view of conflict, while needing to be emotionally and communicatively prepared, are far more likely to promote creative solutions to problems and imaginative approaches to achieving alternative visions of school success. The nature of differing professional perspectives has a lot to do with undiscussables, assumptive worlds, deeply felt ideologies, and conflictual school issues stemming from competing remedies, and fads, for school improvement (Peck & Reitzug, 2012).

Teachers' professional judgment is juxtaposed to demands for school leaders' instructional interventions. Teachers need not be autonomous in their use of pro-fessional judgment, but they may need opportunities for *self-determination*. This expression should be placed in context as collaboratively exploring, inquiring, data gathering, collaborating, and improving. When *self-determination* involves collaborative professional learning, better outcomes are far more likely to occur (Beatty, 2000a). The staff's shared commitment to character education, with its curricular and pedagogical implications, has a chance to promote a culture of care and mutual respect among all members of the school and its community. Under the circumstances, this seems a noble and worthwhile pursuit (e.g., Dean, 2001; Dean et al., 2007; Fullan, 2002a, 2002b; Fullan & Hargreaves, 1998). Teachers need to retain faith in their ability to make a difference in student learning. Dispirited teachers are unlikely to be effective in their classrooms (Leithwood & Beatty, 2008). Teachers' professional judgment, and perspectives, led to the choice of character education as a means to build cohesive and cooperative student–student and student–teacher relationships. The emotions of leading teaching and learning are linked inextricably. "If educational reformers ignore the emotional dimensions of educational change, emotions and feelings will only re-enter the change process by the back door" (Hargreaves, 1997, p. 109). Leaders and teachers need to get beyond contrived collegiality (Beatty, 2011b; Hargreaves & Dawe, 1990), if they are to share in collaboratively creating a way forward that all stakeholders can embrace with conviction.

The superintendent's insistence on attending to academics and accordingly, student test scores, suggests an apparent difference in professional perspectives about how to go about improving student learning.

Over the past 20 years, debates about where to start in school improvement fall between proponents of building from the ground up culturally first, to others who see cultural inertia as only responsive to pressure from the top down (e.g., Evans, 1996). On one side, the school improvement faction argues that culture building is foundational to all change (e.g., Fullan, 2002a; Fullan & Hargreaves, 1998). Meanwhile, *school effectiveness* proponents (e.g., Mortimore, 1993; Teddlie & Reynolds, 2000) have made a strong case for standardized testing and constant comparison. Those who support this latter approach see high-stakes testing as supporting school effectiveness. The emphasis on testing allows schools to establish baseline data and to monitor one kind of evidence of progress. Opponents believe emphasis on test scores has given rise to the use of rankings with unfair comparisons creating humiliating public exposure (Hargreaves, 2004); potential embarrassment has led to various forms of cheating and fraud (Berliner & Biddle, 1995). In Wanda's school, the deterioration of test scores leads her superintendent to view them as evidence of a bad decision, but it may be an implementation dip (Fullan, 2002b; Fullan & Miles, 1992).

The principal and her colleagues may have been prepared for such a dip while remaining committed to attend to cultural conditions first. So how might all stakeholders meaningfully consider such issues? With feelings running high, it is important to acknowledge emotions and the range of perspectives driving these feelings. Next, those involved must explain theories and assumptions they hold dear. Discussions of ideologies are surprisingly rare during professional interactions in schools, despite the omnipresence of their influence (Everhart, 1991). That said, ideologies need not remain unconsidered and undeclared. With a view to making our theories and ideologies text rather than subtext in school leadership, Robinson

(2010) advocated their explicit articulation in her model of *open-to-learning conversations*. In such conversations, the *open-to-learning* modeling leader declares an ideological position as a descriptor of her/his point of departure. Robinson argued that such declarations help to establish the professionalism of the conversation and can serve to promote greater openness to a range of perspectives. Her approach elevates the conversation above the rough terrain of mistaken impressions, mis-understandings, and faulty assumptions about colleagues' reasons for the things they do and say, and the ways they teach and lead. The first step must recognize emotions, else, unacknowledged feelings can drive the discussion into disaster or silence and retreat. When leaders remember to consider *feelings first* and declare their own sense of vulnerability, they can expect to surface and then calmly consider overt issues while effectively addressing some covert matters as well. Leadership decisions reflect the normative culture of control. Getting to know and appreciate styles and prefer-ences, and even the ideologies of the individuals we work with, can be helpful in establishing the foundation for collaboration. Sameness is not a prerequisite, *but understanding is*. In open-to-learning conversations, admissions of feelings and declarations about professional assumptions represent the starting point for collaborative professional learning (Robinson, 2010). According to Fisher and Uri (1991), grounded concepts of acknowledging and working through the emotions and the appreciation of interests can lead to win-win solutions when negotiating contested terrain. The goal is to find and build upon the common ground of mutual understanding, from which informed professional choices can be made.

Some school reform theorists suggest that it is not a matter of either focusing on academic learning or building a constructive learning culture. Hallinger and Heck (2010; 2011) provided empirical evidence of the synergistic merits of multi-level richly interconnected collaborative leadership. Sammons and colleagues (1995) have argued persuasively that culturally conducive conditions are indeed necessary, but *not sufficient* for improved learning. Evans (1996) recommended deliberately destabilizing the status quo to create a sense of urgency. In this case, these leaders' perspectives upon the human side of school change will be influential here. There may be a great deal of common ground between these two leaders, if they can discover it together.

Instructional leadership that can influence teachers to refine their practices depends simultaneously on mutual respect and trust (Tschannen-Moran, 2009). But trust is not enough. There needs to be focus and genuine inquiry in such professional exchanges. Recent international studies have shown demonstrable impact, effect sizes, across a range of instructional practices (Hattie, 2009). Hattie called for an emphasis on *Visible Learning* e.g., from his meta-analysis of meta-analyses he found that the use of timely and appropriately focused feedback yielded an impressive effect size. Hattie encouraged teachers and leaders to meas-ure their practices' observable impacts upon student learning. To address these serious issues with each other, teachers and leaders need to establish the custom of having professionally meaningful conversations as a regular part of their daily routines.

DECIDING HOW TO DECIDE

This case foreshadows further conflict between the principal and her superintendent. Self-awareness is critical for leaders. Support systems abound to assist principals in achieving deeper self and other awareness. Most conflict derives from assumptions and misunderstandings. While conflict is inevitable, negative outcomes are not. Careful management of communication, power, and emotions can lead to better results.

Standing your ground. What are the outcomes for a self-empowered leader? That is, what happens if Wanda decides to stand on principle by resisting the superintendent's power to override her work? Such a position fits the category of reaction rather than that of *considered response*. The mindful leader (Carroll, 2007) acknowledges feelings to remain fully present to both self and situation as well as to choose how best to respond. One consideration is the superintendent's likely reaction to her immovable stance. What could planting her feet suggest about her leadership capabilities within the complexities of the entire system, including the need to acknowledge, listen to, and collaborate with her superiors? These impressions lead to inferences about her suitability for other positions. Wanda may be able to engage creatively in communication with her superintendent, and still be able to retain her position on the matter. Should the two leaders' positions remain fixed, and resolution remains out of reach, there are benefits to having a facilitated discussion. This can be cost effective, quick, and impartial, promoting self-determination of both parties, especially with the use of transformative mediation practices (Busch & Folger, 2005). The skilful transformative mediator knows how to assist the parties in restoring their sense of empowerment so that they can re-engage in the process of mutually satisfactory self-determination (Fenton, 2010).

LEARNING ACTIVITY 2.3

- If the superintendent pulls rank, what opportunities could be lost if Wanda simply acquiesces to the superintendent's wishes instead of promoting the collaborative consideration of the complexities in this case?
- How might Wanda use emotional meaning making and declaration of her own sense of vulnerability to promote a mutual understanding ethic between them?

Recognizing the presence of emotions. Their own thoughts and feelings inevitably influence both the principal and her superintendent, likely interacting in reinforcing spirals. For example, if the superintendent fears that the school's performance on the standardized tests may continue to slip, he also may fear for his own reputation and career. The superintendent may fear that the principal will not cooperate thus undermining his authority, which may be associated with fear that he is not respected, and perhaps even insecurity about his position. The principal may react to lowering test scores with shame about her school's performance, anticipation of her evaluation, and perceptions of disrespect for her perspectives as well as fear of becoming disempowered and overruled by the superintendent. Such feelings of loss can trigger shame. As Scheff and Retzinger (2000) have argued, shame is a master emotion, capable of disabling our attention to other priorities, as we do not tolerate shame. Instead, we transform shame and anticipated shame into fear, anger and blame. Shame leads to anticipated separation from peers. Importantly, at a primal level, anticipated separation can feel like annihilation or impending death. For these emotional reasons, the anticipated interaction between Wanda and her superintendent may evoke deep feelings of anticipated shame and fear that can in turn, compromise her ability to stay engaged and *reflect in action* as she interacts with the superintendent. Thinking and feeling are inseparable; they influence each other. The flood of fear can evoke a neurological response within the brain that can disable one's openness to receiving further information, one's ability to listen deeply, and one's readiness to understand and recognize the merits in another's perspectives. To accomplish what is called a recognition shift in transformative dispute resolution parlance (Busch & Folger, 2005; Fenton, 2010) both parties must feel empowered, which occurs when they experience the feeling of being heard, understood, appreciated and in effect known (Beatty, 2002, 2011a). Each can assist the other in experiencing empowerment, which creates the sense of safety that opens the door to receiving information and assimilating new understandings. This openness can lead to the recognition shift referred to by Busch and Folger (2005). However, these recognition shifts result only with sufficiently mutually empowering communication. Preparation for these moments would wisely include reflective practice and even training in transformative communication (Fenton, personal communication, February 1, 2013).

Overcoming isolation. Classically, educational leaders such as principals and often superintendents remain isolated with the burdens of their concerns and inevitable anxieties, regularly suffering in silence (Beatty, 2002, 2009b). Emotional labor is a term that describes the effort or paid work of professionally suppressing authentic emotions and, instead, simultaneously acting out completely different feelings (Hochschild, 1983). Educators are no strangers to emotional labor. Teachers often project enthusiasm to inspire learning and engagement even when this zeal is hard to muster. Indeed teachers report this as a satisfying aspect of their work. School leaders face fragmented interactions requiring many different emotional frames when for instance, they could be moving from happy students to angry defiant ones who often have equally oppositional parents and then have to face a range of other moment-to-moment interactions with colleagues. They often have to suppress their own emotions and ignore their own needs in order to take care of the next person's cares and concerns. Emotional numbness associated with continuous emotional labor can result in a divided or even disintegrated sense of, self (Beatty, 2002). As Margolis (1998) warned, access to one's emotions is essential if we are to retain our connection with the fabric of the self that is our ethical and moral center.

School leaders need to use emotional meaning making, both alone and in collaborative reflection with others, to ensure that they remain integrated and highly functioning (Beatty, 2002; 2006; 2011a). It is through the connections between the emotional self and the emotional other that deepened capabilities for emotional meaning making or emotional ways of knowing are developed. With reflection in the presence of supportive critical friends, the achievement of a genuinely non-anxious presence (Friedman, 1985) comes within reach. Ideally, Wanda will have a well-established support system. If not, she needs to get one.

It is highly recommended that educational leaders receive coaching and mentorship on a regular basis in a strictly confidential relationship, ideally with a person outside of their immediate professional network. Social workers and psychologists call this supervision. The lack of such support for leaders remains the norm in education and this presents a problem that compromises leaders and their work. Lacking an official coach or mentor, Wanda would be wise to gain access to an ad hoc trustworthy buddy in order to work through this and any other professionally challenging situation in a mindful and constructive way.

Despite a crushing work ethic and the best of intentions, leaders are regularly wounded in the line of duty. This is just as true in education as elsewhere. The research of Ackerman and Maslin-Ostrowski (2002) offered invaluable evidence of the healing power of revisiting, storying, and restorying the wounding experience. With support in place at the outset, the chances of a full recovery from a wounding experience are greatly increased. Importantly, these authors analyzed the stories of hundreds of school principals, revealing a range of responses to inevitable woundings, responses that correlate with the quality of support available at the time, and even after the fact in the process of participating in the research itself. The generative power of storying and restorying can hardly be overstated.

LEARNING ACTIVITY 2.4

- Create a conversation between the superintendent and his confidante/mentor as well as between the principal and hers. What inner meaning making issues might emerge if they took that reflective opportunity with meaningful support prior to meeting with each other?
- Consider the principal's options about addressing staff with the dilemma presented to her by the superintendent. What collaborative problem solving might they undertake to prepare for resolving the situation together?
- Create some sample conversations that might occur among groups of staff as they work in small groups to consider the situation.

THE EMOTIONS OF LEADING TEACHING AND LEARNING

Sooner or later, Wanda and her teachers are going to be delving into the process of improving *academic* instructional practice in their school. Those test scores need to improve and this aspect of leadership in teaching and learning will inevitably involve boundary crossings and the development of new ways of working together. They must transcend political and micropolitical wranglings and their associated feelings to ensure professional progress and academic success.

In schools, as elsewhere, things *political* are emotionally charged. Many of the adults in the building have chosen to spend their days with society's children, which requires a certain devotion. While their purposes are many, including academic learning, schools are where people learn, or do not learn, to get along. Some schools are exciting, happy places, where children and adults feel respected, energized, and loved. Schools can be filled with familiar faces and daily routines that offer opportunities for purpose and satisfaction. They can provide a safe haven from the dangers of an outside world. But schools can also be places of deadening tedium, confusion, humiliation, and even terror and what happens at school comes home. At the end of the day, students, teachers, and leaders take school home with them. They study, they mark, they prepare, they share their stories of woe and joy and they worry, agonizing over failures, frustrations, and fears. For students, teachers, and leaders the world of home and the world of school are mentally and emotionally inseparable.

In recent years, schools have become more pressured places, where test scores claim to measure the entirety of schooling. Studies of some of the effects of such testing report a growing collection of disturbing findings. Since Berliner and Biddle's (1995) discoveries of American educators cheating to boost school scores, the media has reported major examples in Houston and Atlanta, which are only media-sensationalized incidents due to their large scale. Hargreaves' (2004) study of the emotional politics of public displays of school failure showed the exacerbated effects of distinction for the privileged and disgust for the less fortunate. McGuire (2013) explored some of the deleterious impacts on Australian principals from publishing the results of their whole school's performance on high-stakes tests on the national MYSCHOOL website. A court case examining the effects of testing pressures on teachers linked the United Kingdom's school review process to serious health issues and even deaths among teachers (Jeffrey & Woods, 1996, p. 325).

As Hargreaves (1997) has warned, emotions are bound to be a part of educational reform. Whether we try to ignore them or not, emotions are likely to run high when professional territories, job descriptions, assessment policies, and professional affiliations are suddenly and irretrievably changed. In such a politically charged environment it is an emotional challenge to teach and to lead.

Many of the changes that have occurred in schools over recent years have been emotionally demanding. The principal finds her/himself in the middle, pushing for and striving to accomplish performativities[2] (Ball, 1987, 2000, 2003) for a variety of stakeholders who have powerful voices openly critiquing teachers, leaders, and schools. People in schools are expected to practice self and impression management for a larger number of audiences, leading to emotional labor (Hochschild, 1983), which takes its toll.

Policy changes have impacted job descriptions and increased the demands on educators at all levels. For instance, changing to more prescriptive, skills-based curriculum has limited teacher autonomy and creative freedoms, requiring them to focus primarily on preparing students for standardized tests. Changes in funding formulas and limitations on services for children with special learning problems have created the need for retraining so that teachers can provide adequately for a more diverse student population. Policies that involve parents in decision making require leaders to develop new partnerships with parents, with whom they must work more closely than ever before (Sarason, 1995). Feelings of inadequacy and fear of failure can be associated with these changes. Having one's work critiqued and learning to communicate in new ways are emotionally charged endeavors (Southworth, 1998).

One of the ways that such pressures can be managed is in a more collaborative school culture, by sharing the load of responsibility and conferring on best practices. Educational research and theory has advocated for collaborative school cultures (e.g., Anderson & Cox, 1987; Nias, 1989; Nias et al., 1989), shared leadership (Blase & Blase, 1997) and empowered teachers (Blase & Anderson, 1995) for some time. Accomplishing shifts in culture and leadership style and increasing teacher empowerment at the same time as teachers' work becomes more de-professionalized involves conflicting professional identities. Learning to integrate these changes in self-perception presents further emotional challenges. Each shift involves changes in attitude that require the acknowledgment of the value of personal knowledge (e.g., Aitken & Mildon, 1992). In times of reform some of the most influential personal knowledge is emotional.

While the current changes in education can be distressing, the promise of empowerment can be exciting and energizing. As teacher development becomes even more critical, the call for teachers' voices to be heard in directing their own learning (Goodson, 1992) and the emphasis on professional reflection (Grimmett & Crehan, 1992) argues for validating authentic professional selves. Calls for increased emphasis on instructional leadership and clinical supervision (Glickman et al., 1998; Huberman, 1988; Joyce & Showers, 1988) draw attention to the relationship between teachers and leaders and their combined efforts to improve learning for students. In the educational leadership literature, "leaders have to become learners themselves" (Gronn, 1999, p. viii).

Yet creating learning communities demands sharing in new ways, altering relationships and views of the professional self and other. Developing new kinds of relationships is emotional territory, for both leaders and teachers. Changing perceptions, from former autonomy and hierarchical distance to interacting as interdependent professional peers with shared purpose, involves paradigm shifts that are both intellectual and emotional.

Mapping the emotional terrain of schools. Issues of territory, autonomy, responsibility, and participation in school decision making shape and reshape the emotional terrain of schools. The emotional terrain of organizations can be viewed as specialized emotional arenas (Hearn, 1996), or zones of influence (Lortie, 1975), emotional geographies (Hargreaves, 2000b) that provide kinds of emotional mappings, and as professional knowledge landscapes (Connelly & Clandinin, 1995a) with emotional implications. Schools are places of complex, interconnected, intrapersonal, and interpersonal emotional terrain.

Some organizations demand particular professional emotions: "specialist organizations are structured around the organization of the emotions . . . as when bereavement or loss is managed in medical organizations" (Hearn, 1996, p. 160). Schools also require emotional specialization. However, rather than one set of professional emotions that pervades the entire organization, such as a funeral parlour or a soda shop, teachers and leaders must organize their emotions for different audiences, with different sets of expectations of them. There are unpredictable contextual factors that vary constantly. For example, an administrator may be sitting with a bereaved parent one moment, and celebrating with a newly promoted colleague the next. A teacher may demonstrate enthusiasm for a new curriculum imperative with a leader or a parent and, later the same day, participate in professional critique of the same topic with teacher colleagues. Tailoring emotional responses for such varieties of encounters is distinctive from the specialist emotional arena described by Hearn (1996).

Teachers and leaders have traditionally occupied distinct zones of influence (Lortie, 1975) such that they have tended to stay out of each other's territory to a great extent. Indeed classrooms have been characterized as private places where teachers have enjoyed autonomy and creative freedoms but also isolation and loneliness (Lieberman & Miller, 1984). However, recent reform measures have called for boundary crossings. Leaders are now required to be more aware of and actively involved in what happens in their teachers' classrooms. Teachers can experience this as an invasion of territory, creating new tensions. Leaders too, who have been unaccustomed to take direct responsibility for teachers' performance, are experiencing added pressures from published high-stakes test scores and school comparison data. Today, interactions between teachers and leaders are more essential than ever before, though perhaps not any less emotionally demanding.

The notion of patterns of emotional management as articulated by Hargreaves (2000b) represents a collection of emotional geographies from studies of teachers' recalled emotional experiences with colleagues, parents, and students. Hargreaves' emotional geographies framework considers emotional distance and closeness among people in schools embedded in culture, moral purpose, professional norms and roles, political power and status, and physical proximity or separation. Hargreaves argued that not only excessive distance but also closeness can be problematic to optimal professional practice. For instance emotional closeness of friendship can overshadow professional concerns, leaving them unaddressed, while excessive distance can undermine the development of relationships. Hargreaves' framework illustrates some of the stress points that engender emotional tensions and alliances.

Shared moral purpose can relieve tensions and create bonds; however, undiscussables in the form of excessive professional distance, even in the presence of physical closeness, can suppress any negotiation of shared purpose. As seen in the chapter's case, Hargreaves's emotional framework may uncover some *assumptive worlds*.

Teachers' emotional challenges can also be seen as epistemological; that is, differences in professional perspectives and moral purposes. Clandinin and Hogan (1995, p. 37) argued that moral and epistemological dilemmas are inherent in teachers' professional knowledge. They studied discursive differences between teachers' views of their encounters inside and outside of their classrooms. Such interactions generated emotional responses that in their own right became an important dimension noting an "uneasy state of teachers' professional lives" (Clandinin & Hogan, 1995, p. 37). They suggested this tension had "arisen from circumstances, practices, and undergoings that themselves had affective content for the person in question" (Clandinin & Hogan, 1995, p. 37). They distinguished between teachers' internal professional authority within their classrooms and a contrasting sense of their subordinated knowledge outside of their classrooms, an area dominated by external authorities rather than their own. Connelly and Clandinin (1995b) argued that this tension demands different stories for the various knowledge landscapes. *Sacred stories* give prominence and respect to current priorities in policy and practice. *Cover stories*, similar to the notion of performativity, focus on suitable acquiescence to the current sacred policies. *Secret stories* are the private and unshared realities of their classroom practices. Consequently, the dissonance among these different *stories* creates *emotional labor* as teachers act and enact differently across school and knowledge landscapes.

The intrasubjective and intersubjective emotional terrain of schools engages complex emotional processes. Mapping this terrain by appreciating its arenas, zones, domains, territories, geographies, and landscapes can provide complementary schemas to assist in discerning important and interrelated social, political, moral, intellectual, and emotional patterns (Day & Lee, 2011).

Leaders and Emotions. Leaders who want a different working world for themselves and their colleagues need to summon the courage first to break the silence (Beatty, 2000b, 2009b), assume responsibility for surfacing emotions and conflict, and acknowledge their own vulnerability. These steps can create safe spaces for others. What are the factors associated with leaders' emotional preparedness for an integrative approach to sustainable teaching, learning leading and living well in today's schools?

Leaders are the sum of their experiences, which is important because ". . . leaders' overt practices are continuously mediated by their inner lives—their thoughts, feelings, values and dispositions. These internal states act as interpretive fields for leaders as they do for all people" (Leithwood & Beatty, 2008, p. 126).

In Beatty's (2002, 2007a, 2007b, 2009b) research with 25 principals from England, Ireland, Canada, the U.S., Australia, and New Zealand, principals met online for seven months to explore the emotions of their work. Policy pressures emerged quickly as a source of consternation.

> When the LEA (Local Educational Authority) changes its policy to do with special needs . . . leaving me to face parents whose expectations are dashed and leave them nowhere to turn, they focus their anger and frustration on me. I feel as if I have won the lottery but can't have any of the money. This feeling of powerlessness was most acute in my early years as a Headteacher.[3] In the first term, I often wondered why I had taken up the post . . . Having the responsibility without ultimate power can be deadening.
>
> (UK Headteacher)

Perpetual emotional labor causes emotional numbness (Hochschild, 1983). The above quote notes how the leader's self is divided in having to manufacture the emotional strength to embrace her mandated responsibility and mask her own very real frustrations and disapproval of the policy as she *manages* parents' anger. To avoid numbness associated with ongoing emotional labor, the opportunity to reflect with a group of trusted colleagues emerged as invaluable and even transformational. These online reflections yielded stories of joys and sorrows, angers and fears as these principals began to reclaim their whole selves.

> It's all about feeling known.
>
> (UK Headteacher)

> At the beginning, I found it difficult to find time; now it's a "treat" to get online. The conversations have made me reflect so much more, consider my approaches, applaud my colleagues online, wherever they are . . . I've mentioned this forum . . . and the majority response has been "how do you find the time?" Now I know I need to find the time.
>
> (Another UK Headteacher)

Principals can come to identify strongly with their schools. As David Loader (1997) shared in his reflective narrative, principals' identities may be completely entangled with their schools. "My personal failure was that I had no sense of myself as separate from the institution (Loader, 1997, p. 147).

The passion of purpose among online principals was palpable. Work can be a joy, and accordingly bonds are strong. Understandably, workaholism was often not far behind, but for many principals, clearly, their role is a labor of love.

> I would have died for that school! . . . I truly enjoy my work. I cannot think of any other job I'd rather do . . . there is no greater pleasure than seeing a teacher succeed.

Reflecting about their online discussions, the principals realized that they were now feeling differently about their work, and making changes in their leadership practices. Participation in this collaborative reflection and emotional meaning making had had transformational effects.

The "emotions of leadership" has played an important part in my consciousness . . . Just knowing how angry, upset, happy etc., other people get has allowed me to feel OK about the way I feel. I guess the privilege of being part of the conversations has been to legitimize MY feelings, and go with them, rather than try to block them out.

Graduate programs designed to foster emotional preparedness to lead have yielded encouraging results (Beatty, 2006). A graduate reflected upon the surprising outcome of participating in one such two-year, part-time school leadership Master's degree.

You can give lip service to emotions but until you're forced into reflecting and working with people in that way, you don't actually change. And that's what's happened for me over the last two years is that [with emphasis and deep conviction] I've changed!

In further studies, a graduate who had since become a principal and considered himself "not very emotional" reflected on the impact of emotional meaning making on his leadership practice.

A good technical leader without the relationships would be more likely the efficient tyrant, rather than someone who is able to get the best out of their people—because people want to do their best . . . The whole feel of the school is based on relationships. I can't imagine where I'd be in five years from now without the whole development of relationships through emotions.

Another graduate who had since become an assistant principal commented on the courage required and the remarkable rewards from leading and learning through emotional meaning making.

I've—finally, finally, finally—moved into my own as a leader. I've found my own place in terms of how to deal with things. And I've found a place that I'm satisfied with. I've found a place that is a fit for me and is reflective of me. It's not reflective of my mentor and who he is. It's not my previous assistant principal. It's not reflective of anyone. It's who I am! There's a lot of personal pride and joy in that. I'm quite proud of myself, that I actually had the guts.

It takes tremendous courage to lead from a place of authentic emotional attunement to self and others even in the midst of the macro- and micropolitical complexities facing today's school leaders. However, the returns are impressive. Such leaders, many of whom I have had the privilege of working with and learning from over the years, tell me that with experience and practice at leading in this way, their work has become even more satisfying and far more successful.

NOTES

1   Pre-K is short for Pre-Kindergarten, and includes programs for young children and may be referred to as early childhood education or preschool in other jurisdictions
2   Performativity is a concept developed in the context of education by Ball (2000, 2003). The political pressure to seem to be performing absorbs significant time and effort depleting the resources available to be doing the job itself. Teaching-to-the-test can be considered a function of performativity
3   In England and Ireland, principals are referred to as *headteachers*.

REFERENCES

Ackerman, R. & Maslin-Ostrowski, P. (2002). *The wounded leader: How real leadership emerges in times of crisis*. San Francisco, CA: Jossey-Bass.

Aitken, J. L. & Mildon, D. (1992). Teacher education and the developing teacher: The role of personal knowledge. In M. G. Fullan & A. Hargreaves (Eds.), *Teacher development and educational change*. London: Falmer Press.

Anderson, B. & Cox, P. (1987). *Configuring the education system for a shared future: Collaborative vision, action, reflection*. Andover, MA: Regional Laboratory for Educational Improvement of the Northeast and the Islands.

Ball, S. (1987). *The micro-politics of the school*. New York: Methuen.

Ball, S. (2000). Performativities and fabrications in the education economy: Towards the performative society. *Australian Educational Researcher*, *27*(2), 1–25.

Ball, S. (2003). The teacher's soul and the terrors of performativity. *Journal of Educational Policy*, *18*(2), 215–228.

Barth, R. (2004). *Learning by heart*. San Francisco, CA: Jossey-Bass.

Beatty, B. (2000a). Teachers leading their own professional growth: Self-directed reflection and collaboration and changes in perception of self and work in secondary school teachers. *Journal of In-Service Education*, *26*(1), 73–97.

Beatty, B. (2000b). The emotions of educational leadership: Breaking the silence. *International Journal of Leadership in Education*, *3*(4), 331–358.

Beatty, B. (2002). *Emotion matters in educational leadership: Examining the unexamined*. Unpublished doctoral dissertation, Ontario Institute for Studies in Education University of Toronto.

Beatty, B. (2006). Becoming emotionally prepared for leadership: Courage counter-intuition and commitment to connectedness. *International Journal of Knowledge Culture and Change*, *6*(5), 51–66.

Beatty, B. (2007a). Feeling the future of school leadership: Learning to lead with the emotions in mind. *Leading and Managing*, *13*(2), 44–65.

Beatty, B. (2007b). Going through the emotions: Leadership that gets to the heart of school renewal. *Australian Journal of Education*, *51*(3), 328–340.

Beatty, B. (2009a). Toward an emotional understanding of school success: Connecting collaborative culture building, principal succession and inner leadership. In N. Cranston & L. Ehrich (Eds.), *Australian educational leadership today: Issues and trends* (pp. 187–215). Samford Valley, Australia: Australian Academic Press.

Beatty, B. (2009b). Developing school administrators who can lead with the emotions in mind: Making the commitment to connectedness. In Thomas Ryan (Ed.), *Canadian educational leadership* (pp.149–183). Calgary, Canada: Detselig Enterprises.

Beatty, B. (2011a). Leadership and teacher emotions. In C. Day & J. C. Lee (Eds.), *New understandings of teacher's work: Emotions and educational change* (pp. 217–242). London: Springer.

Beatty, B. (2011b). From crayons to perfume. Getting beyond contrived collegiality. *Journal of Educational Change, 12*(2), 257–266.

Berliner, D. & Biddle, B. (1995). *The manufactured crisis: Myths, fraud and the attack on America's public school system*. New York: Perseus Books Harper Collins.

Blackmore, J. (1993). In the shadow of men: The historical construction of administration as a "masculinist" enterprise. In J. Blackmore & J. Kenway (Eds.), *Gender matters in educational administration and policy: A feminist introduction* (pp. 27–48). London: Falmer Press.

Blackmore, J. (1996). Doing "emotional labour" in the education market place: Stories from the field of women in management. *Discourse: Studies in the Cultural Politics of Education, 17*(3), 337–349.

Blase, J. (2006). *Teachers bringing out the best in teachers: A guide to peer consultation for administrators and teachers*. Thousand Oaks, CA: Sage Publications.

Blase, J. & Anderson, G. (1995). *The micropolitics of educational leadership*. New York: Cassell.

Blase, J. & Blase, J. (1994). *Empowering teachers*. Thousand Oaks, CA: Corwin Press.

Blase, J. & Blase, J. (1997). *The fire is back! Principals sharing governance*. Thousand Oaks, CA: Sage Publications.

Blase, J. & Blase, J. (2001). *Empowering teachers: What successful principals do*. Thousand Oaks, CA: Corwin Press.

Busch, B. & Folger, J. P. (2005). *The promise of mediation: The transformative approach to mediation*. San Francisco, CA: Jossey-Bass.

Carroll, M. (2007). *The mindful leader*. Boston: Trumpeter Books.

Clandinin, D. J. & Hogan, P. (1995). Shifting moral landscapes. In F. M. Connelly & D. J. Clandinin (Eds.), *Teachers' professional knowledge landscapes*. New York: Teachers College.

Connelly, F. M. & Clandinin, D. J. (1995a). Educational qualities of the landscape: Desires, tensions and possibilities. In F. M. Connelly & D. J. Clandinin (Eds.), *Teachers' professional knowledge landscapes* (pp. 153–163). New York: Teachers College.

Connelly F. M. & Clandinin, D. J. (1995b). Teachers' professional knowledge: Secret, sacred, and cover stories. In F. M. Connelly & D. J. Clandinin (Eds.), *Teachers' professional knowledge landscapes* (pp. 1–15). New York: Teachers College.

Day, C. & Lee, J. C. (Eds.), (2011). *New understandings of teachers work*, Professional Development in Schools and Higher Education Series. London: Springer.

Dean, S. (2001). *Hearts & minds: A public school miracle*. Toronto: Penguin Press.

Dean, S., Beatty, B., & Brew, C. (2007). Creating safe and caring learning communities: Understanding school based development of social capital. In L. Smith & D. Riley (Eds.), *ACEL yearbook, 2007: Blooming leadership* (pp. 25–50). Armidale: Australian Council for Educational Leaders.

Denzin, N. (1984). *On understanding emotion*. San Francisco, CA: Jossey-Bass.

Dinham, S. (2000). Teacher satisfaction, leadership, and school climate: universal challenges. In A. R. Thomas (Ed.), *Challenges of the principalship* (pp. 34–45). Point Lonsdale (Vic): The Professional Reading Guide.

Ellis, C. & Flaherty, M. (Eds.), (1992). *Investigating subjectivity*. Newbury Park, CA: Sage Publications.

Evans, R. (1996). *The human side of school change*. San Francisco, CA: Jossey-Bass.

Everhart, R. (1991). Unraveling micropolitical mystiques: Some methodological opportunities. *Education and Urban Society, 23*(4), August, 455–464.

Fenton, S. L. (2010). *High conflict behaviors and transformative mediation*. Unpublished doctoral dissertation, LaTrobe University, Bundoora, Victoria, Australia.

Fisher, R. & Uri, W. (1991). *Getting to yes. Negotiating agreement without giving in*. New York: Penguin Books.

Flessa, J. (2009). Educational micropolitics and distributed leadership. *Peabody Journal of Education, 84*: 331–349

Friedman, E. H. (1985). *Generation to generation*. New York: The Guilford Press.

Fullan, M. (2002a). Educational reform as continuous improvement. In W. D. Hawley & D. L. Rollie (Eds.), *The keys to effective schools. Educational reform as continuous improvement* (pp. 1–9). National Education Association. Thousand Oaks, CA: Corwin Press.

Fullan, M. (2002b). The change leader. *Educational Leadership*, The Association for Supervision and Curriculum Development. May 2002. http://pil.numplus.com/SchoolLeadership/04-fullan/Articles/2002/05_02.pdf

Fullan, M. & Miles, M. (1992). Getting reform right: What works and what doesn't. *Phi Delta Kappan, 73*, 745–752.

Fullan, M. G. & Hargreaves, A. (1998). *What's worth fighting for in your school?* (2nd ed.). New York: Teachers College Press, Columbia University.

Gideon, B. & Erlandson, D. (2001). Here's what happens when a principal says "I want you to come up with the ideas." *Journal of Staff Development, 22*(4), 14–17.

Glickman, C., Gordon, S., & Ross-Gordon, J. (1998). *Supervision of instruction: A developmental approach*. Needham Heights, MA: Allyn & Bacon.

Goodson, I. (1992). Sponsoring the teacher's voice: Teachers lives and teacher development. In A. Hargreaves & M. G. Fullan (Eds.), *Understanding teacher development* (pp. 110–121). London: Cassell.

Greenfield, T. B. (1975). Theory about organizations: A new perspective and its implications for schools. In M. Hughes (Ed.), *Administering education: International challenges* (pp. 71–99). London: The Athlone Press.

Grimmett, P. & Crehan, E. (1992). The nature of collegiality in teacher development: The case of clinical supervision. In M. G. Fullan & A. Hargreaves (Eds.), *Teacher development and educational change*. London: Falmer Press.

Gronn, P. (1999). *The making of educational leaders*. London: Cassell.

Hallinger, P. (2003). Leading educational change: reflections on the practice of instructional and transformational leadership. *Cambridge Journal of Education, 33*(3), 329–351.

Hallinger, P. & Heck, R. H., (2010). Leadership for learning: Does collaborative leadership make a difference? *Educational Management Administration and Leadership, 38*(6), 654–678.

Hallinger, P. & Heck, R. (2011). Collaborative leadership and school improvement: Understanding the impact on school capacity and student learning. In *International handbook of leadership for learning* (pp. 469–485). London: Springer.

Hargreaves, A. (Ed.). (1997). *ASCD Yearbook. Rethinking educational change with heart and mind*. Alexandria, VA: Association for Curriculum and Development.

Hargreaves, A. (1998). The emotional politics of teaching and teacher development: with implications for educational leadership. *International Journal of Leadership in Education: Theory and Practice, 1*(4), 315–336.

Hargreaves, A. (2000a). Mixed emotions: Teachers' perceptions of their interactions with students. *Teaching and Teacher Education, 16*(8), 811–826.

Hargreaves, A. (2000b, April). *Emotional geographies: Teaching in a box*. Paper presented at the annual meeting of the American Educational Research Association, New Orleans, Louisiana.

Hargreaves, A. (2004). Distinction and disgust: the emotional politics of school failure. *International Journal of Leadership in Education: Theory and Practice*, 7(1), 27–41.

Hargreaves, A. & Dawe, R. (1990). Paths of professional development: Contrived collegiality, collaborative culture, and the case of peer coaching. *Teaching and Teacher Education*, 6(3), 227–241.

Hargreaves, A. & Fullan, M. (1998). *What's worth fighting for in education*? Buckingham: Open University Press.

Hattie, J. (2009). *Visible learning*. New York: Routledge.

Hearn, J. (1996). Emotive subjects: Organizational men, organizational masculinities and the (de)construction of 'emotions'. In S. Fineman (Ed.), *Emotion in organizations* (2nd ed.) (pp. 142–166). London: Sage Publications.

Hochschild, A. R. (1983). *The managed heart: The commercialization of human feeling*. Berkeley, CA: University of California Press.

Huberman, M. (1988). Teacher careers and school improvement. *Journal of Curriculum Studies*, 20(2), 119–32.

Jeffrey, B. & Woods, P. (1996). Feeling deprofessionalised: The social construction of emotions during an OFSTED inspection. *Cambridge Journal of Education*, 26(3), 325–343.

Joyce, B. & Showers, B. (1988). *Student achievement through staff development*. Albany, NY: Longman.

Leithwood, K. & Beatty, B. (2008). *Leading with teacher emotions in mind*. Thousand Oaks, CA: Corwin Press.

Leithwood, K. & Steinbach, R. (1995). *Expert problem solving: Evidence from school and district leaders*. Albany, NY: State University of New York Press.

Leithwood, K., Harris, A., & Hopkins, D. (2008). Seven strong claims about successful school. *School Leadership and Management*, 28(1), 27–42.

Leithwood, K., Steinbach, R., & Jantzi, D. (2002). School leadership and teachers' motivation to implement accountability policies. *Educational Administration Quarterly*, 38(1), 94–119.

Lieberman, A. & Miller, L. (1984). *Teachers: Their world and their work*. Alexandria, VA: Association for Supervision and Curriculum Development.

Loader, D. (1997). *The inner principal*. London: Falmer Press.

Lortie, D. C. (1975). *Schoolteacher: A sociological study*. Chicago: University of Chicago Press.

Louis, K. S., Leithwood, K., Wahlstrom, K. L., & Anderson, S. E., (2010). *Learning from leading: Investigating the links to improved student learning*. Center for Applied Research and Educational Improvement/University of Minnesota, Ontario Institute for Studies in Education/University of Toronto.

Margolis, D. R. (1998). *The fabric of self: A theory of ethics and emotions*. New Haven, CT: Yale.

Marks, H. M. & Printy, S. M. (2003). Principal leadership and school performance: An integration of transformational and instructional leadership. *Educational Administration Quarterly*, 39(3), 370–397.

Marshall, C. & Mitchell, B. (1991). The assumptive worlds of fledgling administrators. *Urban Society*, 23(4), 396–415.

McGuire, R. (2013). Australian government school principals respond to My School: Principals' cognitive, strategic and emotional responses. *Australian Educational Leader Journal of the Australian Council for Educational Leaders*, 35(1), 12–16.

Mortimore, P. (1993). School effectiveness and the management of effective learning and teaching. *School Effectiveness and School Improvement*, 4(4), 290–310

National Policy Board for Educational Administration (2007, December). *Educational leadership policy standards: ISLLC 2008*. Washington, DC: Author. Retrieved from: www.principals. org/s_nassp/sec_inside.asp?CID=1298&DID=56055

Nias, J. (1989). *Primary teachers talking*. London: Routledge and Kegan Paul.

Nias, J. (1996). Thinking about feeling: the emotions in teaching. *Cambridge Journal of Education*, 26(3), 293–306

Nias, J., Southworth, G., & Yeomans, R. (1989). *Staff relationships in the primary school*. London: Cassell Education.

Ontario Ministry of Education (2010). *School effectiveness framework: A tool for school improvement and student success*. Retrieved from: www.edu.gov.on.ca/eng/literacynumeracy/framework.html

Peck, C. & Reitzug, U. C. (2012). How existing business management concepts become school leadership fashions. *Educational Administration Quarterly*, 48(2), 347–381. doi:10.1177/0013 16X11432924

Pollock, K & Winton, S. (2012). School improvement: a case of competing priorities! *Journal of Cases in Educational Leadership*, 15(3), 11–2

Robinson, V., (2010). *Open to learning conversations*. www.educationalleaders.govt.nz/Problem-solving/Leadership-dilemmas/Open-to-learning-conversations

Sammons, P., Hillman, L., & Mortimore, P. (1995). *Key characteristics of effective schools: A review of school effectiveness research*. London: Institute of Education.

Sarason, S. B. (1995). *Parent involvement and the political principle*. San Francisco, CA: Jossey-Bass.

Scheff, T. & Retzinger, S. (2000). Shame: The master emotion of everyday life. *Journal of Mundane Behavior*, www.mundanebehavior.org/issues/v1n3/scheff-retzinger.htm (accessed February 19, 2013).

Schön, D. A. (1983). *The reflective practitioner*. New York: Basic Books.

Silins, H. (1994). The relationship between transformational and transactional leadership and school improvement outcomes. *School Effectiveness and School Improvement*, 5(3), 272–298.

Silins, H. & Mulford, B. (2004). Schools as learning organizations—Effects on teacher leadership and student outcomes. *School Effectiveness and School Improvement*, 15(3–4), 443–466.

Southworth, G. (1998). *Leading improving primary schools: The work of heads and deputies*. London: Falmer Press.

Teddlie, C. & Reynolds, D., (2000). *The international handbook of school effectiveness research*. New York: Falmer Press.

Tschannen-Moran, M. (2004a). Fostering teacher professionalism in schools—the role of leadership orientation and trust. *Educational Administration Quarterly*, 45(2), 217–247.

Tschannen-Moran, M. (2004b). *Trust matters: Leadership for successful schools*. San Francisco, CA: Jossey-Bass.

Tschannen-Moran, M. (2009). Fostering teacher professionalism in schools the role of leadership orientation and trust. *Educational Administration Quarterly*, 45(2), 217–247.

Townsend, R. (1990). Toward a broader micropolitics of schools: A review of *The micro-politics of the school: Towards a theory of school organization* by Stephen J. Ball. *Curriculum Inquiry*, 20(2), 205–224.

CHAPTER 3

The Politics of School-Level Community Engagement and Decision Making

Timothy A. Drake and
Ellen B. Goldring

CHAPTER OVERVIEW

This chapter is designed to enable learning about the politics of community-school partnerships and the mediating role school leaders can play in forging and nurturing that relationship, with an emphasis on school-level decision making and school-community communication. This unique aspect of school leadership is termed "environmental leadership" (Goldring & Sullivan, 1996). At the end of this chapter, readers should be able to integrate the goals of environmental leadership with an understanding of power and politics and its influence on school-community communication and group decision-making processes. This chapter includes a case study to expand upon and apply learning from concepts outlined in the chapter. Specifically, this chapter will include the following sections: Environmental Leadership; *Case Study: East High School*; Power & Politics; Group Decision Making; and Leading Communication between the School & Community and a chapter summary. Throughout this chapter are opportunities to apply the sections to the case study and application activities. Of course all of these perspectives are an integral part of developing the knowledge, dispositions, and performances associated with ISLLC Standard 6, wherein school leaders are challenged to "[promote] the success of every student by understanding, responding to, and influencing the political, social, economic, legal, and cultural context" (Council of Chief State School Officers, 2008). This chapter is specifically designed to teach the goals of environmental leadership and power relations in schools to aid aspiring principals in acting to influence local, district, state, and national decisions affecting student learning in a school environment (ELCC Building-level 6.2). We also review the principles of group decision making and the school-community relationship to prepare school leaders to understand, anticipate, and assess emerging trends and initiatives in order to adapt school-based leadership strategies (ELCC Building-level 6.3).

THE "NEW LOCALISM" IN AMERICAN EDUCATION

Administrator perspectives about the community-school relationship have undergone considerable change since the 1960s. Prior to that point, an ethic of professional conduct emphasized a managerial distancing from community interactions, notably represented by chest-high counters many schools erected to separate visitors from school staff and faculty. The turbulence of the 1960s, however, catalyzed efforts to place control of the schools into the hands of locally elected residents and representatives. Although many of these efforts were short-lived, their lasting impact included a major shift in thinking from a closed- to an open-systems perspective of school leadership. Specifically, this movement opened schools in the following ways: (a) encouraged the community to more actively participate in school governance through, for instance, school-based management; (b) encouraged schools to recognize the environmental, social, and political context that surrounds each school; and (c) encouraged both communities and schools to recognize that they both comprise an ecology of learning that together act as a network of learning resources and environments (Crowson et al., 2010; Driscoll & Goldring, 2006).

This community-school relationship has also been reshaped by the changing political environment in which state and federal mandates and policies play an increasingly significant role in shaping efforts to strengthen public schools. While these changes reflect a top-down approach to education reform, there is a recognition that, at its most basic level, schooling remains local. Termed *the new localism* in American public education, school leaders now must act locally to respond to new accountability pressures requiring evidence of effectiveness in the instruction of students and measurement and reporting of achievement outcomes for all of them (Crowson & Goldring, 2010). In this environment, the school's community represents both a *challenging partner* and powerful resource for effective schooling. Communities are a challenging partner because, like living organisms, they encounter and respond to changing environments, and are composed of interactive parts, including families, other schools, businesses, public and social services, religious institutions, community and non-profit agencies, and other organizations. They are a *powerful resource* because communities represent a vast array of networks, relationships, and assets and capacities that school leaders can leverage in collaborative arrangements with schools to improve effective teaching (Crowson et al., 2010; McKnight & Kretzmann, 1996).

Given this relationship, scholarly research emphasizes leadership's expanded role in acquiring the skills and abilities and dispositions to navigate the complex ecological environment of communities to forge productive partnerships. Among these skills are the need for political acumen (Cooper, 2009; Murphy, 2000); the importance of using knowledge of social, political, and economic contexts to develop political clarity, capacity, collaboration, and an 'ethic of risk' (Feuerstein, 2001; Hoffman, 2009); knowledge of future trends that can affect schools (Copland, 2000; Hodgkinson, 2003); and an understanding of emerging leadership theories (Moolenaar et al., 2010; Shields, 2010).

ENVIRONMENTAL LEADERSHIP

Students of educational leadership often are met with a barrage of terms and approaches to improving leadership influences upon instruction and student learning, including transformational leadership, distributed leadership, *direct leadership, and instructional leadership*. While some of these (e.g., direct leadership) focus narrowly on work inside schools, most recognize the important role parents and communities can play in improving their school's educational outcomes and furthering its vision and goals. Environmental leadership constitutes leadership that focuses on integrating the external with internal school-based processes and procedures and linking implicitly with the school's community, broadly defined (Goldring & Sullivan, 1996).

As mentioned in the introduction to this chapter, the external environment of schools can be quite challenging to understand and manage. By nature, these external contexts are often unstable, ambiguous, and complex. School board members turn over; school demographics, enrollment patterns, and school zoning change; social service agency leadership and resources vary in their support of schools, for example. School leaders, faced with the challenge of forging productive and lasting relationships within this environment, have traditionally responded with actions that tend to buffer their schools from external clientele and organizations. In a survey of principals in New York City, for instance, Mann (1976) found that, in communicating with the community, most principals considered themselves to be "trustees" of the district; that is, solely representatives of the school rather than the community. They viewed their roles as maintaining and implementing district perspectives and decisions to the parents and the community. Far fewer viewed themselves as "delegates" of the community; that is, representatives of the community to the district. The trustee approach has long been rejected for a more collaborative, open perspective of engaging with parents and the community.

In order to develop an understanding of the role of the environmental leader in leading school and community, we first discuss issues surrounding power relations in collaborative, inter-organizational relationships. Before doing so, we present a case study that will help facilitate our discussion throughout the remainder of the chapter. Use the following question to help guide reading of this case:

How does the school and community context shape the school-community relationship?

To answer this question, consider the following:

- the economic conditions of the community
- the changing population of students and families

- school performance and student achievement
- principal tenure
- teacher perspectives
- parent attitudes
- the school's relationship with external community organizations.

CASE 3.1: EAST HIGH SCHOOL

As a newly hired principal of East High school, you are anxious to learn more about the school. Although you are new to the area, you quickly find out that East High, though currently one of the lowest performing in the district, has been an integral part of the urban community in which it resides. Historically, many of the teachers and administrators have lived in the community and taught at the school. The feeder elementary school is located next door and the middle school across the street. The school boundary covers an area of about 4 square miles.

Recently, there have been a number of changes that have reshaped the school environment and context. Most notable among these changes has been the shifting composition of families living in the area. The economic prosperity of the 1990s and early 2000s led to a large out-migration of middle-class families to suburban areas. As a result, many local businesses were forced either to close or move to outlying areas. This exodus of families and businesses resulted in two demographic changes to the student population—first, the number of students at East High has steadily declined in recent years, making it the smallest school in the district; second, the share of minority students, particularly Latinos, has increased substantially. With this change has also come a greater share of low-income and working-class families.

Along with these environmental changes, district policy and state accountability has shaped the context in which the school operates. In 2002, the school's prestigious STEM magnet program was discontinued. A few years later, the district implemented a program of choice that allows parents and students to choose from a variety of programs across the district. The school's repeated failing status on state accountability reports in past years and low value-added achievement scores has also contributed to the decline in students and resulted in high teacher and administrative turnover. In fact, during the last two years East High had four different principals, the last of which was an interim replacement from central office. Their tenure is as shown in Table 3.1:

Currently, East High has a student population of 824 students, 64 percent of which are African American, 34 percent Hispanic, 1 percent White, and 1 percent other. East High also has the highest number of students designated for special education in the district and a large percentage of ELL. Last year, the school ranked last in the district in value-added achievement scores for reading and math. East High also had the second

Table 3.1 Tenure of Principals

Principal	Tenure	Reason for Exit
Hadley	22 years	Retired
Fox	3 months	Hired into Central Office
Wood	1 year 1 month	Unprofessional Conduct
Carrey	4 months	Interim from Central Office

Note: Pseudonyms used

Table 3.2 East High School, Select Characteristics

Students			
Enrollment	824	Special Education (%)	22.3
White (%)	1.0	LEP (%)	35.0
Black (%)	64.0	Dropout Rate	31.2
Hispanic (%)	34.0	Graduation Rate	75.1
Other (%)	1.0	AYP	No
Female (%)	50.7	Below Proficient (%)	45.6
Free (%)	88.1	Proficient (%)	46.3
Reduced (%)	5.2	Advanced (%)	8.1
Free Reduced (%)	93.3		
Teachers			
White (%)	44.8		
Black (%)	34.5		
Hispanic (%)	15.5		
Other (%)	5.2		
Female (%)	58.1		

lowest graduation rate and the highest rates of student dropout. The district provided you with the following table on some of East High's key student, teacher, and school characteristics (see Table 3.2).

Checking your email one day, you see that the district has sent you the results of the annual, recent survey of students, teachers, and parents in your area. This survey is relatively new in the district and is designed to help leaders use data to make informed decisions. Among the topics covered, you find the following results on parental involvement and participation, as reported by teachers and parents:

• *Teachers* were significantly *less likely* than other district school teachers to (a) indicate trust in parents' ability to help their children with schoolwork; (b) express confidence in parental and community engagement as a means of increasing classroom effectiveness; (c) have time for involving parents and community in useful ways; and (d) indicate that parents give timely responses to teacher requests. Teachers were also significantly less likely than other teachers in the district to consider parental involvement and community engagement to be part of their responsibilities as a teacher, and reported *significantly lower rates* of working closely with parents and community agencies to meet students' needs.

- *Parents* at East High were significantly *less likely* than other district schools to report involvement at the school, represented by PTO/PTA meetings and activities, parent–teacher conferences, academic events, extracurricular school activities, general school meetings, volunteering at the school, fundraising, conversations with teachers by phone or email, and helping their child with schoolwork at home. Parents were also significantly *less likely* to feel appreciated by school teachers and staff, and knowledgeable about the school.

Although these results are not too surprising given your experiences in the school thus far, you have noticed that East High has a number of services and external programs that are noteworthy and seem to be positively contributing to the school. Among these are East High's participation in the federal Teacher Incentive Fund (TIF) where teachers can earn additional compensation for student achievement results, and a district-created teacher effectiveness program, which impose additional academic expectations on the school in return for more resources. Other external organizations that provide significant support for students include the Junior Reserve Officers' Training Corps (JROTC) and the school's participation in the states inter-scholastic activities program. A few years ago, the school teamed up with the Umoja Student Development Corporation, a program designed to meet the needs of troubled African American male students. Umoja's model is to partner with students and equip adults to address social-emotional needs, provide a safe and restorative climate for learning, and connect students' current educational experience to their future aspirations. In your interactions with the Umoja director, you can sense that he has a strong relationship with many of the students and families. East High also has a successful, but very small, Advancement via Individual Determination (AVID) program, a college-readiness system designed to increase the number of students who enroll in four-year colleges.

While teachers have indicated to you that the relatively low socioeconomic status of the community and the relative paucity of businesses in the school's immediate vicinity make community engagement a challenge, faith-based organizations seem to be particularly prevalent in the community. Additionally, the schools programs of choice include partnerships with Bell Helicopter, IBM, and the local community college (LCC) to support the robotics program. An aviation training program is also offered through a partnership with LCC, though you notice that few students are enrolled. Finally, a local railroad company seems to actively recruit graduates from East High.

LEARNING ACTIVITY 3.1

The Environmental Leader and East High School

As the new principal at East High, imagine you just read the previous section on environmental leadership and want to apply some of the concepts and ideas that you learned.

Activity

Using the terms and concepts outlined in the chapter, write down ways in which you might:

- proactively facilitate communication from East High to the community;
- gather and incorporate information about the community into the school;
- maintain existing partnerships and develop new partnerships with community actors by leading school outreach into the community;
- bring parents and other community actors into the school;
- use the community as a resource for instruction.

Application

Find someone who is unfamiliar with the concept of environmental leadership. Explain some of the key concepts, goals, and ideas behind environmental leadership. Then, briefly describe the case of East High and share your ideas about how the goals and principles of environmental leadership might be applied to case.

POWER AND POLITICS IN SCHOOLS

As we mentioned in the introduction to this chapter, school leaders are faced with new organizational environments where traditionally defined non-school actors play a larger role in shaping the work of their schools. Traditionally, non-school actors were defined as parents, community agencies, businesses, and the like. In fact, because schools are increasingly being viewed as not separate from, but part of the community, the term "non-school" may be misleading. Parents, community social service organizations, and other stakeholders are important allies in improving school outcomes. Within this new landscape, school leaders are called upon to mediate relationships between these groups. Successful principals develop the ability to build bridges and span boundaries across sectors, leveraging multiple resources and existing relationships to improve school outcomes and strengthen the community. Successful principals see their schools as integral to the life and success of the whole community. These relationships nurture mutual commitment, joint planning, and problem solving. This is referred to as civic capacity (Henig & Stone, 2007).

In simple terms, the concept of civic capacity is rooted in a notion of social capital and can be summed up in two words: relationships matter (Field, 2003). Social capital refers to "the set of resources that inhere in relationships of trust and cooperation between and among people" (Warren, 2005, p. 136); or, in the words of Putnam and Leonardi, "the features of social organization, such as networks, norms and social trust, that facilitate coordination and cooperation for mutual benefit" (Putnam & Leonardi, 1993). The formation of social capital both within school communities and between schools and the communities in which they are situated should be a very explicit and important goal. Social capital is a popular term. In fact, there is an organization that sums up the essence of its meaning: bettertogether.org. This organization's website, whose tag line summarizes its principles in the words "Connect with others. Build trust. Get involved," suggests 150 things anyone can do to build social capital. For example, one of the items on the list is to collect oral histories from older town residents.

Social capital has become an important concept in explaining the mechanisms by which communities and schools interact. The essential characteristic of social capital is the fact that it resides in the relationships among individuals within a social organization. The educational benefits accrue when the community as a whole values education and shares some degree of oversight for all its children.

The idea of social capital has been extended to include the political and civic networks in communities. Overlapping webs of relationships—what Putnam terms "networks of civic engagement"—enrich the quality of life of any individual residing in the society (Putnam & Leonardi, 1993, p. 173). Such networks foster robust norms of reciprocity, facilitate communication and the development of trust, and "embody past success at collaboration, which can serve as a culturally defined template for future collaboration" (p. 173–174). Although dense social networks may not be focused on the exchange of educational information, they still provide a rich context to sustain and support schooling. Overall, social capital is formed when there are opportunities for students to build social trust and norms of mutual understanding through bonding with adults, sharing information, and forming links with other individuals in various institutions. Evidence for its positive effect is overwhelming (Putnam & Feldstein, 2003).

Thus, civic capacity is defined as the "degree to which a cross-sector coalition comes together in support of a task of community wide importance" (Stone, 1998, p. 234), and civic capacity develops social capital and vice versa. Civic capacity emphasizes the collective role of community stakeholders, going beyond the view that any one single institution, such as a school, can address the needs of its constituency.

> In the education arena, the capacity of any set of stakeholders is limited, and so long as various players think and act in terms of a narrow view of their duty, they miss the full scope of the problem they face and the response to which they could contribute.
>
> (Stone, 1998, p. 254)

It is within this context that we now turn to a brief discussion of the politics of organizations and schools. Simply stated, a study of school politics is a study of power. As environmental leaders working toward successfully integrating the external with internal school processes and procedures and vice versa, school leaders will necessarily need to understand the aspects and function of power. This section will review the research literature on power in organizations, power in schools, and the nexus between the environmental leader and power.

Power in Organizations

In this section we develop the conceptual understanding of power in organizations and then we provide insights into the notion of power in understanding leadership's role in engaging with the community as an environmental leader. The concept of power in organizations has long been debated on a conceptual and empirical level by political scientists, sociologists, psychologists, and economists. While there are many definitions, we refer to Moorhead & Griffin's definition (1998), "Power is the potential ability of a person or group to exercise control over another person or group" (p. 385). In elaborating upon this definition, it is helpful to think about the various dimensions of power, its properties, and use.

Bacharach and Lawler (1980) focus on three specific dimensions of power. First, power has a *relational aspect*. It is clear in the definition above that power is defined in relational terms—one group or individual's potential ability to exercise control over another. As the authors note, a key point underlying the relational aspect of power is that we can begin to analyze the interactional dynamics of power relationships—Who are the key actors and groups? How do organizational subgroups compete for scarce resources? How do organizational elites interact with other (seemingly inferior) subgroups? It is in these interactions that we can begin to understand power relationships in and between organizations or in our case between schools and the community.

For example, a superintendent and school board, faced with the decision about the fate of a historic school building in need of serious repairs, may take an expert-based, school-centered "decide and defend" approach and close the school (Johnson, 2009). This is, in fact, within their jurisdiction and authority. However, it may be that the community feels quite differently about the building and its historical significance. Studying the interaction between the community and school board helps us to understand how they perceive each other. In this case, the school board feels their position of authority and expertise places them in a position to hand down the decision to the community; the community, on the other hand, feels that the building's historical significance gives it the right to make the decision. The process of group decision making will be outlined later in the chapter, but it is important to note how power and group decision making interact to form outcomes.

Second, power has a *dependence aspect*, in that "the power of an actor or group is derived from the function of the other person's dependence on the actor" (p. 20).

In our definition above, one individual or group has the potential to exert control over another, defining the dependent relationship of the latter to the former. Of course, the level of dependence is contingent upon the availability of outcome alternatives (i.e., can I go somewhere else for what I need?) and the degree of value attributed to the outcome (i.e., do I really need this?). In the case of the school building and the "decide and defend" approach, the community is subordinate to the school board and superintendent. That is, while alternative outcomes may be available to individual families (e.g., private school), the community is left with the decision of the school board.

Nonetheless, the community is not left without future recourse, for power also has a *sanctioning aspect*, or actual changes actors can and do make to shape each other's outcomes. In this case, the community may choose to elect a new school board. It is also important to note that our definition highlights the potential for sanction or control, because having the ability to sanction does not always mean that individuals or groups will exercise that power. In addition, the sanctioning aspect does not always need to be viewed as a punishment, as in the case of the community punishing the school board for making the decision. Rather, this sanctioning power can also be exercised to manipulate outcomes through rewards. For instance, in our example it could be that the school board, upon hearing the negative reaction from the community, decides to help local officials repurpose the building into a community recreational or arts center.

Importantly, these aspects of power can be vested in individuals or groups either formally or informally. Scott (1987) notes that the formal power in organizations is, at least in part, by design. Formal hierarchies are often established to define one position as controlling another. One way to think of these formal power structures is to think of authority, or a formally sanctioned right to make decisions and exercise control (Bacharach & Lawler, 1980). Positions in organizations determine lines of authority. The school board, in this case, has the authority to close the school. The community, in turn, has the authority to elect a new school board. Both of these actions are determined by formal lines of authority.

Informal forms of power, on the other hand, are not formally embedded in institutional structures. Rather, informal forms of power are manifested through personal influence. Bacharach and Lawler (1980) note that whereas authority is often unidirectional (e.g., top-down), influence is unbounded, flowing in multiple directions within an organization (e.g., horizontal, upward, downward). In addition, influence may be entirely divorced from formal position, instead related to personal characteristics, expertise, or opportunity. Individuals and groups can have the potential to wield both formal and informal means of power. In our example, it may be that there is a builder who is aware of the discussions about the school and wants to see it closed so that his company can get the contract for the new school. He may use his influence to persuade the school board to close the school because he sees an opportunity for gain.

Power and Schools

The traditionally defined political organization of schools includes centralized bureaucracy, standardized resource allocation, rules, policies and regulations, and bureaucratic incentives that are clearly codified, and lend themselves to clearly defined roles and responsibilities. These formal structures define power relationships between, for instance, administrators and teachers, teachers and students, schools and parents, district leaders and schools, and unions and district leaders. As in other organizational settings, all the actors involved in or engaged with schools, whether it be district administrators, teachers, principals, parents, or community members, broker power relations through both formal and informal means.

Nevertheless, the changing landscape in education has broken down some of these traditionally defined structures. Whereas before school leaders were called upon to broker intra-school power relations with teachers, students, and staff, today's leadership now operates in a cross-sector environment that includes parents, community leaders and social service providers, business leaders, local non-government organizations, and many other stakeholders. Increasingly, actors from more general political environments, like mayors, city councils, state legislatures, and the like, are also becoming involved in the local work of schools and school districts (Henig, 2013).

In this environment, where power relations may not always be so clearly defined or new relationships are frequently emerging, school leaders have the opportunity and challenge of learning how to negotiate these relationships. As hierarchies break down (or are redefined), Susan Auerbach (2012) argues that a principal must learn to share power through authentic partnerships. In her broader conception of leadership for partnerships, Auerbach outlines four categories across a continuum of leadership. At one level, a school leader can *prevent partnerships* by maintaining control over goals, buffering outsiders like parents and community organizations from their children's school and exercising a unilateral "power over" other groups. In these instances, the power differential between school and families/community organizations is large. Much of this approach to preventing partnerships would be a reliance on formal power relationships based on a school leader's tendency to create situational dependence and/or sanction. As the formal leader of the school, for instance, a principal can tell parents how they will share information. Or, the school leader can "pull rank," using positional authority to achieve objectives. Next, under *nominal partnerships*, a principal may be compelled to communicate more with stakeholders through norms and policies. This level of leadership, however, is also characterized by a desire to maintain power, a view of families and community organizers as liabilities rather than assets and the desire to continue to exercise a unilateral "power over" others. The power differential between groups is again large.

Leadership for *traditional* partnerships is geared toward enhancing student achievement, and can include a more "open door" model, where the school begins to cooperate with parents and communities through joint planning and implementation. Under this form of leadership, school leaders seek to enhance home-school communications and family health and wellbeing through school-linked services. Henderson and others (2007) characterized this form of school leadership as creating "family-friendly schools." In traditional partners, power relations with families are a mix of unilateral "power over" and relational "power to" act. Finally, at the other side of the continuum is Auerbach's conception of *authentic partnerships*. Authentic partnerships occur when families and community organizers are viewed as full partners and participants in setting the goals and direction of the school. These relationships are defined by a minimal power differential, where both school leaders and community groups have relational "power to" act. These partnerships include transformative, inclusive, and social justice models of school leadership, which proactively seek equity and cultural responsiveness and reach out to marginalized students and families.

Summary of Power and Politics

In this section, we argued that successfully integrating the external with internal school processes and procedures and vice versa requires an understanding of the aspects and functions of power. We defined power as the potential ability of a person or group to exercise control over another person or group, and focused on the relational, dependence and sanctioning aspect of power (Bacharach & Lawler, 1980; Moorhead & Griffin, 1998). We also described how power can be vested formally through structures or policies, or informally through influence or reputation. In describing power relations in school-community partnerships, we also highlighted the importance of forming authentic partnerships, where school and community groups have relational "power to" act, especially for the benefit of marginalized students and families (Auerbach, 2012).

LEADING GROUP DECISION MAKING

A more open approach to engaging with external communities and environments and a deep understanding of power relationships in schools is an important aspect of environmental leadership. Equally important for the environmental leader are the principles associated with effective group decision making as a mechanism to bridge and bond between school and community. Before discussing some of the issues surrounding group decision making, it is important to briefly discuss the formal decision making process. We also highlight factors that are important to consider when thinking about the potential for group success. In doing so, we draw upon Moorhead and Griffin's (1998) work.

The Decision Making Process

Decision making is the process of choosing between alternatives. Decisions can be "programmed," that is, well-structured, and occur frequently enough or in routine situations to create decision rules or sets of procedures that define how to decide once information has been gathered. Decisions can also be "unprogrammed," or poorly-structured, and infrequent enough to require judgment, creativity, and problem solving. In these situations decisions are also often made with information that may be incomplete or vague and carry a greater degree of risk.

The decision making process, therefore, has several approaches. The *rational approach* is perhaps the most well known of these. Under this approach, individuals or groups follow a logical pattern of steps to arrive at a decision, including (a) stating the goal; (b) identifying the problem; (c) determining the decision type (programmed or unprogrammed); (d) collecting data and information, generating, evaluating, and choosing among alternatives; (e) then implementing the plan. After implementation, the outcomes are then measured and compared to the goal, with adjustments made in the cases of any discrepancy (Moorhead & Griffin, 1998; Wagner, 1978).

Nonetheless, the rational approach often assumes an environment of objectivity and complete information. The *behavioral approach*, on the other hand, recognizes information asymmetries and subjectivity in the decision making process. This recognition often leads to the use of procedures or rules of thumb, acknowledging suboptimization, or accepting the less than best possible outcome, and satisficing, wherein individuals or groups examine alternatives only until a solution that meets minimal requirements, or satisfactory outcomes or decisions, is found.

Of course, in practice decision-making processes can include a mix of the behavioral and rational approaches. In group settings, the power relations within a group will also affect the process. For instance, for programmed and routinized decisions, like preparing a school's budget, the principal can exercise her formal position of power to guide the group decision making process in allocating resources across fiscal categories. *How* these decisions are made, however, will be influenced by a mix of the intra-group power structures, forms of informal and formal power, and group decision-making processes. With respect to a school's budget, the group may have a clear goal in mind and a logical plan to follow, but decisions often need to be made in a timely manner and without full information. In this case, prior experience, rules of thumb, and suboptimization may guide budgetary decisions. The actual outcome of these decisions, however, will be negotiated by the power relations within a group. Does the principal truly have the final say because of her formal position of power? Or does the experienced teacher leader in the science department wield his influence to disproportionately allocate resources to new science curricula and professional development? Thus, both power relations and decision-making processes interact to form outcomes.

Since this interaction is especially relevant in group settings, we turn to a brief discussion of group decision making.

Group decision making. As school decision making becomes shared among a variety of stakeholders, the environmental leader must learn to manage group decision making. To maximize the potential for successful group processes, it is most important to consider first the group's purpose and goals, for these will help select group members and the norms and cohesiveness that result. They will also impact the power relationships within the group. Important questions that will guide this process include: What am I trying to accomplish in the group? How long will the group be together? Is this a standing committee with regular ongoing work and engagement, or an ad hoc committee with a short-term defined purpose? In assessing a group's composition, it is sometimes necessary to think about characteristics that go beyond the descriptive labels associated with various educational stakeholders. That is, beyond forming groups of parents, teachers, and community leaders, one could ask, for example, "What type of teacher should I include in planning the year's professional development? New teachers? Experienced? Someone with formal leadership responsibilities? Someone with a good relationship with parents?" Of course the specific answer to these questions is determined by the group's purpose and the role each member can play in contributing to the group's efforts to make a decision. When considering group composition, it is also necessary to consider the size of the group. What number of members is optimal for making a decision? What is the balance between obtaining adequate representation and being efficient? Again, the group's purpose will help answer these questions. Sometimes it is necessary to include members or representatives of particular role groups or constituencies, such as teachers who are active in the union, or parents who are part of a local community group such as citizens for school choice.

In the case of involving parents in decisions, Goldring and Rallis (1993) suggest that group decision making occurs best when school "principals and parents work together to achieve common goals" (p. 83). To reach this level of collaboration, principals should "view parents as important allies with similar aims and interests and seek to involve them." This type of involvement in group decision making can be based on coalition building and/or cooptation. There is a central difference between these two approaches. Coalition building is focused on working with parents or community members or stakeholders with common goals. Cooptation tends to view parents as "external elements to placate" rather than as "true, equal partners" (Goldring & Rallis, 1993, pp. 84–85). In sum, as community members and parents exert more influence in the school, school leaders must broker and guide those relationships so there is a close fit between the school and the environment.

Having considered group size and composition, we now consider a few more issues around group decision making. First, groups are designed to bring information from a variety of stakeholders to bear on a problem, objective, and/or goal. Unfortunately, as group member share information with each other, group members' attitudes and opinions change during discussion. While this phenomenon, referred to as *group polarization*, is not inherently bad, it is important to recognize that group's average post-discussion attitudes tend to be more extreme than pre-discussion attitudes. For example, members who hold particularly strong views may be persuasive and dominate the group, swaying those who previously might have objected or held differing opinions. Or perhaps the group setting leads some individuals to feel less accountable for group actions, thereby resulting in a decision that individually they would never endorse, but collectively are persuaded to do so. It is important to emphasize, however, that group polarization is defined, not by the ability to yield a consensus or make collective action, but by the extent to which these decisions move toward a more extreme attitude or position than before the discussion. In a school setting, this seems to be especially relevant to faculty

LEARNING ACTIVITY 3.2

East High School's Site-based Council

With approval and encouragement from the district, you have decided to form a site-based council at East High to begin to share power with parent and community actors. You plan on organizing the council with power to make decisions in many areas of the school, including authority to decide on the school's budget, curriculum, new teacher hires and assignment, and general activities and supports.

Activity

With a partner, decide on the *composition* and *size* of your council. Use the following questions to help guide your decisions:

- How many school representatives will sit on the council? Who will they be? What positions, experience level, skills, and background will they have? Why?
- How many non-school representatives will sit on the council? How many will represent parents? Community groups? Are there other members of the community you feel will be important additions to the council? Why?
- How long will council members hold a position on the council? Why?
- Who will lead council discussions? Why?
- How often will the council meet?
- How could you, as a leader, "sell" the council to the school and community? What barriers might you face?
- Are there any other considerations that are important in forming this council?

Application

Compare and contrast your decisions with those of another group.

meetings, where the discussion of a particular student's behavior, for instance, often leads a majority of teachers to be persuaded by the most vocal among them, even when those teachers may have differing opinions or limited contact with the individual.

In contrast to group polarization, groups that are unified and cohesive and tend toward unanimity in thought, often at the expense of appraising alternative courses of action are subject to groupthink. *Groupthink* has a long history in the psychology literature on group dynamics and decision making. It is defined not by group cohesiveness, but by the extent to which it excessively affects a group's ability to weigh options when making decisions. In Janis' seminal work *Victims of Groupthink*

(1972), he argues that group cohesion, though not inherently bad, has a tendency to produce the conditions whereby a group experiences defective decision making. Included among the characteristics he describes are gross omissions in reviewing objectives and alternatives, poor information search, selective bias in processing the information at hand, failure to reconsider originally rejected alternatives, failure to examine some major costs and risks of preferred choice, and failure to work out detailed implementation, monitoring, and contingency plans. Thus, it is not group cohesiveness that is the problem, but a cohesive group's tendency toward behaviors that influence optimal decision making. In educational settings, where it is important to create a sense of common school culture among and between adults and students (Bryk et al., 2010; Lee & Smith, 1995), future school leaders need to make sure that school cohesion and a sense of unity in purpose does not lead to groupthink.

As a leader, the individual is in the important position of either catalyzing or staving off group polarization and group think. If, for example, the school leader insists on dominating the conversation or garnering consensus around his or her own opinions, then that behavior contributes to the conditions of ineffective group decision making. On the other hand, if the school leader encourages participation through structures, norms, and practices designed to account for groupthink and polarization, then that behavior facilitates the conditions that are most associated with successful decision making. For example, consider the outcomes of a school leader who is in charge of organizing a group of teacher leaders to plan the professional development calendar for the school year. If that school leader comes to the first meeting with the calendar already made according to his or her own experiences and preferences, then the decision will not be effective because it really is not a shared decision. If instead a school leader comes to the meeting with suggestions for development based on data from teacher observations and student achievement, and invites others to bring their own data to the meeting, then shared leadership creates the conditions for generating effective group decisions.

Summary of Group Decision Making

In this section we defined decision making as the process of choosing between alternatives. We described two popular models of decision making—rational and behavioral—and argued that a blended model is most often realized in practice and depends upon the power relations within a group. We also discussed the process of managing group decision making by examining group purpose, size, and composition. We also discussed the importance of recognizing group polarization and groupthink.

LEADING COMMUNICATION BETWEEN THE SCHOOL AND COMMUNITY

In our final section, we highlight the environmental leader's role in managing the politics of community engagement through leading communication between

LEARNING ACTIVITY 3.3

Power and Group Decision Making

Visit a local setting in which a group is responsible for making decisions (e.g., local city council, school board, etc.).

During your visit, take notes on:

- The formal power demonstrated within the group. Are there structures, policies, and procedures in place that mark formal lines of power and authority?
- The informal power demonstrated within the group. Who has influence? Why? How can you tell?
- How is the power relations shaped by the size of the group? The group's composition?
- Does the group seem cohesive? Does this cohesion exhibit any of the signs of groupthink or group polarization? How do the power relationships within the group shape this cohesiveness (or lack thereof).

Application

Share your findings with a partner.

the school and the community. Within this, we examine the two-way flow of communication between schools and communities, along with the leadership's role in initiating outreach into the community and leading the community into the school. Additionally, the community may serve as a resource for, and a place of, instruction.

In accordance with an open-systems organizational perspective, or a focus on the interrelationship between schools and their environments, school leaders are now called upon to inform communities of the vision, goals, and instructional programs of the school, and inform districts of the needs, desires, concerns, and interests of the community (Crowson et al., 2010). This flow of information between the school and community is bi-directional, where school leaders are often in a position to mediate its strength, size, and influence. Therefore, one goal of environmental leadership is to help school leadership to develop the necessary skills, competencies, and abilities to perform this role.

Communication from the school to the community. The increased communication of schools to community actors has catalyzed in recent years following new accountability pressures, where school report cards publish information on student achievement, demographics, and teacher quality, such as value-added student achievement measures. Communication is enhanced because of school choice policies, including charter and magnet schools, district-run programs of choice, and vouchers for private schools. These policies allow parents more school options, and making a choice about which programs best meet the needs of individual children is now part of leadership's role. In fact, many school leaders are faced with helping parents make these choices and advocating and marketing their particular school to parents. Highly publicized school violence episodes and other aspects of the social climate of schools remind us that communication between the school and the community can help develop close partnerships and can help prevent future disasters (Gallagher et al., 2005).

There are a number of implicit and explicit ways in which school leaders can communicate with the community. First, a school's teachers and students are the most visible representatives in communicating an image of their school to the community. Teacher-to-parent communiqués, musical and assembly programs, dramatic productions, field trips, athletic events, commencement, work–study programs, and reports on achievements and accomplishments are some of the many ways in which teachers and students represent their school (Gallagher et al., 2005). We argue, however, that, while these are a necessary first step in engaging with the community, they represent a more passive form of communication, in that schools indirectly manage the communication process through individual school actors and that this form of communication tends to be one-way from the school to the community, usually parents.

Increasingly, it is no longer sufficient to employ passive means of engagement. A more active approach is necessary for any school leaders to engage with the surrounding communities in a much more proactive manner to align with school goals and needs. School leaders can effectively and efficiently engage in communicating with the community, and all of these represent more active forms of engagement. Recent examples highlighted in the research literature include:

- In an effort to "sell the school to local residents," the principal led the effort to change the perception of the school by holding coffee-talks with parents and community members, meeting with parents of prospective students, and reaching out to the large, urban community and university to partner for additional resources (Picucci et al., 2002)
- In a chronically underperforming middle school, the principal wanted to "reawaken the hallowed history" of the school. To do so she reignited a sense of community through a large 75th anniversary gala for the local community (Whiteside, 2006).
- The district in a large urban city decided to close a low-performing school. The principal, determined to see the school improve, embarked on a public campaign. With support from faculty, students, and parents, the community persuaded the district to keep the school open and to support the principal's proposed direction for the school's vision and efforts toward reform (Tung & Ouimette, 2007).

In short, while passive forms of engagement help represent, inform, and engage parents and the community about the school, principals who lead communication from the school outward proactively shape the school-community relationship.

Communication from the community to the school. In order to engage with the community, it is important that school leaders look to the community for information about its needs, interests, and concerns. A school that is incongruous with community norms, desires, and behaviors may be counterproductive, not least of which because a one-way flow of information from the school that is decontextualized from the environmental context has a tendency to close out community actors. Instead, school leaders must use a variety of tools and resources to gather a better understanding of the community. These tools include regular, face-to-face interactions with multiple constituencies in the community, and projecting a welcoming approach to the school. Often principals gather more formal information about the community through surveys or measures of public opinion, but visibility and firsthand knowledge of the community cannot be overstated. This often takes place through participation on agencies' steering committees, partnering with community groups to reach mutual outcomes. They might also include more formal changes to school structures through, for instance, the sharing of school management to site-based councils, or a better understanding of the power relations and political structures in a community. A specific examination of some of these will be covered in later sections of this chapter.

Leading outreach into the community. The school leadership can help the school lead outreach into the community by (1) recognizing that the school building is a valuable community resource; (2) mobilizing school members to engage in community service and other forms of assistance; and (3) developing partnerships with other community organizations and services to address the needs of the community. While the first two are often known to principals, the third is more complex and bears further elucidation.

Partnerships with the community have traditionally taken the form of collaborative school-linked service programs and outcomes-based partnerships. Tyack (1992) noted that a goal of the U.S. public school system has been improving the plight of poor children and youth, since the 1890s. *Collaborative school-linked service programs* were designed to help children and families beset by problems of poverty, teenage pregnancy, single parenthood, substance abuse, limited healthcare, and/or inadequate and unaffordable housing by incorporating the provision of health and human services into the function of the school (Wang et al., 1995). Although there is no single model, Wang and colleagues note that collaborative programs can be described in terms of their goals, the services offered, the location of the services, and the service providers. Their popularity ebbed and flowed over the last century, often because their services were linked to top-down approaches of delivery, where information and advice from the community was frequently ignored (Tyack, 1992).

Additionally, school-linked service programs have lost some popularity because they are challenging to manage successfully. These partnerships, by nature, involve cross-sector actors, each with their own norms, regulations, values, training, and professional behavior. In this way, each organization involved in the partnership can be thought of as a boundary. Principals, as environmental leaders, must act as *boundary spanners*. Recent examples of cross-boundary partnerships include Promise

Neighborhoods, a U.S. Department of Education led initiative that focuses on breaking down silos and building a complete continuum of cradle-to-career solutions of both educational programs and family and community supports, and School of the 21st Century, a community-school model that incorporates childcare and family support services into schools with the overall goal of promoting the optimal growth and development of children beginning at birth.

The success (or failure) of these collaborations often hinges on school leaders' ability to act as boundary spanners in helping to bridge the flow of communication between the school and community.

Leading the Community into the School. Along with leading outreach into the community, an environmental leader needs to bring the community into the school. This process goes beyond merely gathering information about the community or inviting parental and community participation through volunteering activities, it involves altering organizational structures, cultures, and capacities to ensure that these external actors are more fully included. Scholarly research in this area tends to highlight two areas of community inreach into the school. First, engage in parental and community involvement by establishing welcoming environments, providing avenues for structured involvement, and initiating contact with families (Hoover-Dempsey & Sandler, 1997). Leaders ensure that the language schools use is not filled with jargon or acronyms specific to the professional field of education (Crowson et al., 2010). Second, principals can include community actors in decision-making processes through formal governance structures like site-based councils. The theory behind these councils is to give non-school actors (parents, community members) a voice in decision making, which should lead to a greater commitment from all groups to improve educational outcomes (Shatkin & Gershberg, 2007). The success of these councils is largely dependent on all council members' ability to broker power relations among the group.

A Note on Instruction

It is important to recognize when considering the importance of school-community relations that schools are not the only organizations that teach the children and youth of a community. While it has long since been recognized by educators and administrators that children's out-of-school experiences profoundly impact learning, school actors have not always viewed the community as an instructional partner. Outside of direct services of instruction (e.g., tutoring services, community centers, museums), surrounding communities have a wealth of information for student learning and development. Importantly, the community represents a setting outside of the walls of the school in which instruction can take place, a setting that is familiar and relevant to students' lives. Advocates of place-based education capitalize on this setting by rooting curriculum and instruction in students' own communities and neighborhoods (Smith, 2013).

Any school also must partner with local businesses, agencies, and organizations to embed instruction in the local landscape. Although this "place-based" education has often been associated with rural schools, increasingly urban school systems are offering choice programs and academies that require partnerships with local organizations to deliver instruction and provide expanded learning opportunities. Often these programs and academies include emphases in the areas of technology and communication, business, law, health services, aviation, hospitality, and management, to name a few. These programs can also include formal structures to involve and incorporate institutional partners from the surrounding community (Driscoll & Goldring, 2006).

CONCLUSION

Community-school engagement is central to school improvement efforts; embedded in the community relationship are issues of power and politics, decision making and communication. Power and politics are not negative, and, are not detrimental to developing strong partnerships. However, an understanding and analysis of the power relationships in schools is crucial for success. Understanding the environmental leadership role in the school as principal can help frame issues for developing strong partnerships, and assist in diagnosing the external environment of the school. Most importantly, acknowledging that the environment outside the school, such as parents and community organizations, requires leadership and attention for developing and implementing a shared vision for strong community–school partnerships.

In developing relationships and partnerships with the community, school leaders want to recognize the importance of civic capacity and social capital. School leaders' understanding of power can help develop and increase civic capacity and social capital. Power has various dimensions. Primarily for school leaders, the following concepts affect all aspects of their work, including: (a) notions of relational power, (b) acknowledging the interdependency of each other in the power relationship, (d) the dependency aspect of power, and (e) the sanctioning reality of school politics. Successful principals focus on both the informal and formal aspects of power in their schools.

Environmental leaders know that power is a natural aspect to all organizations, and schools are not unique; armed with a deep understanding of power relationships, group decision making and communication can become more effective. Common decision-making approaches include the rationale and behavioral approaches, both central tools for environmental leaders to enhance the school-community relationship. Communication with school partners requires two pathways—from the community to the school and from the school to the community. In sum, power, decision making, and communication frame the environmental leader's role and provide the cornerstones for success.

REFERENCES

Auerbach, S. (Ed.), (2012). *School leadership for authentic family and community partnerships: Research perspectives for transforming practice*. New York: Routledge.

Bacharach, S. B. & Lawler, E. J. (1980). *Power and politics in organizations*. San Francisco, CA: Jossey-Bass.

Bryk, A. S., Sebring, P. B., Allensworth, E., Easton, J. Q., & Luppescu, S. (2010). *Organizing schools for improvement: Lessons from Chicago*. Chicago: University of Chicago Press.

Cooper, C. W. (2009). Performing cultural work in demographically changing schools: Implications for expanding transformative leadership frameworks. *Educational Administration Quarterly, 45*(5), 694–724.

Copland, M. A. (2000). Problem-based learning and prospective principals' problem-framing ability. *Educational Administration Quarterly, 36*(4), 585–607.

Council of Chief State School Officers. (2008). *Education leadership policy standards: ISLLC 2008*. Washington, DC: Author.

Crowson, R. L. & Goldring, E. B. (Eds.), (2010). *The new localism in American education: Re-examining issues of neighborhood and community in public education*. National Society for the Study of Education (NSSE) Yearbook, 108th Yearbook, Vol. I. New York: Teachers College, Columbia University.

Crowson, R. L., Goldring, E. B., & Haynes, K. T. (2010). *Successful schools and the community relationship: Concepts and skills to meet 21st century challenges*. Richmond, CA: McCutchan Publishing Corporation.

Driscoll, M. & Goldring, E. (2006). How can educational leadership incorporate communities as contexts for student learning? In W. Firestone and Carolyn Riehl (Eds.), *A new agenda for research in educational leadership*. New York: Teachers CollegePress.

Feuerstein, A. (2001). Selling our schools? Principals' views on schoolhouse commercialism and school-business interactions. *Educational Administration Quarterly, 37*(3), 322–371.

Field, J. (2003). Civic engagement and lifelong learning: Survey findings on social capital and attitudes towards learning. *Studies in the Education of Adults, 35*(2), 142–156.

Gallagher, D. R., Bagin, D., & Kindred, L. W. (2005). *The school and community relations* (8th Edition). Needham Heights, MA: Allyn & Bacon Publishing.

Goldring, E. & Sullivan, A. (1996). Beyond the boundaries: Principals, parents and communities shaping the school environment. In K. Leithwood, J. Chapman, D. Corson, P. Hallinger, & A. Hart (Eds.), *International handbook of educational leadership and administration*, Volume 1 (pp. 195–222). Norwell, MA: Kluwer Academic.

Goldring, E. B. & Rallis, S. F. (1993). *Principals of dynamic schools: Taking charge of change*. Newbury Park, CA: Corwin.

Henderson, A. T., Mapp, K. L. Johnson, V. L., & Davies, D. (2007). *Beyond the bake sale: The essential guide to family-school partnerships*. New York: The New Press.

Henig, J. R. (2013). *The end of exceptionalism in American education: The changing politics of school reform*. Cambridge, MA: Harvard Education Press.

Henig, J. R. & Stone, C. N. (2007). Civic capacity and education reform: The case for school-community realignment. In Rothman, R. (Ed.), *City schools: How districts and communities can create smart education systems* (pp. 117–136). Cambridge, MA: Harvard Education Press.

Hodgkinson, C. (2003). Conclusion: Tomorrow, and tomorrow, and tomorrow: A post-post-modern purview. In P. T. Begley & O. Johansson, (Eds.), *The ethical dimensions of school leadership* (Vol. 1) (pp. 221–231). Houten, Netherlands: Springer.

Hoffman, L. P. (2009). Educational leadership and social activism: a call for action. *Journal of Educational Administration and History, 41*(4), 391–410.

Hoover-Dempsey, K. V. & Sandler, H. M. (1997). Why do parents become involved in their children's education? *Review of Educational Research, 67*(1), 3–42.

Janis, I. L. (1972). *Victims of groupthink: A psychological study of foreign-policy decisions and fiascos.* Boston: Houghton Mifflin.

Johnson, P. A. (2009). And the survey says: The case for community engagement. *Journal of Cases in Educational Leadership, 12*(3), 9–25.

Lee, V. E. & Smith, J. B. (1995). Effects of high school restructuring and size on early gains in achievement and engagement. *Sociology of Education, 68*, 241–270.

Mann, D. (1976).*The politics of administrative representation.* Lexington, MA: D. C. Heath.

McKnight, J. & Kretzmann, J. 1996). *Mapping community capacity.* Report, Institute for Policy Research, Northwestern University, Evanston, IL.

Moolenaar, N. M., Daly, A. J., & Sleegers, P. J. (2010). Occupying the principal position: Examining relationships between transformational leadership, social network position, and schools' innovative climate. *Educational Administration Quarterly, 46*(5), 623–670.

Moorhead, G. & Griffin, R. W. (1998). *Organizational behavior: Managing people and organizations.* Boston: Houghton Mifflin Company.

Murphy, J. (2000). Governing America's schools: The shifting playing field. *The Teachers College Record, 102*(1), 57–84.

Picucci, A. C., Brownson, A., Kahlert, R., & Sobel, A. (2002). *Driven to succeed: High-performing, high-poverty, turnaround middle schools. Volume II: Case studies of high-performing, high-poverty, turnaround middle schools.* Austin, TX: The University of Texas at Austin, The Charles A. Dana Center.

Putnam, R. & Feldstein, L. M. (2003). *Better together: Restoring the American community.* New York: Simon & Schuster.

Putnam, R. D. & Leonardi, R. (1993). *Making democracy work: Civic traditions in modern Italy.* Princeton, NJ: Princeton University Press.

Scott, W. R. (1987). *Organizations: Rational, natural, and open systems* (2nd ed.). Englewood Cliffs, NJ: Prentice Hall.

Shatkin, G. & Gershberg, A. I. (2007). Empowering parents and building communities the role of school-based councils in educational governance and accountability. *Urban Education, 42*(6), 582–615.

Shields, C. M. (2010). Transformative leadership: Working for equity in diverse contexts. *Educational Administration Quarterly, 46*(4), 558–589.

Smith, G. A. (2013). Place-based education. In Stevenson, R. B., Brody, M., Dillon, J. & Arjen, A. (Eds.), *International handbook of research on environmental education* (pp. 213–220). New York: Routledge.

Stone, C. N. (1998). Civic capacity and urban school reform. In C. N. Stone (Ed.), *Changing urban education* (pp. 250–274). Lawrence, KA: University of Kansas Press.

Tung, M. & Ouimette, R. (2007, April). *Promising results and lessons from the first Boston district school converting to pilot status.* Paper presented at the annual meeting of the American Educational Research Association, Chicago, IL. Retrieved December 2007, from www.ccebos.org/BCLA_conversion_study.pdf

Tyack, D. (1992). Health and social services in public schools: Historical perspectives. *The Future of Children, 2*, 19–31.

Wagner, C. (1978). Consensus through respect: a model of rational group decision-making. *Philosophical Studies, 34*(4), 335–349.

Wang, M. C., Haertel, G. D., & Walberg, H. J. (1995). *Effective features of collaborative school-linked services for children in elementary school: What do we know from research and practice?* San Francisco, CA: Jossey-Bass.

Warren, M. R. (2005).Communities and schools: A new view of urban education reform, *Harvard Educational Review*, 75(2), 133–174.

Whiteside, V. B. (2006). *Meeting the challenge of No Child Left Behind: How an inner-city middle school succeeded.* Unpublished doctoral dissertation, Fordham University, New York City.

CHAPTER 4

The Politics of District-Level Decision Making

Lance D. Fusarelli and George J. Petersen

CHAPTER OVERVIEW

This chapter uses the contentious issue of student reassignment and community schools to highlight the ways in which politics impacts decision making at the district level. The learning goals and objectives of the chapter are to help future school leaders understand the political dimensions of district-level decision making. This chapter addresses ISLLC/ELCC Standard 6: District-Level Leadership. Specifically, it addresses ELCC Standard Element 6.1: District advocacy; Element 6.2: local district-level decision making and its effects on student learning; and Element 6.3: the impact of emerging trends and initiatives on district-level leadership strategies.

The case presented in this chapter highlights many of the elements of Standard 6, particularly board conflict, conflict between the board and superintendent, and superintendent turnover. The case highlights how power and politics at the district level influence local policy decisions (Standard 6.2) as well as how this strife-riven political context impacts the ability of district leaders to advocate for equitable school policies and programs (Standard 6.1); it also raises significant questions as to what constitutes equitable policy (Standard 6.3).

With the steady loss of local control over the past three decades, a trend which accelerated greatly under President Bush's No Child Left Behind Act (NCLB) and President Obama's Race to the Top (R2T) initiative, coupled with implementation of the new Common Core curriculum standards in schools throughout the nation. Some are wondering what major domains of decision making remain under true local control (Cross, 2004; DeBray, 2006; Fusarelli, 2009; Fusarelli & Cooper, 2009). However, despite the steady erosion of local control, district-level leadership and decision making play a major role in school improvement and system performance (Petersen, 1999; Petersen & Barnett, 2005).

District leadership varies from system to system depending on the size and complexity of the district. Large districts have assistant and associate superintendents, may be divided into regions, and have several district-level administrators responsible for curriculum development and instructional supervision. Smaller, more rural districts (which still constitute the majority) may have only a skeletal district office and organization. While some large, urban districts operate under mayoral control, most systems have an elected school board with responsibility for hiring personnel, including the superintendent (Maeroff, 2010, notes that they provide literally millions of jobs), setting district policies, approving curriculum policies and materials, and reviewing and approving multi-million dollar budgets (including school construction, which provides multiple jobs outside the school system). Novice board members are often surprised at the number of legal and fiduciary responsibilities they have. With over 100,000 board members governing nearly 15,000 districts, they constitute the largest group of elected officials in the U.S. Collectively, they manage a budget of over $500 million annually (Hess, 2008). On a daily basis, superintendents, district personnel, and school boards play a key role in educating children.

Many superintendents, district leaders, and school boards work well together and earnestly strive to provide the best possible education for children (Kowalski et al., 2011). However, as will be seen in the case study presented in this chapter, controversies and political conflict sometimes occur and can disrupt significantly the educational process. Although the case study profiled in this chapter is a large, countywide system, district-level political conflict between superintendents and school boards (and within boards themselves) occurs in districts of all shapes and sizes (Petersen & Fusarelli, 2008). As the single largest job provider in rural areas and small towns, district governance and leadership can quickly become major centers of political intrigue. In fact, some might assert that politics in rural districts is more malicious because it is more personal—where everybody knows your name and your business. Thus, the district-level politics examined in this case are just as applicable to smaller, less urban districts, as they are to larger districts similar to Wake County.

The domain of local control examined in this chapter is student assignment. Many suburban districts, such as Wake County (NC), Fulton County (GA), and Clark County (NV) are growing rapidly, necessitating the constant construction of new schools and the annual redrawing of local school attendance zones. On the other hand, when schools close or school or districts consolidate, student reassignment becomes a contentious issue as well. Some school districts are concerned about resegregation of public schools, particularly as wider arrays of school choice, such as charter schools and vouchers, gain in popularity. On the other hand, many urban districts continue to lose students and some rural districts are faced with tough decisions to close community schools or consolidate districts altogether. All of these actions, no matter how well rationalized and justified in the name of efficiency and economies of scale, generate intense political conflict with superintendents and their school boards. Sometimes, decisions are made not in the best interests of children but rather are those that upset the fewest number of vocal stakeholders.

Any one of the many decisions school boards make, including the hiring and firing of the superintendent, can serve as a lightning rod for political conflict. All school board decisions can act as a catalyst leading to the creation of interest groups, advocacy coalitions, and the broadening of the scope of conflict from a local issue to one receiving state and national media attention. Often, these rather fluid coalitions form and reform around specific issues of concern. In this chapter, we examine one such decision that has embroiled the Wake County Public School System (WCPSS) in controversy for the past four years—the issue of student reassignment and community schools. The highly public drama led to the resignation and firing of two superintendents, significant board turnover, a switch from Democratic control of the school board to Republican control, and then back to Democratic control (even though school board elections in North Carolina are officially non-partisan). This case generated lawsuits, civil rights complaints, and charges of racism and resegregation—all of which have drawn the attention of major media outlets, including the *New York Times*. It even caught the attention of satirist Stephen Colbert. This is a particularly important issue given that many schools throughout the country are resegregating at alarming rates (Boger & Orfield, 2009; Green, 2008). As a result, the case raises issues of equity and poses several ethical dilemmas for school leaders (Standard 6.2).

CASE 4.1: STUDENT REASSIGNMENT AND COMMUNITY SCHOOLS

The WCPSS is the 16th largest school district in the country, with a mostly suburban composition sprinkled with a few urban and rural schools. It has 169 schools, with two more under construction, and nearly 150,000 students and 9400 teachers. It has become a majority-minority district, with 49 percent of the student population Caucasian, 24 percent African American, 15 percent Latino, and 7 percent Asian. Explosive enrollment growth has necessitated almost yearly construction of new schools and the frequent redrawing of school attendance zones, a trend expected to continue through 2020, with a projected 37,000 new students joining the system between 2013 and 2020. The total budget for 2012–2013 was nearly $1.4 billion dollars.

For several years, the Wake County school system had a reputation of being progressive, with a student reassignment plan designed to prevent any school from having more than 40 percent of students eligible for free or reduced-price lunch. The reassignment plan, which made extensive use of magnet schools, attempted to encourage integration by socioeconomic status and prevent any school from being labeled a high-poverty school. Supporters of the policy "have prevailed in every school board election since the Raleigh and Wake County schools merged into a single system in 1976" (Geary, 2009, pp. 1–2). Support for the policy also comes from the business community, which views it as important to the region's economic growth. The Wake County reassignment model has been touted as one of the most successful in the nation in terms of improving educational excellence and maintaining diversity (Grant, 2011).

However, over the years, this reassignment plan, coupled with uneven growth and expansion in different parts of the county, produced dissatisfaction among some parents, particularly those whose children were reassigned away from their neighborhood schools. A small percentage of district parents also had their children's base or assigned schools switched more than once over the years the plan was implemented. While the percentage of students reassigned each year was relatively low (6–7 percent, sometimes lower), the actual reported number appeared to many to be quite high. Wake County is a district of 150,000, so 5 percent equals 7500 students. Compounding the issue is that in WCPSS, some schools operate on a year-round calendar while others follow the traditional school calendar. Although the rationale for year-round schooling was designed to limit the loss of student learning over the summer, unfortunately, this also created a situation in which some parents with multiple children were following different school calendars, despite efforts by the district to minimize the number of families in such situations.

Despite these challenges, Wake County had been relatively immune to significant strife and factionalism on its school board; few members publicly identified or aligned themselves with either the Democratic or Republican Party. According to Kevin Hill, former chair of the school board (2011–2012), he didn't even know the party affiliation of other board members when he was first elected in 2007. That situation and level of nonpartisanship appeared to change as mostly suburban parents unhappy with student reassignment became vocal in their opposition to the policy.

In 2009, a newly elected slate of four Republicans (all of whom were vocal in their party identification and who received support from the national Republican Party) took control of the Wake County school board and promptly sought to dismantle or significantly modify the existing reassignment plan, allowing for more community or neighborhood schools and less busing. At this point, Republicans held a slim 5–4 majority on the board and were brought into office largely by "suburban voters fed up with frequent reassignment and long bus rides" (Goldsmith & Hui, 2012, p. 1) coupled with dissatisfaction of the "frequent reassignments and widespread discontent with former school board practices (Hui et al., 2012, p. 3).

One of the first actions of the new board majority was to remove all references to diversity from Board Policy 6200, the student assignment policy (Geary, 2012). Shortly after the new Republican majority took control of the school system, the Wake County superintendent, Del Burns, who was very much an insider (a veteran Wake County district leader) and strong supporter of the reassignment plan, resigned, citing his inability to support the directives of the new board's leadership. Interestingly, Wake County has a history of insularity, preferring to hire district and school leaders accustomed to the "Wake County way," which generally consists of agreement on student reassignment and of allowing school leaders with significant educational experience to run the school system with minimal interference from the board.

With Burns' resignation, the new Republican majority had an opportunity to hire a superintendent of its liking and, in a radical departure from precedent, went outside the educational establishment and hired Tony Tata, a former Army general and Broad Foundation graduate with minimal educational experience. None of the Democrats on the board supported his hire.

Upon Tata's hiring in December 2010, the new Republican majority directed him to develop a new student assignment plan; this, in turn, triggered a storm of protest, when interest groups such as Great Schools in Wake, a coalition of concerned citizens banded together to fight efforts to return to community or neighborhood schools, became actively involved in unseating the Republican majority in the next school board election. The local chapter of the National Association for the Advancement of Colored People also got involved and filed a complaint of resegregation with the U.S. Department of Education's Office for Civil Rights that triggered a federal investigation of the school district (Hui et al., 2012).

In October 2011, at the urging of Superintendent Tata, the board voted 6–2 to approve the new, choice-based student assignment plan, which gave preference to community schools (Goldsmith & Hui, 2012). A month later, a Democratic candidate whom the superintendent had publicly criticized for putting inaccurate information in a press release and of making untrue statements about staff members, won a seat on the board, part of a Democratic sweep of five seats that flipped control of the board back to Democrats. Both national political parties contributed financial resources as well as technical expertise (campaign commercials, lobbying, and technology and media support) to the campaign. The most costly board election in Wake County history, "Candidates, political parties, and independent groups poured at least $500,000 into mailers, TV and radio advertisements and other get-out-the-vote efforts in the five races" (Hui et al., 2012, p. 1). Voter turnout (21 percent) was nearly twice that of 2009, when Republicans took control of the board.

A few months later, in February 2012, Superintendent Tata charged two of the new Democratic board members with potential ethics violations over their ties with Great Schools in Wake, a citizen group often critical of Tata. In May, Tata again complained in a board meeting that the new board members were disrespectful toward staff and had been "throwing the staff under the bus" (Goldsmith & Hui, 2012, p. 1). One month after that, in June 2012, the new Democratic majority directed the superintendent to come up with a new student reassignment plan that mandated diversity as a component.

Triggering Event

In the midst of all this turmoil, at the beginning of the 2012–2013 school year, a major busing fiasco erupted. Earlier in the year, in an action approved by the Democratic-majority board, Tata had removed 52 of 933 buses as part of cost-saving measures (ridership/capacity was lower on many bus routes than state guidelines, which could have resulted in less state aid for district transportation in the future). In July, with the start of the year-round school calendar, minor busing issues occurred, including "complaints about late or missing buses" (Hui, 2013a, p. 1). However, several weeks later when the majority of WCPSS students began school under the traditional school calendar, the busing problem exploded. Some buses were 1–2 hours late picking up children; some dropped children off at the wrong stop; others didn't arrive at all. This situation affected thousands of students, as they also encountered difficulty getting home from school as well (some children got home 2–4 hours after school ended and at least one was dropped off in the wrong town).

A firestorm of protest erupted, as angry parents and board members vented their frustrations with anyone who would listen, including swarming media reporters. More than 2000 calls flooded the superintendent's office during the first few days of school. One angry parent stated, "It took the Cary Police Department to figure out that the school had put my son on the wrong bus . . . The kicker is he's got a tag on his book bag that says he's supposed to be on route one" (ABC11 Investigates, 2012).

Democratic board members were quick to blame Tata and his staff (and by not-so-subtle implication, the choice-based neighborhood schools plan) for the mess. "Democratic board members blamed the choice-based student assignment plan that Tata helped develop for aggravating the situation by increasing by 20 percent the number of daily miles buses traveled" (Hui, 2013a, p. 1). Martin called for an audit of the transportation department; Superintendent Tata requested then-board chair Kevin Hill to conduct the audit using a bipartisan panel, since three of the Democratic board members had already been sharply critical of the situation. Yet, three weeks into the school year, some buses were still dropping off children after the school day began (Brown, 2012). Shortly thereafter, Don Haydon, chief facilities and operations officer, resigned because of the busing fiasco.

LEARNING ACTIVITY 4.3 Think About It!

Scapegoating

When crises occur, the public often demands change. Sometimes, the change is legitimate, while at others a scapegoat must be found. In this case, defenders of the superintendent were convinced Haydon was made a scapegoat while the crisis provided Tata's opponents with an opportunity to remove him as well. What do you think?

Republicans countered, with then-school board member Chris Malone writing to a constituent, "They [Democratic board members] were waiting like a coiled rattlesnake waiting for a moment of vulnerability for purposes of political cover to strike" (Hui, 2013a, p. 1). But former board member Beverley Clark asserted that, "The bus disasters of the last week are directly related to the inefficiency of the choice plan. You can't fix the bus problem without fixing the choice problem" (Hui, 2012b, p. 1). In the end, nearly all the buses went back in operation, although the district had to scramble to find and train qualified drivers.

As the relationship between Superintendent Tata and the new Democratic majority continued to deteriorate, members expressed frustration at the lack of detail offered in the revised reassignment plan developed by the superintendent. In September 2012, after less than 20 months on the job, the board voted to fire Superintendent Tata. The 5–4 vote was strictly along party lines. In part, the new board blamed Super-intendent Tata for the transportation crisis at the start of the 2012–2013 school year, as the district's transportation system was unable to adjust effectively to the modifications of the student reassignment plan. Tata received a severance package in excess of

$250,000—a particularly hard pill for voters to swallow in light of the district's need to pass a $1 billion bond issue.

Tata's firing brought a stream of criticism of the new Democratic-controlled board, particularly when his supporters pointed to improved test scores and several new programs, including single gender academies, initiated during his brief tenure. In response, the Wake County Taxpayers Association, which had previously filed a complaint about the Democratic majority's plan to scrap community schools with AdvancED, the organization that accredits the district's high schools, amended its complaint to include the firing of Superintendent Tata. Russell Capps, president of the taxpayers association, stated, "This wasn't really about student assignment. The whole thing was about getting rid of Tata. This was a vengeful action against Tata" (Hui, 2012a, p. 3M).

In May 2013, the board, by a 7–1 vote, approved a modified reassignment plan that tries to "minimize high concentrations of low-performing students and students from low-income families" while also keeping students in schools near their homes and at schools they currently attend. The modified reassignment plan isn't quite as comprehensive as the old reassignment plan and reflects some degree of compromise from the lingering effect of the 2009 election.

Future Issues

Due to explosive growth, Wake County needs approximately $1 billion in new school bonds, a very large amount that would require approval by an increasingly skeptical public. The board asserts that passage of the bond is essential because the district must build 16 new schools, fully renovate six schools, and partially renovate others (Hui, 2013b). Tata's firing, and his quarter million dollar severance package, has delayed efforts of the school board and county commissioners to put a bond issue on the ballot (projected for a vote fall 2013). To complicate matters, Wake County Republican Party has threatened to publically oppose this bond issue. In North Carolina, the county commissioners are responsible for financing public schools; as such, in many counties, school boards members and county commissioners are often at odds over spending, with school board members wanting more and more money, and county commissioners reluctant to approve tax increases.

In fact, in Wake County, where conflict between the school board and county commissioners is decades-old, the Republican-controlled county commissioners have asked the Republican-controlled state legislature to grant county commissioners ownership of all school buildings and to control the construction of future schools (Huntsberry, 2013). The county commissioners have asked the legislature to require four of the nine school board members to stand countywide, rather than by district or precinct. Both initiatives would strip away much of the school board's power and would shift voting power from inner Raleigh to the more conservative suburbs (Huntsberry, 2013). Both the school board and county commissioners have hired competing lobbyists to make their case in the state legislature; the county commissioners allocated $25,000 for a lobbyist, while the school board allocated $100,000 to their lobbying firm (Huntsberry, 2013).

It is likely that the proposal to give county commissioners control over school buildings, at least in select counties such as Wake, will pass, while the proposal to move four seats on the school board from district to countywide seats is less likely to pass. It is entirely possible that the proposal for countywide seats has been offered as a leverage point—not unlike how vouchers have been used as leverage to obtain passage and expansion of charter schools (Fusarelli, 2003). Fundamentally altering how nearly half of school board members in Wake County are elected would be a devastating blow to a board that has historically been liberal and attentive to the needs of urban, predominantly minority voters. This worst case scenario might give county commissioners the leverage they need to take control and ownership over school buildings and future school construction. Such power could be used in the future as leverage for board concessions or at least for significant input from the county commissioners over a wide array of local education policies.

Another issue that is unlikely to go away is the rising cost of school board elections, which may further limit the available pool of candidates to those who have the wealth, means, and political connections to seek countywide office. For example, Kevin Hill stated that when he first ran for the board in 2007, he raised approximately $6000 for his successful campaign. In 2011, he spent nearly $70,000 in his re-election bid. The demand for constant fund raising and campaigning led Hill to announce that he planned not to seek re-election when his current term expires.

With respect to further turnover on the school board, in 2013, only Republican-held seats are up for re-election; thus, the board is certain to remain under Democratic control at least until 2016. With a new superintendent to be hired summer 2013 and Democrats expected to gain at least one more seat in the fall 2013 election, we expect board-superintendent-community relations to be more calm and smooth, at least until the fall 2015 election.

THE POLITICS OF DISTRICT-LEVEL DECISION MAKING

School Boards and Superintendents

Pivotal to the success of any school district is the positive relationship between the board of education and the district superintendent. For over two centuries, the public has relied on elected boards to govern public education. As legal extensions of state government, board members are public trustees acting on behalf of all residents of the school district to set policy and ensure the implementation of state laws and regulations. The superintendent, as the top-level administrator, is to make policy recommendations, ensure policy enforcement, and provide leadership and management for the day-to-day operation of the district. Although this may appear to be a simple and straightforward model of local governance, in practice the line separating policy development and administration is often blurred and sometimes invisible. Unfortunately, as the Wake County case demonstrates, relations between the superintendent (actually, between two superintendents) and board members were strained, with factions largely identifiable by party affiliation.

The Dissatisfaction Theory of Democracy, developed by Lutz and Iannaccone (1978), asserts that when school boards make decisions that run contrary to public or community opinion and values (at least, among likely voters), then at some point voters will become dissatisfied enough to defeat incumbent board members, replacing them with members more aligned to their preferences. These new board members, in turn, often fire the superintendent, which produces new (and more aligned) policies (see also Lutz and Iannaccone, 2008). The case study presented in this chapter supports the basic propositions of this theory, although since many board elections have single digit rates of voter participation (anything beyond 12 percent may be considered high), it is reasonable to question the very notion of community values or preferences. It is not even clear who is the community. Still, the cycles of board and superintendent turnover presented in the case lend support to Lutz and Iannaccone's theory.

Research has demonstrated that school board members come to their positions with a limited understanding of their policy role or the role of individual members as a governing body (Spillane & Regnier, 1998). Other research has shown that board members do not necessarily enter into the policymaking processes with their opinions and preferences already formed and ordered (Asen et al., 2013), and consequently they are vulnerable to an array of external, social, economic, and political influences over which they have little control (Boyd, 1976). Because of this, policy analysts have perennially questioned boards' potential to deliberate about local needs and values and to translate community goals into district policy (Trujillo, 2012).

Of course, novice superintendents also sometimes get confused over what their role is in the school system (Petersen et al., 2008), a situation that can be exacerbated when the novice superintendent has little experience working in educational settings (Fusarelli, 2005). Whether personal conviction, vengeful politics, or the need to demonstrate he was in charge, Tata went beyond his role as appointed manager working for an elected board when he leveled ethics charges against two board members and accused another of spreading untruths (Geary, 2012). By making politics personal and alienating a third of the elected board, Tata severely undermined his position and effectively sealed his own fate. Tata lost the trust of the board, and it was clear that the board did not trust Tata would fully and faithfully implement their desire for a student reassignment plan that incorporated diversity into the plan.

Although mandates by the federal government continue to have greater levels of influence on education in the U.S., state and local levels still make key policy decisions that affect the daily environment of the school, and school board members as both community members and elected officials embody this component of local decision making (Tracy, 2010). What we also know is that, provided the dispersion of decision making, research has shown that local officials do not implement federal mandates in a uniform manner. For example, local policy makers may or may not regard research as salient for district issues. Their understanding of what constitutes research or how it may inform local issues may differ from the purposes articulated by federal policy makers (Asen et. al., 2013).

Decision Making and Conflict

The influential work of Cyert and March (1992) argued that organizations are made up of coalitions of individuals and that these coalitions form and reform around specific issues of concern. They demonstrated that it is important to understand that members of coalitions include both internal and external stakeholders who have an interest in the organization. This view of organizational decision making recognizes the role of conflict and conflict resolution. In a discussion of boards of education and decision making there is an overwhelming body of evidence that reveals that school boards often form coalitions of opposing factions and the goals of a school district are often displayed by the goals of competing interest groups.

Other research by Hung (1998) offers a typology describing the roles of corporate boards that makes an important distinction between extrinsic and intrinsic forces that shape board dynamics and orientations. Extrinsic issues are those that come from the external environment, issues that, at least in the short term, the board has to take as a given (e.g., organizational context variables, characteristics of elections, etc.). Intrinsic factors derive from institutional choices, characteristics of the board members, and board practices. These factors result in disagreements, which are often the result of fundamental differences over values and preferences. The values of organizational members contribute to the framing of core questions and the articulation of educational policy. When values differ, they often create conflict among members. For example, one area of classic conflict between boards and superintendents occurs when the role of the superintendent and board become ill defined and blurred. Confusion about the separation of responsibilities between the superintendent and school board significantly erode institutional stability and morale while promoting dysfunction in communication and decision making (Fusarelli & Petersen, 2002).

The case of Wake County presents a clear case of board-manager conflict whereby the board sets policy and the superintendent is supposed to execute it (Geary, 2012). Former superintendent Del Burns resigned because he did not believe he could carry out the Republican majority's policy to move toward community schools. The school board terminated former Superintendent Tata because members did not believe he would properly implement and execute their plans to incorporate socioeconomic diversity as a major component of student reassignment. The board also had issues of lack of trust, respect, and conflict over "who is in charge" of the school system with Superintendent Tata. As Geary (2012) stated, "If the two [board and superintendent] aren't on the same page, the board's only recourse is to replace the manager with someone who will be" (p. 2).

Contributing to potential areas of conflict are the make-up or type of school board and the leadership decisions of the superintendent in working with them. In 2001, Björk and Lindle presented characteristics of school boards (dominated, factional, pluralistic, or inert) and how superintendents choose to work with them. The Wake County school board is clearly a factional board. While Björk and Lindle found that 19 percent of superintendents identified their boards as factional, less than 2 percent adopted the role of political strategist (i.e., work to get a majority of board support on district initiatives). They concluded that superintendents tend to assume roles incongruent with community power structures and suggested that many superintendents are politically naïve when dealing with boards of education.

Yet, nowhere is the relational dynamics of superintendent-school board played out in a more public arena than the board's acceptance or rejection of a superintendent's policy recommendation. Recent research has shown that school boards

---

LEARNING ACTIVITY 4.4

1. Observe a school board meeting in your area. Take note of the setting: the structure of the room; the location of significant cultural markers (flags, nameplates, seating of board and audience, etc.); and the time and frequency of board meetings. Comment on the process and conduct of the meeting. Who spoke and on what issues? Was the meeting structured to encourage community participation? What was the tone of the meeting? Was it welcoming to outsiders and did it encourage community participation? Were substantive issues discussed? Why or why not?

2. Trace the party identifications of members of your local school board over the last decade. How easy is it to identify the party affiliation of board members? How has the composition of the board changed over time and why? Have any elections generated controversy or spurred unusually high voter turnout? How competitive are local board elections and what does it cost for successful election to the board?

3. Study media accounts (including videos, newsprint, and blogs) of a controversial issue in your school district. What is the tone of the reporting? How were issues presented? Could you detect any bias in media coverage? What impact, if any, do you believe the media played in the controversy?

4. Identify any coalitions or factions present in the controversy you examined in activity #3 above. What stakeholders are involved in these coalitions? What role did the coalitions play, if any, in shaping the outcome of the conflict? If the conflict remains unresolved, what role do you think they will play in the future?

are inclined to approve a significant majority of superintendent recommendations (Kowalski et al., 2011). Nonetheless, evidence in this case points to a situation where the Wake County board of education's initial decision to approve the superintendent's policy recommendation for choice-based student assignment eventually led to political division, accusations of insensitivity and racism, and the eventual dismissal of the superintendent. As one can imagine, the situation was rife with political conflict and unintended consequences. One example of a smoldering issue becoming a brush fire was the reassignment plan not taking into consideration the multiple and different calendars under which schools operated. Traditional and year-round school schedules required some parents with multiple children to follow different school calendars. While school schedules were not the focus of the conflict among board members and between the board and superintendent, this aspect of the reassignment plan generated a great deal of attention and conflict among the board, community and the superintendent.

The Role of the Media

School board member Hill blamed the media for politicizing school board decisions with its constant identification of decisions by party affiliation. However, John Drescher (2012), editor for the *News & Observer*, the major newspaper serving Raleigh and surrounding areas, stated that the reason they "often describe the board in partisan terms [is] because party affiliation is relevant to almost every significant decision the board makes. The parties support candidates during elections. Once on the board, members tend to vote with their bloc" (p. B1). Because the state capital is in Wake County and WCPSS is one of the largest school districts in the country, conflicts between the superintendent and the school board, and within the school board itself, generate a great deal of state and national attention. The complex racial dimensions of the issues received significant media attention but so did the lack of solidary between the board, the community and the superintendent when the district's busing went awry and each turn of events was so partisan that it provided ideal fodder for news coverage and therefore, was extensively covered in a wide variety of media outlets.

The Role of Technology in Political Conflict

Technology played a role in the expansion of the conflict between various superintendents and school board members; specifically, email blitzes, blogging, online message boards, and social networking sites. Chandler (2009) observed that in a growing number of school districts, web-savvy parents have become grassroots activists unafraid to pressure superintendents or board members to support their cause. By utilizing technology, such parents are able more quickly and efficiently to keep other parents informed by closely monitoring pending changes in policies or programs. Often, parents will get information out to the community before the school district does (Chandler, 2009). This nimble use of communication channels empowers parent coalitions and attracts much media attention. In the case of Wake County, bloggers, most of them conservative, were vocal and visible participants in the political drama.

STANDARDS ADDRESSED

This chapter addresses ISLLC/ELCC Standard 6: District-Level Leadership. Specifically, it addresses ELCC Standard Element 6.1: District advocacy; Element 6.2: local district-level decision making and its effects on student learning; and Element 6.3: the impact of emerging trends and initiatives on district-level leadership strategies.

This case highlights many of the elements of Standard 6. The political conflict generated by increased partisanship on the school board, and a shift from a Democratic majority to a Republican majority, then back to a Democratic majority within the span of four years has lead to Wake County having three superintendents in three years, an unconscionable disruption in leadership stability, which severely constrains district-level leadership initiatives. Thus, the case highlights how power and politics at the district level influence local policy decisions (Standard 6.2— knowledge) as well as how this strife-riven political context impacts the ability of district leaders to advocate for equitable school policies and programs (Standard 6.2—skills); it also raises significant questions as to what constitutes "equitable."

With respect to stakeholders and the community, parents want many things from the school system, but most of all they want stability. They want to know where their children are going to school, when, and on what calendar. Change can be good and necessary, but constant change and flip-flopping on major policies affecting school children, coupled with partisan bickering and board and super-intendent turnover, creates so much turbulence that parents want to opt out. Further, with the state legislature under unified Republican control (both the House, Senate, and Governor) and expansion of charter schools, Wake parents will have more opportunities to opt out of the school system.

The media was a player in the drama between the superintendent, school board members, and the community as well. It was vocal in its opposition to the Democratic-majority board's decision to fire Superintendent Tata, asserting that he had "calmed a system in turmoil . . . and had provided a powerful example of effective public leadership" (Drescher, 2012, p. B1), although it was supportive of the Democratic majority's decision to return to diversity by socioeconomic status in its student assignment policy.

The pressing need for Wake County to pass a large bond issue to meet explosive growth and expansion, in light of the political tensions and conflicts exposed in this case study, highlights how politics and emerging issues impact leadership strategies (Standard 6.3—knowledge and skills). At the very least, the case situation delayed placing the bond referendum on the ballot. The delay stemmed from the change in the superintendent's office, required appointment of an interim superintendent (a veteran insider who did not even apply for the permanent position), and a national search for a new superintendent. The new superintendent will have four short months to reestablish trust in the school system and lead the charge to pass the bond referendum whose outcome is very much in doubt given the politics of delays and change in superintendents.

DISCUSSION QUESTIONS

Superintendents believe they need to stay out of board politics and you might well assert that the superintendent erred in inserting himself in board politics by making ethics allegations against two Democratic board members. However, imagine you were a highly ethical, moral absolutist type leader. If you truly believed board members were acting unethically, wouldn't you have an obligation to call them out on the behavior or file ethics charges? Or would you weigh the benefits and rewards and the short- and long-term consequences of such actions when deciding what action to take?

In a similar vein, if you were elected to the school board, and you had what you considered as legitimate differences with the superintendent, differences that created a superintendent-board relationship that was unworkable, would you fire the superintendent? Would you act to fire knowing the following four contingencies: (1) how important passage of the upcoming school bond issue was to students in the district; (2) that the firing would create leadership instability and would undoubtedly appear in the media and to the public as petty politics; (3) that firing the superintendent would cost a quarter of a million dollars (in addition to the cost of hiring an interim superintendent, hiring a search firm, and conducting a national search for a permanent superintendent) knowing that you will be asking taxpayers for a nearly billion dollar tax increase (bond) a few short months later; and (4) that the decision might decrease public confidence in the leadership of the district? What decision is ethical in such a situation, given all of these contingencies, and what is your justification for such a decision?

On the other hand, if you take such factors into consideration and do not fire the superintendent, to what degree, if any, might that harm or create a less-than-beneficial circumstance for the education of students in the district? Would you wait until after passage of the bond to fire the superintendent and if so, how would you ethically justify such a decision?

REFERENCES

ABC11 Investigates. (2012, August 29). *Money at root of Wake County bus issues*. Accessed at: http://abclocal.go.com/wtvd/story?section=news/abc11_investigates&id=8789963

Asen, R., Gurke, D., Conners, P., Solomon, R., & Gumm, E. (2013). Research evidence and school board deliberations: Lessons from three Wisconsin school districts. *Educational Policy*, 27(1), 33–63.

Björk, L. & Lindle, J. C. (2001). Superintendent and interest groups. *Educational Policy*, 15(1), 76–91.

Boger, J. C. & Orfield, G. (Eds.), (2009). *School resegregation: Must the South turn back?* Chapel Hill, NC: University of North Carolina Press.

Boyd, W. L. (1976). The public, the professionals, and educational policy: Who governs? *Teachers College Record,* 77(4), 539–578.

Brown, J. (2012, September 11). *Problems persist for Wake County school buses.* Accessed at: http://abclocal.go.com/wtvd/story?section=news/local&id=8805160

Chandler, M. A. (2009, January 30). Well-connected parents take on school boards. *The Washington Post,* p. A01.

Cross, C. T. (2004). *Political education: National policy comes of age.* New York: Teachers College Press.

Cyert, R. M. & March, J. G. (1992). *A behavioral theory of the firm* (2nd ed.). Englewood Cliffs, NJ: Prentice Hall.

DeBray, E. H. (2006). *Politics, ideology, and education: Federal policy during the Clinton and Bush administrations.* New York: Teachers College Press.

Drescher, J. (2012, September 29). Politics and the school board. *News & Observer,* p. B1.

Fusarelli, B. C. (2005). When generals (or colonels) become superintendents: Conflict, chaos, and community. In G. J. Petersen & L. D. Fusarelli (Eds.), *The politics of leadership: Superintendents and school boards in changing times.* Charlotte, NC: Information Age Publishing.

Fusarelli, B. C. & Cooper, B. S. (Eds.), (2009). *The rising state: How state power is transforming our nation's schools.* Albany, NY: State University of New York Press.

Fusarelli, L. & Petersen, G. J. (2002). Changing times, changing relationships: An exploration of current trends influencing the relationship between superintendents and boards of education. In G. Perreault & F. C. Lunenburg (Eds.), *NCPEA 2002 Yearbook: The changing world of school administration* (pp. 282–293). Lanham, MD: Scarecrow Press.

Fusarelli, L. D. (2003). *The political dynamics of school choice.* New York: Palgrave Macmillan.

Fusarelli, L. D. (2009). Improvement or interference? Reenvisioning the "state" in education reform. In B. C. Fusarelli & B. S. Cooper (Eds.), *The rising state: How state power is transforming our nation's schools* (pp. 243–270). Albany, NY: State University of New York Press.

Geary, B. (2009, July 1). Wake school board race taking shape. *Indy Week* [online version], 1–3.

Geary, B. (2012, September 26). Wake school board says ta-ta to Tata. *Indy Week* [online version].

Goldsmith, T. & Hui, T. K. (2012, September 26). Wake school board fires Superintendent Tata. *News & Observer* [online version].

Grant, G. (2011). *Hope and despair in the American city: Why there are no bad schools in Raleigh.* Cambridge, MA: Harvard University Press.

Green, P. (2008). The politics of (de)segregation. In B. S. Cooper, J. G. Cibulka, & L. D. Fusarelli (Eds.), *Handbook of education politics and policy* (pp. 388–410). New York: Routledge.

Hess, F. M. (2008). Money, interest groups, and school board elections. In T. L. Alsbury (Ed.), *The future of school board governance: Relevancy and revelation* (pp. 137–154). Lanham, MD: Rowman & Littlefield Education.

Hui, T. K. (2012a, December 23). Board defends dropping choice plan. *News & Observer-Midtown Raleigh News,* p. 3M.

Hui, T. K. (2012b, September 5). *Wake County school board members argue over what's to blame for bus problems.* [blog]. Accessed at: http://blogs.newsobserver.com/wakeed/wake-county-school-board-members-argue-over-whats-to-blame-for-bus-problems.

Hui, T. K. (2013a, March 7). Emails show distrust in Wake County school bus fiasco. *News & Observer* [online edition].

Hui, T. K. (2013b, May 12). Board OKs $940M in projects. *News & Observer*, p. 3M.

Hui, T. K., Goldsmith, T., & Garfield, M. (2012, June 6). Democrats again control Wake school board. *News & Observer* [online edition].

Hung, H. (1998, April). A typology of the theories of the roles of governing boards. *Corporate Governance*, *6*(2), 101–111.

Huntsberry, W. (2013, February 20). Wake County commissioners call on legislature to neuter school board. *Indy Week* [online version].

Kowalski, T. J., McCord, R., Petersen, G. J., Young, I., & Ellerson, N. (2011). *The American school superintendent: 2010 decennial study*. Arlington, VA: Rowman & Littlefield Education and the American Association of School Administrators.

Lutz, F. W. & Iannaccone, L. (Eds.), (1978). *Public participation in local school districts*. Lexington, MA: Lexington Books.

Lutz, F. W. & Iannaccone, L. (2008). The dissatisfaction theory of American democracy. In T. L. Alsbury (Ed.), *The future of school board governance: Relevancy and revelation* (pp. 3–24). Lanham, MD: Rowman & Littlefield Education.

Maeroff, G. I. (2010). *School boards in America: A flawed exercise in democracy*. New York: Palgrave Macmillan.

Petersen, G. J. (1999). Demonstrated actions of instructional leaders: An examination of five California superintendents. *Education Policy Analysis Archives*, 7(18), 1–24.

Petersen, G. J. & Barnett, B. G. (2005). The superintendent as instructional leader: Current practice, future conceptualizations, and implications for preparation. In L. G. Bjork & T. J. Kowalski (Eds.), *The contemporary superintendent: Preparation, practice, and development* (pp. 107–136). Thousand Oaks, CA: Corwin Press.

Petersen, G. J. & Fusarelli, L. D. (2008). Systemic leadership amidst turbulence: Super-intendent-school board relations under pressure. In T. Alsbury (Ed.) *The future of school board governance: Relevancy and revelation*, (p. 115–136). Lanham, MD: Rowman & Littlefield Education.

Petersen, G. J., Fusarelli, L. D., & Kowalski, T. J. (2008). Novice superintendents' perceptions of preparation, adequacy, and problems of practice. *Journal of Research on Leadership Education*, *3*(2), 1–22.

Spillane, R. & Regnier, P. (1998). *The superintendent of the future: Strategy and action for achieving academic excellence*. Gaithersburg, MD: Aspen.

Tracy, K. (2010). *Challenges of ordinary democracy: A case study in deliberation and dissent*. University Park, PA: Pennsylvania State University Press.

Trujillo, T. M. (2012, December). The disproportionate erosion of local control: Urban school boards, high-stakes accountability, and democracy. *Educational Policy*. Retrieved from http://epx.sagepub.com/content/early/2012/12/11/0895904812465118

CHAPTER 5

Politics, Culture, Social Conditions

Gerardo R. López

CHAPTER OVERVIEW

This chapter discusses a case study that focuses on the various changes that occurred in a suburban city in the Deep South following a major natural disaster. The demographics shifts that occurred not only placed enhanced demands on school officials to meet the needs of an increasingly diverse student population, but forced school leaders to deal with racial tensions that were prompted by these demographic shifts. The case connects to ISLLC (2008) Standard 6.1, which states that leadership "candidates understand and can advocate for . . . students, families, and caregivers."

Grounded in actual events, the case begins with a description of the community context, describes the hurricane that devastated the area, and discusses the changes that took place in the aftermath of the storm. The case also describes the challenges faced by an immigrant student who is trying to navigate the cultural and academic terrain of his new school and community, while dealing with the pressures of being an "outsider" in a social context that is not understanding of him or his family. The chapter concludes with a set of activities that are useful to preparation programs for aspiring leaders to better understand the complexity of social change and the importance of cultural understanding and advocacy.

CASE 5.1: JAMBALAYA CON SAZÓN[1]

Political contexts for schooling are an amalgam of social and cultural history in any given location. In the U.S., histories of places include phases of cultural dominance by one group or groups, which are often replaced as populations of other groups grow. Communities are formed as legal jurisdictions such as municipalities, counties (or parishes). Magnolia Parish and the nearby City of Bayou share histories, but also share conflicting histories, as their proximity impacts each other. This set of histories is a dish of jambalaya with some spice: Jambalaya con Sazón.

Magnolia Parish

Ever since its founding in 1825 as a working-class suburb of a large southern port city, Magnolia Parish has historically prided itself as a hub of the working class. Adjacent to the City of Bayou, and easily accessible via multiple forms of transportation, Magnolia's quiet streets, generous open spaces, and proximity to the city, was instantly appealing to the early settlers—particularly to those seeking an alternative to the hustle and bustle of city life. In fact, within ten years of the parish's founding, Magnolia grew from a small suburb of 14 sugar plantations to well over 1500 single unit family homes.

By the late 1800s, Magnolia had a thriving port terminal and had become a major hub for cattle processing, dairy farming, and other waterfront businesses. As development continued westward, Magnolia Parish radically transformed into a thriving suburb that greatly benefited from its proximity to the City of Bayou. By 1925, Magnolia was providing educational services to well over 5000 students. Yet, the pressure for new schools continued in order to meet the educational needs of an ever-expanding population of working-class individuals.

By the early 1950s, Magnolia Parish Public Schools were providing educational services to nearly 12,000 students. Magnolia's reputation as a great place for employment, excellent schools, and burgeoning shopping, naturally drew more workers and their families into the city. Like their predecessors, most of the new residents were primarily White families who were fleeing from the City of Bayou, searching for a slice of suburban life. Unlike their predecessors, however, these new residents were also trying to avoid the forced racial integration of Bayou schools following the 1954 *Brown v. Board of Education* federal decision.

Given the rampant *White flight* from the City of Bayou in the 1950s and 1960s, the population of Magnolia was practically bursting. In fact, by 1960, the city's population was slightly above 200,000 residents with 32,000 students crowding into 38 schools.

During the next two decades, the parish nearly doubled in size, stabilizing at about 450,000 residents by 1980. Data suggests that, while Magnolia Parish became Whiter, Bayou had become more densely populated and non-White during this same period. Distrust and animosity between the two neighboring cities arose rampantly, as racial tensions led to racial animus, hostility, and general suspicion between African American and White populations.

By 1989, this reputation solidified when the people of Magnolia elected a well-known racist and former Grand Wizard of the Ku Klux Klan, who also expressed staunch anti-Semitism, to serve as their representative to the state legislature. The election of a declared racist tarnished the parish for many years thereafter.

Tragedy Strikes

In August of 2005, one of the strongest hurricanes to ever land on U.S. soil hit the entire Gulf Coast region. The National Weather Service named the huge, Category 5 storm, Katy, and it made landfall just east of the City of Bayou with winds gusting at over 175 miles per hour. Given Hurricane Katy's size, the federal government declared a state of emergency 24 hours prior to the storm's landing, mobilizing thousands of National Guard troops to the region. A hurricane warning was finally issued 19 hours before the storm, prompting mandatory evacuations in the City of Bayou (residents who could not leave because of transportation or health issues would be able to seek shelter in the city's professional football arena). The Magnolia Parish President also issued a mandatory evacuation for residents in low-lying areas, but strongly encouraged voluntary evacuation for all other residents in the parish.

As Hurricane Katy inched its way closer to landfall, City, parish, and other government officials—along with emergency personnel and National Guard troops—all had contingency plans in place. They were prepared for the worst and knew that the sheer size and force of the hurricane would leave behind a trail of destruction along its path. Despite their preparations and advanced knowledge, they could not anticipate, nor plan, for what happened once the storm made landfall.

Hurricane Katy made landfall at approximately 5:00 a.m., as a Category 4 storm. As powerful wind surges and heavy rainfall put enhanced pressure on the city's levee system, water levels immediately peaked, and water started pouring over the levees into the City of Bayou. By 8:00 a.m. that morning, several flood warnings had been issued. By 11:00 a.m., several portions of the City of Bayou were already under 10 feet of water. It was clear that at least one levee had been breached. By 2:00 p.m., three other levees in the city had also given way. Water was now flowing into the city at a rapid pace, winding its way among homes and through streets, consuming everything in its path: homes, cars, trees, fences, telephone and utility poles. The city had become a virtual swimming pool as pumping station after pumping station began to fail due to the sheer stress of trying pump out all of the water flowing into the city.

Within the first 24 hours, over 53 levees in the City of Bayou been breached. Over 85 percent of the city was flooded and there was no way to stop the flow of water from one of the levees. Residents of Bayou who chose to weather the storm, or could not leave for personal, material, physical, or health reasons, now needed evacuation. As images of individuals helplessly trapped on rooftops amidst rising floodwaters flashed over television screens across the world, it was clear that the majority of these individuals were Black and poor. With flood levels ranging from 20 feet nearest the levee to 1.5 feet in other parts of the city, Hurricane Katy was one of the most catastrophic natural disasters in the country's history.

Immediate Aftermath

For four days following the flood, residents of Bayou waited for help to arrive, but their patience wore thin. The city was in crisis, several thousand more National Guard troops mobilized, and federal emergency crews sustained around the clock efforts to rescue victims from their flooded homes. Yet, despite these search-and-rescue efforts, thousands of residents remained trapped in their homes or on rooftops without any assistance whatsoever. All of these victims were desperate, tired, hungry, and weak. Some gave up all hope of rescue and began to search for dry land on their own. Others held on for dear life but did not make it; their bodies were too weak from spending days floating in bacteria-infested water without food or drink.

This feeling of deep hopelessness and abandonment quickly festered into anger and desperation. The tens of thousands of individuals who had taken refuge in the Bayou Football Arena and Civic Center had no food and very little potable water. Bathroom facilities had run out of toilet paper and sewage backed into the restrooms due to the flooding. Parents ran out of diapers and baby formula for their children. Moreover, the small amount of emergency supplies ran out, and replenishment of supplies delayed. Although residents were promised that they would be relocated to a neighboring state, the process was painfully slow. After days of waiting, their patience evaporated.

On the fifth day following the storm, residents simply decided to take matters into their own hands. Some treaded water to a local Wal-Mart store and forcefully proceeded to take the supplies they needed. Others tried to steal vehicles, perhaps in an impulsive attempt to find some mode of transportation out of the flooded city. The looting and chaos only added to the stress of the search-and-rescue mission underway by federal, state, and local officials. In nearby Magnolia Parish, the situation was markedly different. While crime and chaos swept the City of Bayou, things were relatively calm and orderly in Magnolia Parish. While residents of Bayou were visibly frustrated and anguished, the streets of Magnolia were relatively empty—the majority of residents left the parish prior to the storm's arrival. While the City of Bayou was almost completely submerged under water, the flooding in Magnolia was largely contained to one section of the parish. Certainly, the stark contrast between Magnolia Parish and the City of Bayou was not lost, particularly on the residents of Bayou who felt desperately trapped and under police surveillance in their own city.

As frustration grew among those marooned in the City of Bayou, some residents crossed the river into Magnolia's West Bank to board buses that would shuttle them to a different state. About 6000 Bayou residents initially received permission to cross this bridge, patrolled by Magnolia Parish Police. Once transportation and fuel supplies in Magnolia became exhausted, evacuation of Bayou residents over the Magnolia jurisdiction discontinued abruptly.

Without knowing about the cancellation of the Magnolia evacuation route, a group of approximately 200 Bayou evacuees attempted to cross the bridge. This time, however,

Magnolia Parish Police met them at gunpoint and advised them to turn away. The evacuees refused to turn back, fully recognizing that the city they were fleeing from was not only under water but was in utter chaos. Not wanting to turn back, and prevented from moving forward, the evacuees decided to sit on the bridge in protest. After several hours of this faceoff, Magnolia Police decided to put an end to the civil disobedience by firing a warning shot to disperse the persistent crowd.

Scattering from the scene, evacuees came to conclusion that in their hour of greatest need their city, state, and federal government abandoned them; moreover, a judicial system more intent on maintaining law and order than in protecting and serving blocked their route to safety. Adding insult to injury, Magnolia Police defended their actions, blaming the City of Bayou for failing to manage its own crisis effectively. As far as they were concerned, they were hired to protect and serve Magnolia Parish not the City of Bayou; from their point of view, they were simply doing their job.

Post Hurricane Rebuilding

It would be several months before the City of Bayou could resume regular operations after the devastating storm. In total, there were over 1800 deaths associated with Hurricane Katy from the City of Bayou alone—the majority were flood victims. In addition, over 400,000 Bayou residents were displaced from their homes. Several could not return, because they simply had no home or family to return to. Those who did return found their homes practically destroyed by the storm and flood waters. Most homes were simply uninhabitable due mainly to mold and other structural damage.

Some residents took shelter in government-issued, Federal Emergency Management Agency (FEMA) trailers, while others were forced to look for rental properties outside the city while their homes were repaired. An unfortunate consequence of the storm was that it destroyed many of the city's apartment complexes resulting in a lower number of available rental units coupled with higher rental prices. Many of these families decided to move into nearby Magnolia Parish, along with hundreds of other families who no longer wished to live in the city. The outflow of Magnolia residents, who moved away and/or decided not to return after the storm, provided an abundance of affordable housing stock for these prospective residents.

In addition, the need to rebuild spurned a wave of immigration into the greater Bayou metropolitan area. Most of these newcomers were undocumented young men from Mexico, Honduras, and other Latin American countries who had been lured to the city with the reconstruction boom. The federal government enabled this demographic shift by lifting employer sanctions on companies who knowingly hired undocumented workers (Hew, 2006). In fact, construction jobs were so plentiful that many employers began to recruit workers from New York, Chicago, and Los Angeles. Many of these new recruits were not Mexican, but from other parts of Latin America: Brazil, Dominican Republic, and El Salvador. Most of these newcomers found the City of Bayou to be too expensive and chose to settle in nearby Magnolia Parish where multiple men shared a single home or apartment complex.

The massive hiring of Latinos to rebuild the City of Bayou fostered resentment among the African American community. Many African Americans desperately needed jobs, but most of the jobs went to younger, non-local Latino workers, perceived to work longer hours for less pay. In general, African Americans were upset that they now had to compete with a newcomer workforce for jobs in their own community. They were also angry that employers would intentionally seek out undocumented workers, rather than hiring an equally competent U.S. Citizen. This angered many civic leaders in the Black community and led to racial tensions between lifelong African American residents and their recently arrived Latino counterparts.

Two years following the devastating storm, Magnolia Parish transformed from being an almost exclusively White suburb to more diversity with over a 30 percent Black and Latino population. Although the parish lost a sizeable number of its White residents during this time, it gained many more new residents. These residents had complexions and accents that parish residents had never experienced. Spouses, children, and extended family members later joined many of the men, who went to Magnolia to work in the rebuilding efforts. They enrolled in local schools, shopped at local grocery stores, and went to local church services. Eventually, businesses that catered to the Latino community—grocery stores, meat markets, restaurants, beauty salons, repair shops, etc.—started appearing in Magnolia Parish imparting a distinct Latino flavor in different pockets of town.

Because these new residents were not concentrated in one particular section or barrio within Magnolia, but rather were dispersed throughout both the West and East banks of the parish, their impact was particularly felt within the Magnolia Parish Public School System (MPPSS). Schools not only had to educate many student from different countries (Mexico, Dominican Republic, Honduras, Brazil, etc.), but quickly learned that the students had a wide range of linguistic, instructional, and curricular needs. They spoke and understood different levels of English, had different literacy rates, and demon-strated different challenges in the classroom. Teachers quickly learned that Latinos were not a homogenous group. More importantly, school leaders quickly learned that they did not have the staff, skills, training, or resources necessary to work with this newcomer population— especially across a number of different schools in the parish.

A School System in Transition

By 2013, eight years after Hurricane Katy, Magnolia Parish had all but rebounded from the storm's devastation. The parish had not only recovered its population loss, but managed to lure new businesses, including several big-box stores, large chain restaur-ants, and a thriving medical plaza. The school district has also seen its fare share of changes in the aftermath of the hurricane: a host of local and state policy initiatives ushered radical changes in the form of charter schools, vouchers, and partnerships with alternative teacher and administrator preparation providers (e.g., Teach for America, Broad Foundation, etc.).

The ethnic composition of the district also changed dramatically in the eight years following the storm. In 1994, White students comprised nearly 70 percent of the enrolled student population at MPPSS. By 2006, one year after the storm, Whites comprised only 35 percent of the student enrollment, with African Americans comprising over 50 percent of the total student population. In 2013, the Latino population had grown to over 5000 students (10 percent of the student population), most of whom were children of Latino newcomers to the area. These demographic shifts necessitated substantive changes in staffing and curricular programming at MPPSS.

In fact, nearly every school in MPPSS underwent a major restructuring effort since the storm. The district office has become leaner in terms of overall staffing, while building-level administrators now have much more autonomy over fiscal, administrative, and curricular decisions. School principals, for example, have more discretion over personnel and staffing matters and have significant control over their respective school budgets. Although this is a welcome change from a bureaucratic standpoint, the changes have also brought a number of challenges to school principals—particularly for those administrators whose schools are impacted by non-White and English as Second Language (ESL) students. These principals must find creative ways to fund services and learning opportunities for these populations, while simultaneously provide support and professional development opportunities for teachers.

West Magnolia High School, for example, has had to do more with limited resources. In 2006, the high school of 1400 students enrolled only five ESL students. By 2013, the ESL population grew to over 250 students. Yet, despite this growth, the principal could only hire three ESL teachers and two bilingual paraprofessionals. While part of this staffing dilemma is due to a general lack of available certified ESL teachers in the state, a second challenge is learning how to navigate and balance the language and pedagogical needs of the ESL student population with the educational needs of non-ESL students at the school. This has not been an easy undertaking—particularly since there now are multiple stakeholders and interests groups at the school. Therefore, a third challenge faced by school leaders deals with the political landscape of the school itself, and how school leaders must navigate the social, cultural and political conflicts for the best interest of students (ISLLC Standard 6).

Marvin Perez

Marvin Perez is currently a senior at West Magnolia High School. He has an older brother, Dennys, and a younger sister Jomayra. Marvin's father is a construction worker who moved to Magnolia three months after Hurricane Katy left its path of destruction. Marvin and his family arrived in 2007 after his father earned enough money to send for Marvin's mother and two siblings. Their family is originally from the Dominican Republic. In fact, Marvin was born on the island and raised with his two siblings by his grandmother until Marvin was in the fourth grade. Marvin's parents were in New Jersey when their three children joined them. All the children struggled to fit in as newly-arrived immigrants. However, the fact that the family was once again united made the transition to the U.S. much more palatable for everyone, especially for Marvin.

While in New Jersey, Marvin struggled in school. He felt that schools in the U.S. and his beloved Dominican Republic were very different. He simply could not grasp many of the lessons that were taught to him, despite the fact that he was placed in an ESL classroom. Fortunately, he made very good friends and hung out with them during lunch and after school. These friends were also *Dominicanos*: children of African and Spanish ancestry, with prominent African features, and beautiful dark cinnamon skin. It is important to note that Marvin considers himself to be "*Latino*" or "*Dominicano*" and does not self-identify as "Black" (though he does find the term "*moreno*" to be a more culturally accurate signifier). This unique identity is grounded in the troubled post-colonial reality of the Dominican Republic, which is somewhat different from the experiences of African Americans in the U.S. For example, to be "*negro*" in the Dominican Republic is not the equivalent of being "Black" in the U.S.—for there are racial hierarchies, caste systems, and varying degrees of stigma that emerge from the Dominican Republic's historical past. In fact, one of Marvin's pet peeves concerns others viewing or labeling him as an "African American," which not only negates his cultural heritage and linguistic roots, but also rubs against a deeply ingrained—although unconscious—caste ideology.

Marvin's school records indicate that his command of English language is well below average. Since enrolling at MPPSS, he has consistently scored at the "Beginning" level in reading, writing, and comprehension in English, while ranking slightly higher ("Lower Intermediate") in his listening abilities. In contrast, Marvin's English speaking abilities are quite developed. In fact, his English Language Development Test (ELDT) scores suggest he is at the "Advanced" level in his ability to speak English. Marvin's ELDT scores have remained pretty consistent since his arrival in 2007. In effect, despite the fact that he can speak English quite fluently, Marvin remains unable to fully comprehend the totality of the English language and has not made much progress in his English language development.

Furthermore, Marvin has been struggling academically since entering West Magnolia High School in 2009. He has consistently received Ds and Fs in his report card (both interim and final reports), and his teachers consistently indicate that he does not complete his homework assignments and that he is not an active participant in class. In fact, Marvin received straight Fs during his 9th grade year, with the exception of art where he earned a C. Despite this absolutely dismal performance, Marvin was promoted to the 10th grade as well as the next sequence of courses in math, science, English, and social studies. Not surprisingly, Marvin received straight Ds in all of his courses and an F in physical education. However, because a D is considered a passing grade at MPPSS, once again, Marvin was promoted. In the 11th grade, he received a lighter academic load during the first semester: a physical education course, an ESL course, and a three-hour vocational training course in auto body repair. (Marvin failed the latter two courses, but received a C in physical education.) Unfortunately, instead of offering Marvin the opportunity to take courses that would solidify his understanding of those courses that he had failed, yet again, Marvin received promotion to the next sequence of courses in math, social studies, and science during the second semester of the 11th grade. Not surprisingly, Marvin failed all of his courses during the second semester of his junior year.

Because of his poor academic performance, Marvin was held back in the 11th grade. He received a lighter load during the first semester of his encore year—which included no math or science courses whatsoever. This seemed to work well for Marvin, because he received three Cs and one D that semester. During his second semester, Marvin added two science courses and finished the year with a cumulative Grade Point Average of 3.25 for the year; indeed, it would appear that Marvin was finally getting his act together. During his 12th grade year, Marvin kept a scaled down course load: a remedial math course, an English course, and a work–study course. Marvin initially struggled in both his English and math courses, but was able to pass them both with a D and C respectively.

Despite having marginally completed all of his coursework, Marvin could not graduate, because he could not pass the required state graduation examination. Starting in 10th grade, Marvin took the exam nine times, but received a score of *Unsatisfactory* on all portions of the examination each time. Marvin's school counselors realize that there are very few options available and now encourage him to submit the necessary paperwork to withdraw formally from school.

Marvin's mother fully recognizes that Marvin is not perfect, but also sees a problem with the high school administration that keeps socially promoting her child while doing very little to address his academic challenges. As far as she is concerned, Marvin has struggled every year since arriving at MPPSS, but the system pushed him through despite his poor academic performance and his pitiable scores on the state standardized tests. She believes he was promoted to the next grade and to successive courses in math, science, social studies, and English/language arts without the requisite foundation to be successful in those courses. In her view, the school set up Marvin to fail within a system in thoughtlessly promoting him to the next grade without consideration for his overall readiness and grasp of the course material.

After speaking with other Latino parents who also have children at the high school, Marvin's parents concluded that the problem of social promotion was widespread, particularly for Latino students in the ESL program. Marvin's mother is now threatening to sue the school district and has enlisted the assistance of a powerful non-profit civil rights organization to demand justice and put an end to this type of systemic social promotion.

Racial Tensions at West Magnolia High

Adding to the complexity of the situation with his academic progress is a series of events at MPPSS directly involving Marvin Perez. When Marvin arrived at West Magnolia High School, he knew he was different from the rest of the other students. His black skin set him apart from the other Latino students, who constantly teased him by calling him "*El Negro*" ("The Black one"). Moreover, his inability to speak English set him apart from the African American students, who also berated Marvin by saying things like: "*You're Black. Why do you speak Spanish? You're not Mexican!*" This teasing and bullying from Latinos and African American students alike continued throughout Marvin's first three years at West Magnolia High.

By the time Marvin was a senior, he had learned to shrug off the taunts. He befriended two other *Dominicanos* in the 10th grade and the three of them not only looked out for each other, but gave each other courage, confidence, and bravado. While the Latino students eventually stifled their teasing, there was a group of African American boys who relentlessly taunted Marvin and his friends for speaking Spanish. Buoyed by the confidence his friends gave him, Marvin learned to retaliate by flipping them the middle finger and/or holding his crotch while uttering some choice curse words in Spanish.

One day, an ESL paraprofessional observed this exchange and warned one of Marvin's ESL teachers. The teacher followed up with Marvin after class, but Marvin shrugged it off and said that he and friends could take care of the situation if it got out of hand. Later that same day, Marvin and his friend went to use the restroom. The same group of African American boys who had taunted Marvin earlier in the day was waiting inside; one of them uttered: "*Hey wetback! This is America—learn to speak English.*" Without looking at them, Marvin instinctively responded "*Hijos de puta*" ("Sons of bitches") to his friend; they both laughed and approached the urinals.

With their backs to the boys, Marvin and his friend exchanged commentary in Spanish while standing at the urinal. It was clear, that they were talking about the African American boys. What happened next occurred as an absolute blur: one second, Marvin was standing talking to his friend, and the next second, he lay unconscious on the floor. When Marvin regained consciousness, he was in a hospital room. According to his friend, Marvin received "*un puñetazo inesperado*" (sucker punch) by one of the African American boys. However, according to the African American boys, Marvin had turned around, gestured toward his penis, and told them something vulgar in Spanish, provoking one of them to punch Marvin in the face.

Without a definitive answer to what actually transpired in the restroom, school officials had no choice but to suspend both Marvin and the African American boy who had punched him. Marvin was given a 3-day suspension for lewd conduct, while the other boy was given a 7-day suspension for fighting. This only angered Marvin and his family, who insisted on his innocence. It only reinforced their belief that both school personnel and students systematically discriminated against Latinos. This incident united the Spanish speaking community in interesting ways, as they collectively grew to see themselves as victims and targets of discrimination at the school.

The racial tension between Latinos and African American students at West Magnolia High is now at a tipping point. Numerous incidents surrounding bullying and nativist/xenophobic commentary by African American students have been much more common as reported by students and teachers alike. In the same vein, Latino students have also grown increasingly intolerant of these types of taunts and are outwardly pushing back. There have also been reports that small gangs of Latinos threatened African Americans students without any justification or prompting whatsoever. Unfortunately, these types of threats, taunts, and intimidation tactics have become the norm at West Magnolia High School and they are coming from both Black and Brown students alike. School officials have absolutely no idea how to intervene or put an end to the animus between Latinos and African American students.

Clearly, larger social and community issues are seeping into the daily life of the school. As such, school leaders must not only have an understanding of the history of racism that has plagued Magnolia, but must understand current political challenges in light of this broader historical context. The Latino community is not only demanding treatment with respect and dignity, but that genuine opportunities exist for their children to succeed at school. The threat to sue the school and district for engaging in academically questionable education practices (such as inadequate ESL staffing, lack of academic progress checks, social promotion, etc.) is real. Latino parents have found a political voice—aided, in part, by local community organizations, the Spanish language newspaper, and a prominent legal aid and civil rights organization, which is interviewing parents (while simultaneously generating awareness) about the problems with the ESL program and the escalated violence at the school and district. Obviously, there is a need to provide a cogent and comprehensive response to these concerns.

However, school leaders must walk a fine line in their response. For example, they cannot blame or implicate African American students for their role in fights, but they also cannot ignore the fact that that the fights *are* grounded in racial tensions and cultural misunderstanding. School leaders also cannot alienate or downplay the concerns of White constituents who are worried about the increased violence in their community and the safety of their children. Many of the constituents—White, Black, and Latino alike—are now threatening to put their children into charter schools run by national providers (KIPP, GreenDot, etc.), unless MPPSS gets its proverbial act together.

DISCUSSION OF COMPLEXITIES WITHIN THE CASE

This particular case study is rife with issues of cultural conflict and misunderstanding, highlighting the importance and centrality of inter- and intra-cultural awareness and cultural sensitivity (Banks, 2008; Sleeter & Grant, 1987). Indeed, a more holistic appreciation of the larger cultural, social, political, and economic contexts in which schooling happens is needed in order to better understand the particular nuances of this case. The case itself underscores the impact of socioeconomic and cultural mobility—including immigration—and the various ways in which shifting demographic patterns often are instigated by larger events, yet have real effects at the local level (Stull et al., 1995; Suarez-Orozco & Paez, 2008; Suarez-Orozco et al., 2008).

The history of Magnolia is particularly important to understand because the parish was founded as a refuge from the neighboring City of Bayou. This history of racism provides an important backdrop for understanding this case (Anderson, 1988). For nearly two centuries, Magnolia catered to a largely homogenous population; it never had to wrestle with the realities of integration, racial differences, cultural sensitivity, and/or multicultural understanding. For all intents and purposes, as long as African Americans remained in Bayou, residents of Magnolia did not have to think about issues related to race whatsoever. It was not until Hurricane Katy fundamentally altered the social landscape that the residents of Magnolia had to deal with this new political reality.

The changing demographic landscape in Magnolia, coupled with the introduction of new educational rules and policies following the hurricane, provided a host of new challenges for district and building leaders. Not only were building leaders directly responsible for providing the requisite staffing for culturally and linguistically diverse students, but they also needed to have at least some foundational knowledge of the breadth, scope, and goals of the various ESL instructional models available. At MPPSS, this type of deliberate and intentional programming and staffing seemed to be missing. Instead, ELL students were seemingly pushed through the educational pipeline without much regulatory oversight or supervision.

With respect to the law, it is important to note that under *Lau v. Nichols* (1974), the U.S. Supreme Court made it clear that school districts must not only provide a meaningful education to language minority students, but that school authorities must take significant steps to deal with the language deficiencies of these students. Moreover, under *Castaneda v. Pickard* (1981), the courts ruled that the academic programming offered to ESL students must be "based on sound educational theory" and be "effectively implemented with the requisite resources for personnel, instructional materials, and space." Lastly, Title III of the No Child Left Behind Act (2001), provides specific guidelines and regulations surrounding evaluation, instruction, assessment, and accountability provisions for limited English proficiency students. In other words, schools must not only demonstrate that they are providing a sound instructional program for language minority students, but that the resources and staffing they provide to students ensure that these students are learning.

To be certain, school administrators must not only be knowledgeable of federal and state requirements, but must also have a firm understanding of ESL program regulations and policies for students—including, but not limited to, student assessment and placement, content delivery (Bailey, 2007; Echevarria & Short, 2009; Short & Fitzsimmons, 2007), and tracking of student progress (August & Hakuta, 2005). They must also have a firm understanding of instructional programs for ELL students (Gandara, 2005; Moughamian et al., 2009), including knowledge of best practices for Limited English Proficient (LEP) students, which necessitate one or more of the following:

- within classroom, content-based English language instruction;
- push-in support from a specialist who works with LEP students within the regular classroom;
- pull-out support from a specialist who provides targeted instruction outside of the regular classroom;
- formal dual language or bi-literacy programs;
- structured English immersion or Sheltered English instruction practices;
- out-of-school enrichment programs; and/or
- newcomer centers and schools to specifically support recently arrived students.

(López et al., 2013, p. 272)

School leaders must also keep in mind that Latinos are not a homogenous entity. Issues of race, class, caste, and immigration status intersect the Latino diaspora in unique ways (Wortham et al., 2001). Moreover, countries in Latin America each have unique traditions, accents, foods, music, and forms of expression. Therefore, in order to effectively meet the needs of different Latino groups, educators must first understand their unique traditions and customs, including their experiences and history within the U.S. (Millard & Chapa, 2004; Valdes, 1996). Furthermore, educators must have a firm understanding of language development theories, since individuals may speak a particular language, but may not be able to read or write in that same language. This last point is particularly important, because it has direct implications for issues of student placement, instruction, curriculum development, and program evaluation. Clearly, the need for trained ESL teachers who understand the particular nuances of language development cannot be over-emphasized in this particular case (Garcia, 1991; Menken & Atunez, 2001; Menken & Holmes, 2000).

The issue of racism is also a prevalent theme that is interwoven throughout the narrative. The racial tensions and divisions between residents of Bayou and Magnolia have deep historical roots. However, the arrival of Latinos into the area has added a new dimension to this racial equation: Some Latino groups express a particular form of racism toward individuals of African descent (both from Latin America and the U.S.) that is grounded in internalized oppression and emerges from a post-colonial reality. In this regard, racism within the Latino community is similar to, but not necessarily the equivalent of, White racism within the U.S. (Valdes et al., 2002). Meanwhile, African Americans may have their own assumptions about Latinos and/or Spanish speaking populations, and their racial animus toward Latinos (particularly immigrant communities) may have social, economic, and psychological underpinnings as well (Valdes et al., 2002). Moreover, the White community of Magnolia (including administrators and teachers at the school) may have a difficult time understanding and recognizing racism outside of the Black/White binary—in part, because this is the type of racism with which they are familiar and also because they don't recognize or see it outside of its most egregious forms (Bell, 1995). This may be a reason why school officials struggle to understand the tensions between Dominicanos and African Americans at the school (Valdes et al., 2002).

All of these issues converge on politics: the politics of race (Bell, 1995; Ladson-Billings, 1998; López, 2003), the politics of immigration (Perea, 1996; Suarez-Orozco et al., 2008; Wortham et al., 2001), the politics of change (Iannaccone, 1977), and the politics of language (López & Vázquez, 2006; May, 2012). The issues raised in this case study also connect to more established concepts within the politics of education such as conflict and power (Blase, 1991). Not only is there conflict in the form of violence at the school, but Latino parents, community groups, and legal organizations are applying pressure on the district to address and rectify its educational practices toward Latino ESL students. The conflict, in other words, has been "socialized" (Schattschneider, 1960) and awareness of school discrimination has moved beyond the person at the center of the controversy. Such political awareness not only provides the Latino community with a sense of power and agency (Lukes, 1974; Lutz & Iannaccone, 1978), but requires school leaders to address these concerns and grievances in a way that respects and honors their concerns.

Conflict (Stout et al., 1994) is also present among many White members of the community who believe that their values and way of life have deteriorated. Many are exerting political pressure to "vote with their feet" by threatening to leave the school district for alternative educational providers. On the flip side, conflict between the African American community and the larger city of Magnolia has a complex history that dates back to the founding of this country. The racism and bigotry African Americans experience in the Deep South is so deeply ingrained that the violence being manifested against the newcomer population may emerge from a space of "internalized racism" (Fanon, 1952).

Connections to ISLLC Standard 6.1

The ISLLC Standards for district and building-level leaders suggests that leadership candidates must "understand and can advocate for . . . students, families, and caregivers" (ISLLC Standard 6.1). This requires that leadership candidates not only know about the various policies, laws, and regulations that govern the education of cultural and linguistically diverse students, but also know about the "effects of poverty, disadvantages, and resources have on families, caregivers, communities, students, and learning" (ISLLC Standard 6.1).

This particular case study helps illustrate this Standard in practice, as it requires leaders to understand issues of multiculturalism and diversity (e.g., Banks, 2008,

---

LEARNING ACTIVITY 5.2

Professors using this case for instructional purposes should employ a problems-based approach with their students, first identifying the objectives students are to achieve, and then getting students to individually and/or collectively work on particular project(s) that emerge from this case (Bridges & Hallinger, 1995).

Some examples of projects include:

- Developing ideas, approaches, and strategies for teaching students, staff, and community members about the challenges and complexity associated with change.
- Developing ideas, approaches, and strategies for working through the various levels of difference in the school and/or district.
- Developing a conflict resolution or intervention strategy to deal with the racial tensions in school and broader community.
- Developing curricular, instructional, and/or pedagogical approaches that focus on community, relationship-building and unity—with particular emphasis on how to make every member of the community feel valued and included.

Grant & Sleeter, 2007), systematic racism (e.g., Bell, 1995), linguistic racism (e.g., López & Vázquez, 2006), the history of African Americans in the South (e.g., Anderson, 1988), Latino immigration (e.g., Suarez-Orozco et al., 2008), Latino intra-cultural differences (e.g., Wortham et al., 2001), second language learners (e.g., August & Hakuta, 1997), and knowledge of relevant school law (e.g., *Lau v. Nichols*; *Castaneda v. Pickard*, Title I, Title III).

This case also calls on leaders to think through the complexities of working in a changing social, economic, and political context, and the need to navigate the inevitable tensions that can erupt when change happens and/or when cultures collide. It calls on leaders to put themselves in the role of advocates—and to think about the ways they can work though the various issues within the case to make schools productive places of learning for all children.

LEARNING ACTIVITY 5.3

Instructors/programs using this case for assessment purposes of the ISLCC Standard (6.1) can use the problems-based approach referenced above, but employ a more action-based protocol, which requires that the leadership candidate collaborate with members of the broader community to gauge the efficacy of their approach. Some examples of projects include:

- Work with relevant constituents at the school and/or district to develop and implement a "climate survey" that focuses on issues of inclusion. Results from this survey can be used to generate a 3–5 year strategic plan for diversity.
- Form a task force of relevant constituents in the broader community to sponsor a town hall meeting on issues related to diversity, difference, and bullying-prevention. Issues raised in the town hall can be used to generate a community-based protocol that aims to delve further into respective issues.
- Form a task force of relevant constituents to develop and conduct an "equity audit" (Skrla et al., 2004) in the school and/or district. An equity audit is a data collection project to determine gaps or inequities in a particular area (e.g., student achievement rates, passing rates, graduation rates, suspension rates, dropout rates, tracking, teacher quality, etc.). The purpose of the audit is to determine whether gaps exist both within and across schools, and whether particular students are being differentially impacted. Results from an equity audit can be used to generate an action plan for equity and social justice.

NOTE

1   The case study was derived from a "real life" case. While it was not part of a research project, the facts in the case are real. The case was a part of a lawsuit where I was called to testify as an expert witness. Because I am using a real life case, the attorneys for the plaintiffs have asked that I use pseudonyms throughout—not only to protect the identity of the student, but also of the school district involved in this case.

REFERENCES

Anderson, J. D. (1988). *The education of blacks in the South, 1860–1935*. Chapel Hill, NC: The University of North Carolina Press.

August, D. & Hakuta K. (1997). *Improving the schooling of language minority students*. Washington, DC: National Research Council.

August D. & Hakuta, K. (2005). Bilingualism and second-language learning. In M. M. Suarez-Orozco, C. Suarez-Orozco & D. B. Qin (Eds.), *The new immigration: An interdisciplinary reader* (pp. 233–248). New York: Routledge.

Bailey, A. L. (2007). *The language demands of school: Putting academic English to the test*. New Haven, CT: Yale University Press.

Banks, J. (2008). *An introduction to multicultural education*, (4th ed.). New York: Pearson.

Bell, D. A. (1995). Racial realism after we're gone: Prudent speculations on America in a post-racial epoch. In R. Delgado (Ed.), *Critical race theory: The cutting edge* (pp. 2–8). Philadelphia: Temple University Press.

Blase, J. (1991). *The politics of life in schools: Power, conflict, and cooperation*. Newbury Park, CA: Corwin Press.

Bridges, E. M. & Hallinger, P. (1995). *Implementing problem based learning in leadership development*. Eugene, OR: ERIC Clearinghouse on Educational Management.

Brown v. Board of Education, 347 U.S. 483 (1954).

Castañeda v. Pickard, 648 F.2d 989 (1981) U.S. App.

Echevarria, J. & Short, D. (2009). Programs and practices for effective sheltered content instruction. In D. Dolson & L. Burnham-Massey (Eds.), *Improving education for English learners: Research-based approaches* (pp. 250–321). Sacramento, CA: California Department of Education Press.

Fanon, F. (1952/2008). *Black skin, white masks*. New York: Grove Press.

Gandara. P. (2005). Learning English in California: Guideposts for the nation. In M. Suarez-Orozco, C. Suarez-Orozco, & D. B. Qin (Eds.), *The new immigration: An interdisciplinary reader* (pp. 219–232). New York: Routledge.

Garcia, E. (1991). The credentialing of language minority teachers: Practice and policy issues. In U.S. Office of Bilingual Education and Minority Language Affairs (Eds.), *Policy issues for LEP students* (pp. 265–294). Washington, DC: U.S. Office of Education.

Grant, C. A. & Sleeter, C. E. (2007). *Doing multicultural education for achievement and equity*. New York: Routledge.

Hew, M. Jr. (2006). Prosecutorial discretion: An opportunistic defense to employer sanctions following Katrina, 31 *T. Marshall L. Rev.* 463.

Iannaccone, L. (1977). Three views of change in educational politics. In J. D. Scribner (Ed.), *Politics of education* (pp. 255–286). Chicago: University of Chicago Press.

Ladson-Billings, G. (1998). Just what is critical race theory and what's it doing in a nice field like education? *International Journal of Qualitative Studies in Education, 11*(1), 7–24.

Lau v. Nichols, 414 U.S. 563 (1974).

López, G. R. (2003). The (racially neutral) politics of education: A critical race theory perspective. *Educational Administration Quarterly, 39,* 68–94.

López, G. R., Harvey, L., & Chesnut, C. (2013). Latino English language learners in a changing demographic landscape: Critical issues for school leaders to consider in implementing best practice. In L. C., Tillman and J. J. Scheurich (Eds.), *The handbook of research on educational leadership for equity and diversity* (pp. 257–286). New York: Routledge.

López, G. R. & Vázquez, V. A. (2006). "They don't speak English": Interrogating (racist) ideologies and perceptions of school personnel in a Midwestern state. *International Electronic Journal for Leadership in Learning, 10*(29). Retrieved from www.ucalgary.ca/~iejll/volume 10/lopez_vazquez.htm

Lukes, S. (1974). *Power: A radical view*. London: Macmillan.

Lutz, F. W. & Iannaccone, L. (1978). *Public participation in local school districts: The dissatisfaction theory of American democracy*. Lexington, MA: D. C. Health.

May, S. (2012). *Language and minority rights: Ethnicity, nationalism and the politics of language* (2nd ed.). New York: Routledge.

Menken, K. & Antunez, B. (2001). *An overview of the preparation and certification of teachers working with limited English proficient (LEP) students*. Washington, DC: National Clearinghouse for Bilingual Education.

Menken, K. & Holmes, P. (2000). *Ensuring English language learners' success: Balancing teacher quantity with quality*. Washington, DC: National Clearinghouse for Bilingual Education.

Millard, A. V. & Chapa, J. (2004). *Apple pie and enchiladas: Latino newcomers in the rural Midwest*. Austin, TX: University of Texas Press.

Moughamian, A. C., Rivera, M. O., & Francis, D. J. (2009). *Instructional models and strategies for teaching English language learners*. Portsmouth, NH: RMC Research Corporation, Center on Instruction. Retrieved August 1, 2010, from www.centeroninstruction.org/files/ Instructional%20Models%20for%20ELLs.pdf

No Child Left Behind (NCLB) Act of 2001, Pub. L. No. 107–110, § 115, Stat. 1425 (2002).

Perea, J. F. (1996). *Immigrants out: The new nativism and the anti-immigrant impulse in the United States*. New York: NYU Press.

Schattschneider, E. E. (1960). *The semisovereign people: A realist view of democracy in America*. New York: Holt, Rinehart & Winston.

Short, D. & Fitzsimmons, S. (2007). *Double the work: Challenges and solutions to acquiring language and academic literacy for adolescent English language learners: A report to Carnegie Corporation of New York*. Washington, DC: Alliance for Excellent Education. Retrieved August 1, 2010, from www.all4ed.org/fi les/DoubleWork.pdf

Skrla, L., Scheurich, J. J., Garcia, J., & Nolly, G. (2004). Equity audits: A practical leadership tool for developing equitable and excellent schools. *Educational Administration Quarterly, 40*(1), 133–161.

Sleeter, C. E. & Grant, C. A. (1987). An analysis of multicultural education in the United States. *Harvard Educational Review, 57*(4), 421–445.

Stout, R. T., Tallerico, M., & Scribner, K. P. (1994). Values: The "what" of the politics of education. In J. D. Scribner & D. H. Layton (Eds.), *The study of educational politics: The 1994 commemorative yearbook of the Politics of Education Association (1969–1994)* (pp. 5–20). Washington, DC: Falmer.

Stull, D. D., Broadway, M. J., & Griffith, D. (Eds.), (1995). *Any way you cut it: Meat processing and small-town America*. Lawrence, KA: University Press of Kansas.

Suarez-Orozco, C., Suarez-Orozco, M., & Todorova, I. (2008). *Learning a new land: Immigrant students in American society*. Cambridge, MA: Belknap Press.

Suarez-Orozco, M. M. & Paez, M. M. (Eds.), (2008). *Latinos: Remaking America*. Berkeley, CA: University of California Press.

Valdes, F., Culp, J. M., & Harris, A. P. (2002). *Crossroads, directions, and a new critical race theory*. Philadelphia: Temple University Press.

Valdes, G., (1996). *Con respeto: Bridging the distances between culturally diverse families and schools: An ethnographic portrait*. New York: Teachers College Press.

Wortham, S., Murillo, E. G., & Hamann, E. T. (2001). *Education in the new Latino diaspora: Policy and the politics of identity*. New York: Ablex.

CHAPTER 6

The Politics of Community Collaboration

Bonnie C. Fusarelli and Cathy Chada Williams

CHAPTER OVERVIEW

The purpose of this chapter is to help school leaders understand the political ecology of schooling specifically focused on the complex interconnectedness of schools and other social service agencies. It examines the complex interactions of external communities and schools and discusses how principals can maximize the benefits of community engagement while understanding the potential pitfalls of such engagement. The chapter also describes the benefits of creating a sense of community within schools and provides suggestions on ways principals can make schools more welcoming. By reading this chapter and completing the related field assignments, school leaders should be better prepared to dive into the messy political arena of community engagement and hopefully develop new pathways to improve the lives of at-risk children.

In this chapter, the suggested Learning Activities and assessments were selectively derived from elements and sub-elements of ISLLC Standards 6.2, 6.2, and 6.3. The case presented in this chapter highlights important elements of ELCC Standard Element 6.1 and its sub-elements: specifically, the importance of school leaders working together with members of the community and other stakeholders (both inside the system and external to it) in crafting sound policy to mediate the effects of poverty, disadvantage, and lack of resources (6.1—knowledge). Doing so requires school leaders to move beyond being managers or even instructional leaders and into the role of vocal advocates for children (6.1—skills). To be effective in such roles, school leaders must understand the complexity of poverty and other disadvantages and work with others to influence the development of systemic, comprehensive policies that address the powerful impact of poverty on schooling (Elements 6.2 and 6.3). The dilemmas and issued raised in the immediately following case will bring each of these elements to light.

CASE 6.1: THE NEW NORMAL—LEADERSHIP FOR KIDS IN CRISIS

It was a typical day at Green Valley Middle School. Clive Watson, the principal, had started the day by walking around the school greeting staff and interacting with students. After the morning bell, he returned to his office to check email and retrieve voicemail messages. Clive kept his eye on the clock because he had a meeting at 9:30 a.m. with what he referred to as his Kid Talk Support Team, which consisted of three grade-level assistant principals and two counselors.

Though he met with this group regularly to discuss administrative matters, this meeting was different. He had started these meetings several years ago to discuss severe or unusual academic problems of students and as a team, brainstorm additional strategies to help these students be successful. Over the last two years, these meetings had morphed, as the discussion no longer focused only on in school issues. With increasing frequency, the discussions focused on students who were experiencing significant problems outside the realm of the school, but which were negatively impacting their ability to learn.

The number of unusual cases steadily increased over this period and Mr. Watson was not sure how this happened. The school had not changed significantly. Green Valley Middle School was located in a small town that was fiercely proud and supportive of its school. The demographics of the school had been stable for the past seven years. Of the 1200 students, 60 percent were eligible to receive federally supplemented meals, known as free and reduced-price lunch. The racial composition had remained stable with 50 percent African American, 25 percent Hispanic, 22 percent Caucasian, and 3 percent Asian students in the school. It had a stable staff; in fact, several of the teachers had been at the school over 20 years.

Over the three years that Mr. Watson had been principal, the student achievement scores on the state-mandated year-end assessments had climbed from 52 percent to 74 percent proficiency. Overall, the school was on the right track and Mr. Watson was proud of its accomplishments.

He glanced at the clock. It was 9:25—time to get to his Kid Talk Support Team meeting. He gathered his belongings and headed toward the conference room. Mr. Casey, the 6th grade administrator, and Ms. Bustos, the school counselor, were already there. The others trickled in, greeting each other and commenting on the unusually mild winter day. Mr. Watson started the meeting promptly at 9:30.

He asked Mr. Casey and Ms. Bustos to present their information on 6th graders first. Ms. Bustos explained that she had met with a 6th grade student, Miguel Garza, whose teacher, Ms. McDonald, had mentioned to Ms. Bustos. The teacher had been circulating around the classroom while the students were working on an assignment when she noticed a cockroach crawling out of Miguel's backpack. She had Miguel take the bag into the hall where he ran into Ms. Bustos. She helped him empty his book bag and several more roaches scurried out. Ms. Bustos was concerned and tried to call his mother but the phone number on file was no longer in service. Ms. Bustos decided to make a home visit instead. She reported that it was obvious that the family was in distress. Miguel and his three sisters lived in a one-room apartment with their mother, who was unemployed and spoke very limited English. Ms. Bustos noticed no source of heat in the home, and the mother reported that the water was not working. The open shelves in the kitchen exposed a lack of available food. Ms. Bustos attempted to help the mother talk to her landlord and access free county resources, but the parent was resistant to her help.

Mr. Casey also gave an update on 6th grader James McLamb, a student previously identified as in need of mental health treatment. James had lived in an abusive home and had watched his stepfather beat his mother. Even though his mother had recently left this stepfather and had a restraining order against him, James was a very angry young man who continued to struggle to control his behavior at school. The only local assistance available to James was day treatment, and his mother had agreed to send him. Mr. Casey reported that they had run into a snag. James' mother had a full-time job so she was not eligible for financial assistance even though she only earned minimum wage. Without assistance, she could not afford the cost of day treatment for her son. James was going to be staying at school. Mr. Casey reported that he was concerned that James was a "ticking time bomb" and that he was in the process of reconvening the special education team to adjust James's Individual Education Plan (IEP) and discuss other options.

Mr. Watson turned his attention to the 8th grade team, led by Ms. Holmes, the assistant principal, and Ms. Bustos, and asked them for an update. Ms. Holmes reported that they were not making any progress in accessing help for Mark Crumb. Mark identified himself as transgendered. Two weeks ago, he wore a dress to school and used the girls' restroom. He got into a physical altercation with a girl who was in the restroom at the time. That altercation meant Mark's suspension for five days with the girl suspended for two days. When he returned to school two days ago, one of his teachers, Ms. Martin, noticed he was pulling up his sleeves and picking at his arms. To her horror, she saw self-inflicted razor wounds across Mark's entire forearm. Ms. Martin reported the incident to Ms. Bustos. When Ms. Bustos contacted Mark's mom she said she would immediately come to the school. To her surprise his mother withdrew Mark from school, saying she would home-school him from then on. Early this morning, Ms. Martin received an email from Mark that she forwarded to Ms. Bustos. In the email, Mark said that if his mother kept him out of school he was going to commit suicide. Ms. Bustos said she would contact Mark's mother, but Ms. Bustos also warned that the mother was difficult to work with because of her own emotional/mental health issues. Though Mark would no longer be in school, Ms. Bustos hoped to try to get help for Mark.

The meeting continued until 11:00 a.m. with the staff offering suggestions about new strategies to help these students. "Thanks for the updates and for your hard work," he told his staff as he adjourned the meeting.

Mr. Watson started back to his office. As he walked through the school, he pondered about how much the job had changed over the years. When he took his first job as an administrator, these types of issues were the exception. His job was primarily working with the teachers and managing the facility. "I wasn't prepared for this kind of work," he mumbled to himself as he sank into his office chair. Several thoughts were racing through his mind. He was deeply grateful for the work of his Kid Talk Support Team. They always held the best interest of students in their care as being the most important part of their job—all of the students, even the most difficult. He realized, however, that the problems these students were experiencing were beyond the area of expertise of his Kid Talk Support Team, and that he needed additional partners at the table. But he did not know how to begin to access this help or if the superintendent would even support an initiative to try to partner with social services agencies. He quickly jotted down a few ideas and decided he would call the principal at the neighboring middle school for some shared thinking, but when he checked the time he realized he had four minutes to get to Mr. Tim Daniels' class. Mr. Daniel's formal teacher observation was due, and they had previously set the time for this day. He grabbed his electronic tablet and a clipboard with the required paperwork and headed down the hall.

ANALYSIS OF THE CASE

School leaders need an understanding of the rapidly changing social environment in which children are currently being raised. This understanding is essential to appreciate the politics of the development and implementation of coordinated school-linked services programs in schools. Ideally, families and communities should provide children with "all that they need—love, a secure childhood, adequate housing, access to health care, a good education, discipline of character, a sense of personal responsibility, and a commitment to their communities and their country" (White House Task Force for Disadvantaged Youth, 2003, p. 1). However, today's children and their families often live in communities experiencing an ecology of peril (Cottle, 2003), where they confront multiple and co-occurring hardships. As Garbarino (1995) observed, Americans are raising children in a socially toxic environment polluted by the combined effects of poverty, the breakdown of families and communities, and the neglect of children. Drawing from a variety of national and international demographic data, Fusarelli (2011) found that in the past 30 years, children in the U.S. have declined on most measures of child wellbeing.

As a result, an increasing number of students come to school not ready to learn. Their experiences reflect current grim statistics about America's children. Almost one in four (23 percent) of American children live below the poverty level (The Annie E. Casey Foundation, 2012). More than half a million children are living in foster care; about 1.5 million have parents in state and federal prisons; about 12 percent live in families whose dire circumstances qualify them to receive nutrition or food assistance; and estimates are that almost 1 million children are seriously abused or neglected each year. Concurrently, 15 percent of school-age children are seriously overweight; more than 2.6 million teens use illicit substances each month; 3 million are current smokers; and 47 percent of high school students have had sexual intercourse (60 percent of whom used a condom but an alarming 13 percent did not use any method to prevent pregnancy or disease transmission), putting themselves at-risk for unplanned pregnancies and sexually transmitted diseases (YRBSS, 2011). The National Institute of Mental Health estimates that 11 percent of adolescents receive a clinical diagnosis of depression. Moreover, "10–30 percent have subclinical but significant symptoms of depression, meaning that in any given classroom, as many as six students are probably suffering from depression to some degree" (Huberty, 2012 as cited in Desrochers & Houck, 2013, p. 12). Another alarming number: nearly 70 percent of fourth graders cannot read at a proficient level.

Such childhood statistics as these help spur caring individuals to search for creative, integrative policy solutions. A necessary prerequisite to creating effective policy solutions is having a clear understanding of the nature of the problem to be solved (Spillane et al., 2009). How a problem is framed or defined dictates the policy solution to that problem. If the identified source of the problem is incorrect, the proposed solutions will fail (Copland et al., 2009). Simply put, without data-based information, brainstormed solutions shoot at the wrong target. Similarly, overly simplistic solutions just tinker around the edges and fail to get at deep root causes, while overly complicated strategies rarely get implemented with fidelity, and thus, fail. The task of identifying the most promising approaches to address complex social problems is complicated by a lack of political consensus on the appropriate role of governmental agencies or services (including public schools) in addressing issues of poverty and child welfare.

An enduring challenge in American politics is to find consensus on the true nature of the problems that negatively impact students and their academic performance. An even greater challenge is to design and implement systematic social policy solutions to address these enduring problems. For many policy makers the locus of delivery is clear. Since these problems place children at-risk for academic failure, they place public schools at the nexus of interconnected social problems (Wang et al., 1997).

As Koppich (1993) explained:

> The topic of integrated children's services has come to occupy an increasingly prominent place on the political and public policy agenda. The reason seems relatively straightforward: "Report cards" for children and families, whether examined from national, state, or local levels, reveal a steady decline in the life situations for many of the USA's young people.
>
> (Koppich, 1993, p. 51)

Research indicates that this trend has endured over time. Income inequity, the gap in income between high-income and low-income families, has reached historic highs (Saez, 2012); rising dramatically over the last 30–40 years (Reardon, 2013). Historically, high-income families spend more on their children's development (an estimated four times as much in 1972), and this trend has steadily increased, with high-income families now spending nearly seven times as much on their children's development as low-income families (Kornrich & Furstenberg, 2013).

Further, although both remain high, economic inequality now exceeds racial inequality in education outcomes (Reardon, 2013).

> A related trend during the last 20 years is the growing social class gap in other important measures of adolescent "soft skills" and behaviors related to civic engagement, such as participating in extracurricular activities, sports, and academic clubs; volunteering and participating in community life; and self-reports of social trust.
>
> (Putnam et al., 2012 (as cited in Reardon, 2013, p. 12))

In sum, although the dream of upward mobility still exists, it has become far more difficult for many to accomplish (Neuman, 2013).

LEARNING ACTIVITY 6.1

Case Study Application Questions/Activities

1. How could Mr. Watson enhance his support team with resources already available in his school?

2. If you had the power to provide additional resources for Mr. Watson's school that would impact the cases in this study, what would they be? Be specific.

3. How could Mr. Watson work with his local community to better support his students like those in this case study?

See the website for additional activities to use in your school.

UTILIZING THE SCHOOL SITE

Schools remain the only enduring institution in many distressed communities. Thus, policy makers often design policy solutions that utilize schools and their staffs. Every morbidity and epidemic generates its own preventive curriculum, further displacing the academic curriculum. Unfortunately, very few of these curricular interventions have proven to impact vulnerability over time. Psychiatrists, psychologists, counselors, social workers and social science researchers long have realized that piecemeal programs are not powerful enough to change high-risk behaviors; such programs must be combined with other more individualized interventions. One-stop coordinated interventions stem from attempts to address the negative experiences of youth when they are forced to shop around for services. As Dryfoos explained, "This fragmentation—the patchwork quilt of unrelated problems—does not solve their problems" (Dryfoos, 1998, p. 28).

Piecemeal solutions are inadequate and schools cannot (and conceivably should not) respond to the myriad of social problems alone. Therefore, the creation of inter-agency health and human service programs that link schools and other service agencies is a strategy designed to provide a high-quality response to at-risk children without overburdening the school and/or the other agencies. Despite the seemingly rational notion that health, education, and social services ought to be readily available to students where they spend a large portion of their days (in schools) the collaboration between schools and other community agencies has a long history of political tensions (Fusarelli & Lindle, 2011; Smrekar & Mawhinney, 1999). Nevertheless, most academics and practitioners agree that student success is tied to social and political conditions that demand multiple services, from health to jobs and economic development, in both urban and rural communities (Blinn-Pike, 2008; Dryfoos, 2002). Educators and other social service providers must develop strong alliances for the benefit of all students.

However, for policy makers trying to craft appropriate policies and for policy analysts dealing with analytically challenging policy issues, one implication from the need for building strong alliances is to focus not only on conducting a high-quality, technical analysis (such as a benefit-cost analysis) but also on developing a nuanced understanding of the political context of the problem (Weible, 2006). As Weible (2006) noted, most policy analysis textbooks agree that understanding political systems is an important step in recommending alternatives (Weimer & Vining, 2005). Unfortunately, no well-established theoretical framework exists to guide policy analysts (and school leaders) in understanding politically contested policy disputes.

UNDERSTANDING POLITICAL SYSTEMS

Stakeholder analysis can be utilized to understand systems and is utilized to determine the likelihood that a strategy, venue, or alternative will be successful in initiating or preventing a policy change. Weible (2006) explained:

> Almost all applications of stakeholder analysis address a similar set of questions that can lead to a mapping of activities of multiple stakeholders (Brugha & Varvasovsky 2000; Crosby 1991). These questions include:
>
> 1. Who are the stakeholders to include in the analysis?
> 2. What are the stakeholders' interests and beliefs?
> 3. Who controls critical resources?

4. With whom do stakeholders form coalitions?
5. What strategies and venues do stakeholders use to achieve their objectives?

(Weible 2006, p. 96)

Stakeholder analysis differs from political feasibility analysis, which tends to focus on the probability of successfully implementing a particular policy alternative for a particular problem (May 1986; Meltsner 1972; Weible, 2006). Stakeholder analysis helps identify political roadblocks and develop strategies for achieving objectives. Some researchers would suggest that as policy participants, school leaders (and directors and program managers) can benefit from a careful stakeholder analysis to develop a systemic map of a political community and develop long-term, politically feasible strategies. They would argue that an understanding of political contexts (Bardach, 2005; Stokey & Zeckhauser, 1978; Weible, 2006; Weimer & Vining, 2005) or political competency is essential for successful leadership.

However, as Weible (2006) observed, some criticisms of stakeholder analysis have been noted. Among these critiques are the following three: (a) rapid changes in stakeholder coalitions quickly outdates any analysis (Brugha & Varvasovsky, 2000); (b) analysts create typologies, but rarely specify theoretical bases to illuminate causes (Crosby, 1991; Meltsner, 1972); and (c) most analyses focus on a single alternative, which limits policy conclusions and their utility over time (Crosby 1991; Ramirez, 1999).

Stakeholders typically are not concerned with only one policy alternative but with the outcomes of an entire policy subsystem sustainable over time. Therefore, many policy analysts ground stakeholder analysis in an advocacy coalition framework (Sabatier, 1988; Sabatier & Jenkins-Smith, 1993, 1999). Weible notes that the advocacy coalition framework is frequently used to explain stakeholder behavior and policy outcomes in intense political conflicts over periods of a decade or more (Sabatier & Weible, 2005). Therefore, the appropriateness of such a framework would need to consider the local context.

LEARNING ACTIVITY 6.2

Applications of Community Services Political Analysis

1. Investigate and report on local community groups/resources school administrators can utilize to assist these students and their families.
2. Interview a school administrator and ask if they experience situations similar to these within the case study. How do they access assistance for students?
3. Investigate local, state, and/or federal government assistance agencies. What is their role within the schools in your community?
4. Prepare a presentation that you will make to your local school board about additional resources needed to serve all students.

Advocacy coalition framework differs from stakeholder analysis because advocacy coalition framework defines a policy subsystem—not a specific alternative —as the most useful unit of analysis (Sabatier & Jenkins-Smith 1999; Weible, 2006). Stakeholders in a policy subsystem include local, state, and federal government officials, interest groups, nongovernmental organizations, community groups, researchers, members of the media, and target groups. These stakeholders often carry out multiple strategies to influence the decisions in different venues. For example, stakeholders seeking an integrated approach to social service provision might simultaneously pressure political figures and school system leaders, utilize the media, and try to convince opponents to support their views in public meetings (Weible, 2006).

THE NEED FOR COMMUNITY COLLABORATION

Since the passage of the NCLB Act, schools have been called to engage in district-wide, systemic reform efforts and educate all children to proficiency, regardless of ethnicity, income, or family background. This shift in federal educational priorities, from equal opportunity to (near) equal outcomes, is dramatic and unprecedented (Fusarelli & Fusarelli, 2005). Unfortunately, while expectations for educational excellence have risen, public support (particularly in the form of increased financing) has not increased, forcing schools to do more with less.

School leaders can do more with less by effectively influencing others to act in accordance with shared vision and goals. They must exert influence in a variety of forums—including the larger environment in which the school functions. Contemporary school leaders can no longer solely focus on what occurs in the schoolhouse; they are expected to tap into local resources more effectively to meet the needs of their students. Since greater expectations have not resulted in increased funding, school leaders must engage the entire community in school reform initiatives: tapping existing resources more effectively while simultaneously creating or building stronger communities (and families).

Fusarelli and Fusarelli (2005) noted that three significant, distinct, yet inter-related, policy and ideational currents have come together to shape current leadership practice. The three currents include: (1) powerful demographic and societal changes that challenge efforts at school improvement; (2) systemic reform initiatives such as NCLB that emphasize "the well being and learning of all children" so that no children are left behind; and (3) changes in the federal educational agenda that now focuses simultaneously on improved academic achievement, and equity and social justice. Although distinct, each ideational current draws from and is affected by the other two currents. Ideally, the three currents should be addressed concurrently, otherwise, the reform effort only tinkers around the edges of the problem and fails to create sustainable change. However, the admitted weakness in any reform approach that connects educational, health, and social services in communities is an inability to account for improvement or change in local needs or conditions (Cibulka, 1996; Crowson & Boyd, 1993a; Fusarelli, 2008; Haertel & Wang, 1995).

Indeed, the difficulty in documenting program effects contributes to the iterant cycles of coordinated services reform efforts.

Documenting program effects is complicated. First, the transient nature of at-risk populations can undermine the accuracy of pre-post assessments of coordinated services efforts. Individuals or populations who received services, may not be the same individuals or populations assessed as part of a time-delayed program evaluation. Second, increased coordination can result in increased utilization of social services. However, an increase in the number of clients utilizing a service can indicate to some policymakers that conditions are deteriorating thus resulting in a higher rate of use. It is difficult to determine in the short-term if increased number of clients is indicative of an increased need for the service or a more purposeful utilization of that service (and thus an indicator of progress in addressing at-risk families' needs).

A similar situation can occur with schools and standardized testing results. Successful inter-agency efforts to increase school attendance may inadvertently cause a dip in student achievement scores. As students who would historically be absent on testing days, (often students most likely to be low-performing because of historic truancy) are now reflected in the school's achievement data and report cards. Thus, depending on what metrics of success are used, such efforts are politically vulnerable to attacks of ineffectiveness. A coordinated-services or inter-agency program's ability to identify appropriate effectiveness measures and survive potentially negative short-term evaluations can determine the effort's long-term viability—especially in such politically contested terrain as the appropriate role of government in individual lives and community development.

Within this contested political terrain, the idea of creating connections with the community surrounding the school and community agencies to help improve student outcomes is not new. The waxing and waning of popular support for such efforts will be discussed throughout this chapter, but it is important to note that historically, a variety of specialized private and public agencies provided financial, medical, psychological, and employment assistance to those in high-risk circumstances. Unfortunately, these agencies often worked in a virtual vacuum—not knowing what services other agencies were or were not providing. This results in two major problems: (1) underutilization of the resources available and cracks in the system through which children and families could fall; and (2) inefficiency from a duplication of similar services by multiple agencies (Johnson, 2003).

To address the issue of fragmented, disconnected services, inter-agency collaborative programs were developed[1.] Researchers, school personnel, neighborhood organizations, religious groups, volunteers, and service providers began to combine the resources available to more effectively meet the needs of children and further enhance school reform efforts. The desire for a comprehensive or holistic approach to solve the multifaceted problems of today's youth has led to efforts to restructure service provision and the formation of increasing numbers of school-linked programs or community schools.

Every version of coordinated services has unique features and fall on a continuum from simple to complex administrative arrangements (Crowson &

Boyd, 1994; Dryfoos, 1998). A change in the physical location of the service delivery is straightforward (for example, providing physical space for mental health services in the school building). However, more promising, and much more complicated strategies, where the school becomes a true community school in which the school and the supporting intervention agencies are completely integrated and operate collaboratively, require a purposeful focus from school leaders who may be challenged to tap into different skill sets to successfully support such efforts.

PROFESSIONAL JARGON AND POLITICAL BARRIERS TO COORDINATED SERVICES EFFORTS

One challenge school and agency leaders face with efforts to coordinate is effective communication. As will be noted throughout this chapter, differences in professional jargon create barriers to effective cross-agency communication. For example, mental health services and other social service providers will often use the term multi-tiered system of support (MTSS) framework to describe efforts to engage school-based and community providers. The MTSS framework encompasses prevention and wellness promotion, universal screenings for academic and behavioral barriers to learning, evidence-based interventions that increase in intensity as needed, ways to monitor students' responses to implemented interventions, and systematic decision making about programming and services (Desrochers & Houck, 2013, pp. 13–14). They note that:

> The MTSS framework also mirrors the multi-tiered problem-solving models for academics and behavior that are commonly used in schools, such as response to intervention (RTI) and positive behavioral interventions and supports (PBIS). This alignment is important because it not only facilitates early identification and intervention but also enhances the link between mental health, behavior, and learning, and establishes a familiar forum for staff members to communicate, solve problems, and evaluate the effectiveness of the interventions.
>
> (Desrochers & Houck, 2013, p. 14)

It is not surprising then that, in recent years, public service agencies have sought greater access to schools because they believe they can more effectively provide services in a community school than in agency offices (Blinn-Pike, 2008; Brener et al., 2007; Cornwell et al., 2007; Slade, 2003; Tashman et al., 2000; Weist et al., 2006).

However, in communities distrustful of the educational establishment, one could question if the school is the appropriate location for coordinated services efforts. Similarly, concerns have been raised about using school sites for dealing with young people who no longer attend school. Should school-based centers serve out-of-school youth, as well as siblings and parents of current students? To address these concerns, some reformers have put forth a model that places services in a building run by community-based organizations. They believe this may make children and families more comfortable and therefore increase the likelihood they will utilize such services.

Regardless of the actual service delivery site, efforts to coordinate services for at-risk youth and their families are ripe with both intra- and inter-organizational political conflict. Contested topics include the following: (a) confidentiality (how much information agency personnel can share with school officials and vice versa); (b) space (Who gets the office with the window?); (c) turf (Whose job is it? Whose case is it? If it is shared work, who gets the credit/blame?); (d) professionalism (What is the proper role of the professional?); and (e) releasing students from class (or new hours for clinical staff to work before or after school with students). These contested topics all take time, energy, and a particularly skilled principal to navigate the morass and create appropriate policies and practices to better serve students.

Researchers have found that principals with strong interpersonal skills, who engender trust and are able to build respectful relationships with both agency and school personnel, are most successful in leading collaborative efforts (Dryfoos, 1998; Johnson, 2001). The leader plays a key role in establishing trusting relationships both within the organization and between organizations. With such trusting relationships, issues of confidentiality, space, turf wars, and professionalism are greatly diminished (Johnson, 2001).

A NEW ECOLOGY OF SCHOOLING

Over the last two decades there has been a new and increasing appreciation for the interdependencies (a "new ecology" of schooling) between schools, families, and communities (Fusarelli & Lindle, 2011; Goodlad, 1987). These two decades also generated a growing recognition that actively reaching out from school to community (building social capital) may be a necessary step in order to strengthen communities (thus building social competency in youth) if the school is to educate children successfully (Coleman, 1988).

Implicit in the design of many coordinated services efforts are concepts drawn from psychology and from Urie Bronfenbrenner's (1979) ecology of child development schemes, as well as concepts from John Dewey, Eric Erikson, Jean Piaget, and others. Simply put, all the schemas are anchored in the belief that children cannot fully develop without systems of support. When schools seek to connect the multiple systems a child encounters, they are utilizing Bronfenbrenner's ecological systems theory that focuses on the context (and to a lesser degree, the quality of that context) of a child's environment. The key question being: How does a child's world help or hinder continued development?

Bronfenbrenner's ecological systems theory explains child development within the context of children's relationships, social networks, and institutions. This set of contexts form onion-like layers surrounding an individual's development. This nesting imposes a social net for the individual and simultaneously represents societal order. The layers may operate independently but their combined impact can be either positive (builds human capital and healthy stable social systems) or negative (erodes self-efficacy, lowers social competence, creates dysfunction). Bronfen-brenner delineated five layers of nested systems: the microsystem (such as the family or classroom); the mesosystem (two microsystems in interaction); the exosystem (external environments, which indirectly influence development, such as parental workplace or community-based resources); the macrosystem (the larger socio-cultural context); and the chronosystem (the evolution of the external systems over time). These systems, individually and collectively, shape development. Changes or conflict in any one system will ripple throughout other systems. Therefore, multiple systems and the interactions between those systems shape a child's development.

Bronfenbrenner's model may help explain why efforts to establish coordinated, school-linked services for at-risk children and their families are often politically sensitive and open to misinterpretation and distrust from the intended beneficiaries (Crowson & Boyd, 1995a, 1995b; Schutz, 2006). For example, cultural expectations of the macrosystem (parents should raise their own children) may conflict with the real and present needs of families (microsystem) or local norms that include communal approaches to child rearing. Furthermore, each partnering agency may possess its own institutional norms inconsistent with community expectations or, what Ogbu (1974) termed, discontinuities of culture.

POLITICS OF COMMUNITY COLLABORATION

Effective educators know that they must connect both to the individual student and to the community in which the student lives. However, an awareness of the interdependencies necessary to support students' development and learning does not diminish the historical political tensions among social agencies and schools (Boyd, 1979, 1983; Wood & Boyd, 1981). These political tensions have long simmered—given that the childhood social services movement dates to the settlement houses and urbanization of the progressive era at the turn of the 20th century (Fusarelli & Lindle, 2011; Halpern, 1995; Zetlin & Boyd, 1996). (*For a more in-depth overview of the history of coordinated services for at-risk youth, please see the online component connected to Chapter 6.*)

Creating new links among schools, families, and communities, revisit tensions in the American political system for which historically there has been no clear resolution (Cibulka, 1996). Cibulka (1996) identified four tensions that constrain coordinated services efforts in education and impede strong support for coordination efforts. First, a tension exists between different visions of the proper role of schooling. Should schools fulfill a social role or should they focus solely on their academic purpose? What are the appropriate roles of parents, educators, and other professionals in children's development? Second, there is debate over the role of laypersons in service provision. Is it a threat to professionalism? Third, there are conflicting assumptions about the extent of protection that should be offered children and families. In other words, how broad should the safety net be and what mixture of public and private provision should define the institutional characteristics of that net? Fourth, there is tension over the primary goal of coordinating services. Is the major goal efficiency or should equality of opportunity or outcome be the chief concern?

Crowson and Boyd (1993b) contributed to our understanding of these challenges. They noted that integrative or collaborative efforts often require a change in the school's governance structure. Such changes pose additional organizational problems such as the following:

(a) problems of space and facilities management;
(b) funding issues and resource mingling;
(c) differing salary and personnel policies;
(e) new roles and relationships between educators and other agency personnel;
(f) leadership issues;
(g) deficits and differences in professional preparation programs and training;
(h) issues of communication, information sharing, confidentiality, and information retrieval; control issues; and
(i) legal and turf issues.

(Crowson & Boyd, 1993a; 1994; Johnson, 2001; Kirst, 1991)

Fusarelli and Lindle (2011) noted additional challenges. First, collaboration requires a new way of thinking about social problems. The historical division of an individual, at-risk client's needs into distinctive problems, or deficits, often viewed as amenable to treatment by the application of an agency's staff energy and expertise, proved to be ineffective at altering outcomes. The multiple co-morbidities facing many youth cannot adequately be addressed by using isolated and specialized experts to unilaterally address each problem (Fusarelli & Lindle, 2011). The first glimmer of this shift in thinking emerged from the field of psychology in the 1970s. Since that time, there has been a growing, and more nuanced, understanding of the complexity of the problems that confront at-risk youth and their families. Contemporary social service agencies have a more comprehensive focus and use a holistic approach to address the needs of at-risk families, thus they are better positioned to collaborate with schools (Fusarelli & Lindle, 2011).

As social scientists and practitioners began developing and adopting more holistic approaches in the late 1970s and early 1980s, both state and federal legislators introduced bills that mandated comprehensive, collaborative social service delivery. Examples included: Maternal and Child Health Block Grants; the Bureau of Primary Health Care; New Jersey's School-Based Youth Services Program (1987); Kentucky's School-Based Youth Service Centers (1988); California's Healthy Start Support Services for Children Act (1991); New York City Beacons Program (1992)—(Beacons was identified as a Family and Community Endeavors prototype in the 1994 Crime Bill).

Even so, legislative mandates were not widespread, presumably due to the deep political divides over many social issues. Philanthropic organizations also started to focus energy and resources on comprehensive strategies to address the needs of at-risk families. Foundations like The Robert Wood Johnson Foundation, Dewitt-Wallace Readers Digest, Carnegie Corporation's Turning Point initiative, The Hogg Foundation for Mental Health, Anne E. Casey, Kaufman, Kellogg, Stuart, and more recently the Bill and Melinda Gates Foundation, all funded or still fund efforts to coordinated services for at-risk youth and families. The soft-funding nature of most of these types of reforms meant that they could not create dramatic organizational or institutional change. The soft revenue streams relegate such efforts to a peripheral and temporary task or project and do not become a part of the organizational operating budget (Crowson & Boyd, 1996a).

Even when fully funded, mandated coordinated services efforts face challenges common to top-down initiatives. Institutional theorists (March & Olsen, 1975; Bidwell, 1975; Weick, 1976) offered a term for the diffuse governance and organization of schools: loose coupling. As loosely coupled systems, schools often lack complete buy-in for any mandate. Understanding an organization as a loose coupling of actors, rewards, and technology may explain how organizations resist change, yet remain adaptive to environmental pressure and shifts. Weick (1976) observed that loosely coupled systems occur in situations where: (a) several means can produce the same result; (b) there is a lack of coordination; (c) an absence of regulations; and (d) highly connected networks with very slow feedback times. These loosely coupled characteristics sustain the organization in the following ways: by allowing the organization to temporarily persist through rapid environmental fluctuations; by improving the organization's sensitivity to the environment; by allowing local adaptations and creative solutions to develop; by allowing subsystem breakdown without damaging the entire organization; and by allowing more self-determination by participants (educators). Loosely coupled systems permit the old adage of the right hand not knowing what the left is doing to occur without creating much damage or change in the organization.

Another perspective on how coordinated services have influenced schools comes from Crowson and Boyd (1995a; 1996b), who utilized new institutional theory. Their application of institutional theory explained how institutional forces induced enough fragmentation to protect the technical core activities of schools, that is, teaching and learning. Crowson and Boyd explained that schools forced to collaborate with other agencies often react by protecting technical activities and reducing efficiency in a phenomenon termed decoupling by institutional theorists (Zucker, 1987). The institutional response to pressures to collaborate is to retreat to its specialized societal position and disengage, i.e., decouple, from any alliance (Crowson & Boyd, 1995a, 1995b). An alternate response in schools is to *pedagogize* any innovations in service delivery by making them more school-like, institutional practices and that often results in a lack of fidelity to the program design (Crowson & Boyd, 1995a, 1995b; Smrekar & Mawhinney, 1999).

However, institutions (especially public institutions) and their revenue streams are changing. "Contemporary de-differentiation tendencies have engendered a high degree of inter-dependence between and among organizations, institutions and aspects of them, and other forms of life . . . Institutions are becoming more organic, flexible, and subject to more rapid changes than ever before" (Crowson & Boyd, 1994, p. 200). The "formerly fuzzy boundaries between the private lives of families and the public responsibilities of schools are redrawn" (Smrekar, 1994, p. 29). In our rapidly changing social and cultural landscape, during this era of increased school accountability, it seems reasonable to believe that schools will respond with an increased willingness to coordinate with other agencies to do whatever-it-takes to improve the lives of underserved and vulnerable children and youth (Fusarelli & Lindle, 2011).

FROM COORDINATED SERVICE TO COMMUNITY DEVELOPMENT

The academic development of each student is linked indivisibly to mental and physical health and wellbeing. Similarly, schools are inseparable from their community's social and economic health and wellbeing (Fusarelli & Lindle, 2011). Therefore, community development is emerging as an alternative strategy to coordinated services. This contrasts sharply with Waller's (1932) notion, still widely held by many today, of schools as institutions with capacity for independently building a new social order. Contemporary school reformers argue that if public education is to be saved, then U.S. schools must figure out a way to ensure that schools are central to the life of the community (Schlechty, 2001). When the U.S.' system of public education was built, the purpose of schools was to serve the community, but since then the idea of community has changed substantially and some question whether a community remains to be served. As Schlechty asked: "Is there a public for public schools?" (p. 19). At the extreme, reformers call for schools to be agencies intended to build communities rather than agencies intended to serve communities (Schlechty, 2001).

Just as technology has created new ways to access information and new forms of social connections (Facebook, tweeting), such media simultaneously created the potential for disconnection (reduced face-to-face personal interactions), and new forms of aggression (cyber bullying). Humans want to belong to a community. At an accelerated rate, today's children are desperately pursing artificial belongings because their affiliation needs are not being met by families, schools, and neighborhoods (Brendtro & Long, 1995, p. 53). When youth experiences a loss in family or a loss of community they either create substitutes for this loss or attempt to exist alone, which has accompanying negative psychological consequences (Brendtro & Long, 1995). Young people inevitably create surrogate families or communities despite some inherent dysfunctional characteristics among these substitutes (i.e., gang affiliations, promiscuity, cult involvement, detachment, extreme dependency, mass school shootings). Though youth seek surrogates to provide security, affection, and a sense of belonging that they miss, these substitutes may be inadequate leading to even more dire consequences.

Norms (how things are usually done and what is considered normal and acceptable) are important to young people and in schools powerful and extensive norm systems develop that constitute a student subculture (Sergiovanni, 1990). While participation in an identifiable student subculture is a healthy part of the transition from adolescence to adulthood, when a student subculture distances itself from the mainstream norms of society it can have a profound negative impact on how students think and behave and thus negatively impact school culture. A school with a toxic culture, where students do not feel safe, respected or connected, is incapable of supporting student learning and efforts to coordinate services and build healthy communities.

Schools cannot replace families or communities but they can help diminish the loss of connection felt by many of today's youth. As schools work to build a sense of community in the school and provide a safety net that includes one-stop access to a variety of social services, they are also facilitating the strengthening of families and communities. The effective school leader helps build the community students need—both in and out of the school. (See the related activities chapter website on how school leaders can assess the school environment as well as strategies to build healthy school climates.)

A NEW IDENTITY: THE COMMUNITY PRINCIPAL

An important and enduring political question is: Should schools even be involved in efforts to coordinate services for at-risk youth and build community—both in and out of the school building? This has been a perplexing issue since the progressive era and continues to be a major lightening rod issue in some communities. Dryfoos (1998) provided an illustrative example: "When school-based clinics with mental health counseling were first proposed in Arkansas, state health department personnel were accused of being 'child snatchers.'" Militant opposition groups who loudly claim they are protecting the sanctity of the family almost never include parents of the children in the school (Dryfoos, 1998, p.40).

While the controversy has dwindled in most communities over the last decade, (due in part to depressed economic conditions), principals must be aware of the types of deep philosophical questions about the proper role of schools and schooling that such efforts inevitably evoke. As school and community leaders become activist in their activities aimed at creating a sense of community in schools and creating links between schools and community agencies, schools increasingly become positioned as politicized, cold, bureaucratic government agencies where once they were viewed as a special kind of place—an idyllic schoolhouse detached from the contentious world of politics. An unintended consequence of such a shift is that the public may have less confidence in schools that are viewed as politicized and local school boards may see themselves as losing control of their schools and resort to top-down control strategies to reassert their authority.

The mission of schools as promulgators of a common democratic culture is not much talked about nowadays (Schlechty, 2001, p. 29). The operation of many school boards today reflects this loss of a democratic culture. No longer populated with public benefactors, school boards are increasingly fractious—serving the rising influence of special interest groups and, for some, serving as stepping-stones for more powerful public offices. Too many boards symbolize and exacerbate the ways many communities are torn and divided against themselves (Schlechty, 2001). (See Chapter 4 in this volume for a more in-depth discussion of school-board politics.)

As numerous researchers have observed, "rather than serving the community, modern educators must serve many communities, factions, interest groups, and organized lobbies—each of which is in a position to make demands and assert expectations"—often competing expectations on the school (Schlechty, 2001, p. 19; Fusarelli & Fusarelli, 2005). Schlechty (2001) summarized the challenge to public school survival as dependent on school leaders becoming community leaders and community organizers:

> . . . school leaders, including boards of education, must find ways of building and leading community as well as ways of representing and responding to diverse interests and beliefs that characterize so many local school districts. Skill in building communities and skill in creating a sense of the common good is what is now needed in schools.
>
> (Schlechty, 2001, pp. 19–20)

Even as proactive leaders focus on coordinating social services and establishing community schools, which are more friendly learning communities focused on the whole child, some reformers call for even bolder change. Community development or grassroots activism is emerging as an alternative to coordinated services. These efforts embrace the language of market systems and frequently utilized terms include, enterprise, self-reliance, indigenous leadership, entrepreneurship (Crowson, 1998), and more recently, *greenfielding* education (Hess, 2010).

The extent to which market-based solutions will be acceptable to social services providers is unclear. Given the "deep progressive era roots with a focus on protecting the poor (particularly women and children) from the ravages of the market there is a residual distrust against market-based solutions among human service professionals" (Crowson, 1998, p. 60). Nevertheless, market solutions are on the rise, creating the possibility of a new national shift from services to self-help and entrepreneurship.

It is important to note that a central and significant difference exists between servicing and enterprising, which may be similar to the previously outlined differences between traditional mental health services and wraparound services. Crowson (1998) pointed out that providing added (even coordinated) services to families and children can proceed with only a minimal involvement of the client in decision processes. However, the passive client vanishes in a market-based model that typically includes consumer empowerment. Consumers form new coalitions typically to change corporate practices and reflect market conditions. In a truly empowered community, new tensions (and possibly historically old wounds) can emerge as the community engages in the politically laden process of moving from supplying and servicing (e.g., needs) to meeting and responding (e.g., to increased demands for political control) (Crowson, 1998; Fusarelli & Fusarelli, 2005).

Over 50 years ago, Milton Friedman (1962) argued that schools are no different from other institutions in a capitalist market system and that only choices in a free-market environment can produce the highest quality of any service—including educational and social services. School choice advocates want to switch the control of educational placements to parents creating market systems that may lead to the continuing erosion of traditional notions of community. A probable consequence of a market-based approach is that like-minded individuals will separate themselves from the larger public and create new communities in idiosyncratic and isolating ways. Such strategies may result in a de facto segregation of high-need children, youth, and families, thus creating new political dynamics around efforts to provide coordinated services. Conversely, some market-built schools will find their isolation resource-starved and they may not be able to provide social infrastructure for their families who need services beyond the school. To a degree, some public systems have seen this play out in requirements to include home-schooled youth in their athletic teams.

Despite all this, schools are still the best-positioned institutions to provide integrated services to children as well as connect adults to each other in a common democratic culture. Principals and teachers must understand the motives (and apathy) students bring with them to school and design the school experience in such a way to capitalize on these motives and engage students in the intellectual life of school. In developing learning experiences for their students, principals and teachers must consider both their students' local lived experience with their uncensored access to a virtual world with seemingly unlimited information. Ideally, they will use community history and norms to motivate students to engage in a school experience restructured to better meet non-academic needs and better reflect the evolving nature of knowledge and knowledge production.

QUESTIONS AND REFLECTION ACTIVITIES

Assuming it is the proper role of a school leader to address the non-academic needs of their students—including building a sense of community both inside and outside of the schoolhouse—then we need leaders who are social scientists and social architects (Fusarelli & Fusarelli, 2005). As you review the case presented at the beginning of this chapter, use the following questions to help you focus on how Standards 6.1, 6.2 and 6.3 can be applied to the situation at Green Valley Middle School.

For assignments and activities to further explore the topic of coordinating social services for at-risk youth and their families, please see the online extension and enrichment activities for Chapter 6.

LEARNING ACTIVITY 6.3

1. How does a principal create a safety net of integrated social services for at-risk students at their school, one that helps bolster student performance?
2. How does a principal foster a deep and genuine sense of community in their school?
3. How can schools become places where community members want to be actively involved?
4. How can we create schools where students wake up every day, excited about going to school and excited about learning?

NOTE

1   In this chapter, the terms "coordinated," "collaborative," and "integrated" services are used interchangeably. However, as Crowson and Boyd (1993a) noted: "Precise usage of these terms would place them on a continuum ranging from terms referring to minimal cooperation between agencies to terms implying full integration of agencies' programs, governance, and funding streams" (p. 173).

REFERENCES

The Annie E. Casey Foundation, (2012). *KIDS COUNT data book: State trends in child well-being.* Available at: www.aecf.org/KnowledgeCenter/Publications.aspx?pubguid={68E8B2 94-EDCD-444D-85E4-D1C1576830FF}

Bardach, E. (2005). *A practical guide for policy analysis* (2nd ed.). Washington, DC: CQ Press.

Bidwell, C. E. (1965). The school as a formal organization. In J. G. March (Ed.), *Handbook of organizations* (pp. 972–1019). Chicago, IL: Rand McNally.

Blinn-Pike, L. (2008, February). Sex education in rural schools in the United States: Impact of rural educators' community identities. *Sex Education, 8*(1), 77–92.

Boyd, W. L. (1979). Educational policy making in declining suburban school districts: Some preliminary findings. *Education and Urban Society, 11,* 333–366.

Boyd, W. L. (1983). After word: The management and consequences of decline. *Education and Urban Society, 15,* 255–261.

Brendtro, L. & Long, N. (1995). Breaking the cycle of conflict. *Educational Leadership, 52*(5), 52–56.

Brener, N., Wheeler, L., Wolfe, L., Vernon-Smiley, M., & Caldart-Olson, L. (2007, October). Health services: Results from the school health policies and programs study 2006. *Journal of School Health, 77*(8), 464–485.

Bronfenbrenner, U. (1979). *The ecology of human development.* Cambridge, MA: Harvard University Press.

Brugha, R. & Varvasovsky, Z. (2000). Stakeholder analysis: A review. *Health policy and planning, 15*(3), 239–246.

Cibulka, J. (1996). Conclusion: Toward an interpretation of school, family and community connections: Policy changes. In J. G. Cibulka & W. J. Kritek (Eds.), *Coordination among schools, families, and communities: Prospects for educational reform* (pp. 403–435). Albany, NY: State University of New York Press.

Coleman, J. S. (1988). The creation and destruction of social capital: Implications for the law. *Journal of Law, Ethics, and Public Policy, 3*, 375–404.

Copland, M. A., Knapp, M. S., & Swinnerton, J. A. (2009). Principal leadership, data, and school improvement. In T. J. Kowalski & T. J. Lasley II (Eds.), *Handbook of data-based decision making in education* (pp. 153–172). New York: Routledge.

Cornwell, L., Hawley, S., & St. Romain, T. (2007, June). Implementation of a coordinated school health program in a rural, low-income community. *Journal of School Health, 77*(9), 601–606.

Cottle, T. J. (2003). *At peril: Stories of injustice*. Amherst, MA: University of Massachusetts Press.

Crosby, B. L. (1991). *Stakeholder analysis: A vital tool for strategic managers*. Washington, DC: USAID.

Crowson, R. L. (1998), Community empowerment and the public schools: Can educational professionalism survive? *Peabody Journal of Education, 73*(1), 56–68.

Crowson, R. L. & Boyd, W. L. (1993a). Coordinated services for children: Designing arks for storms and seas unknown. *American Journal of Education, 101*(2), 140–179.

Crowson, R. L. & Boyd, W. L. (1993b). Structures and strategies: Toward an understanding of alternative models for coordinated children's services. In K. L. Alves-Zervos & J. R. Shafer (Eds.), *Synthesis of research and practice: Implications for achieving schooling success for children at-risk* (pp. 61–94). Publication Series #93–5. Philadelphia: Temple University, National Education Center on Education in the Inner Cities. (ERIC Document Reproduction Services No. 364652).

Crowson, R. & Boyd, W. (1994). *Achieving coordinated school-linked services: Facilitating utilization of the emerging knowledge base* (Publication Series #94–6). Philadelphia: Temple University, National Education Center on Education in the Inner Cities. (ERIC No. 400350)

Crowson, R. & Boyd, W. (1995a, June). *The constraints to coordinating services for children: A new institutionalism perspective*. A paper presented at the annual meeting of the American Educational Research Association, San Francisco, CA.

Crowson, R. & Boyd, W. (1995b). Integration of services for children. In L. C. Rigsby, M. C. Reynolds, & M. C. Wang (Eds.), *School-community connections: Exploring issues for research and practice*. San Francisco, CA: Jossey-Bass.

Crowson, R. & Boyd, W. (1996a, June). *Achieving coordinated school-linked services: Facilitating utilization of the emerging knowledge base*. Publication Series #94–6. Philadelphia: Temple University, National Education Center on Education in the Inner Cities. (ERIC Document Reproduction Services No. 400 350)

Crowson, R. & Boyd, W. (1996b, June). Achieving coordinated school-linked services: Facilitating utilization of the emerging knowledge base. *Educational Policy, 10*(6), 253–272.

Desrochers, J. E. & Houck, G. M. (2013). *Depression in children and adolescents: Guidelines for school practice*. Silver Spring, MD & Bethesda, MD: National Association of School Nurses & National Association of School Psychologists.

Dryfoos, J. G. (1998). *Safe passages: Making it through adolescence in a risky society, what parents, schools, and communities can do*. New York: Oxford University Press.

Dryfoos, J. (2002). Full-service community schools: Creating new institutions. *Phi Delta Kappan, 83*(5), 393–400.

Friedman, M. (1962). *Capitalism and freedom*. Chicago: University of Chicago Press.

Fusarelli, B. C. (2008). The politics of coordinated services for children: Inter-institutional relations and social justice. In B. S. Cooper, J. G. Cibulka, & L. D. Fusarelli (Eds.), *Handbook of research on the politics of education* (pp. 350–373). Mahwah, NJ: Erlbaum.

Fusarelli, B. C. & Fusarelli, L. D. (2005). Superintendents as applied social scientists and social activists. In L. G. Björk & T. Kowalski (Eds.), *The school district superintendent: Role expectations, professional preparation, development and licensing* (pp. 187–206). Thousand Oaks, CA: Corwin Press.

Fusarelli, B. C. & Lindle, J. C. (2011). The politics, problems, and potential promise of school-linked social services: Insights and new directions from the work of William Lowe Boyd. Special Issue: A fifty-year retrospective on education politics and policy: Examining the intellectual leadership of William Lowe Boyd. *Peabody Journal of Education, 86*(14), 402–415.

Fusarelli, L. D. (2011). School reform in a vacuum: Demographic change, social policy, and the future of children. *Peabody Journal of Education, 86*(3), 215–235.

Garbarino, J. (1995). *Raising children in a socially toxic environment*. San Francisco, CA: Jossey-Bass.

Goodlad, J. I. (1987). *Ecology of school renewal*. Chicago: University of Chicago Press.

Haertel, G. D. & Wang, M. (Eds.), (1997). *Coordination, cooperation, collaboration: What we know about school-linked services*. PhiladelphiaThe Mid-Atlantic Regional Laboratory for Student Success at Temple University.

Halpern, R. (1995). *Rebuilding the inner city: A history of neighborhood initiatives to address poverty in the United States*. New York: Columbia University Press.

Hess, F. M. (2010). *Education unbound: The promise and practice of greenfield schooling*. Alexandria, VA: Association for Supervision & Curriculum Development.

Huberty, T. J. (2012). *Anxiety and depression in children and adolescents: Assessment, intervention, and prevention*. New York: Springer.

Johnson, B. C. (2001). *Coordinated services and urban school reform: A comparative study of three school districts*. Unpublished doctoral dissertation, Pennsylvania State University, State College, PA.

Johnson, B. C. (2003). Coordinated, school-linked services and principal preparation. In F. C. Lunenberg & C. S. Carr (Eds.), *Shaping the future: Policy, partnerships, and emerging perspectives* (pp. 329–339). Eleventh Annual Yearbook of the National Council of Professors of Educational Administration. Lanham, MD: Scarecrow Education.

Kirst, M. W. (1991). *Integrating children's services*. Menlo Park, CA: Ed Source.

Koppich, J. E. & Kirst, M. (1993, February). Editors' introduction. *Education and Urban Society, 25*(2), 123–128.

Kornrich, S. & Furstenberg, F. (2013). Investing in children: Changes in parental spending on children, 1972 to 2007. *Demography, 50*(1), 1–23.

March, J. G. & Olsen, J. P. (1975). The uncertainty of the past: Organizational learning under ambiguity. *European Journal of Political Research, 3*, 147–171.

May, P. J. (1986). Politics and policy analysis. *Political Science Quarterly, 101*(1), 109–25.

Meltsner, A. J. (1972). Political feasibility and policy analysis. *Public Administration Review, 32* (June/December), 859–867.

Neuman, S. (2013). The American dream: Slipping away? *Educational Leadership, 70*(8), 18–22.

Ogbu, J. U. (1974). *The next generation: An ethnography of education in an urban neighborhood*. New York: Academic press.

Putnam, R. D., Frederick, C. B., & Snellman, K. (2012). *Growing class gaps in social connectedness among American youth*. Cambridge, MA: Harvard Kennedy School of Government.

Retrieved from: www.hks.harvard.edu/saguaro/research/SaguaroReport_DivergingSocial Connectedness20120808.pdf

Ramirez, R. (1999). Stakeholder analysis and conflict management. In D. Buckles (Ed.), *Cultivating peace: Conflict and collaboration in natural resource management* (pp. 101–126). Ottawa, CA: International Development Centre.

Reardon, S. F. (2013). The widening income achievement gap. *Educational Leadership*, 70(8). 10–16.

Sabatier, P. A. (1988). An advocacy coalition model of policy change and the role of policy-oriented learning therein. *Policy Sciences, 21*, 129–168.

Sabatier, P. A. & Jenkins-Smith, H. C. (Eds.), (1993). *Policy change and learning: An advocacy coalition approach.* Boulder, CO: Westview Press.

Sabatier P. & Jenkins-Smith, H. (1999). The advocacy coalition framework: An assessment. In P. A. Sabatier (Ed.), *Theories of the policy process* (pp. 117–68). Boulder, CO: Westview Press.

Sabatier, P. A. & Weible, C. M. (2005). *Innovations in the advocacy coalition framework.* Paper presented at the annual meeting of the American Society for Public Administration, Milwaukee, WI.

Saez, E. (2012). *Striking it richer: The evolution of top incomes in the United States (updated with 2009 and 2010 estimates).* Berkeley, CA: Department of Economics, University of California. Retrieved from http://emlab.berkeley.edu/~saez/saez-UStopincomes-2010.pdf.

Schlechty, P. C. (2001). *Shaking up the schoolhouse.* San Francisco, CA: Jossey-Bass.

Schutz, A. (2006). Home is a prison in the global city: The tragic failure of school-based community engagement strategies. *Review of Educational Research*, 76(1), 691–743.

Sergiovanni, T. J. (1990). Adding value to leadership gets extraordinary results. *Educational Leadership*, 47(8), 23–27.

Slade, E. (2003, June). The relationship between school characteristics and the availability of mental health and related health services in middle and high schools in the United States. *Journal of Behavioral Health Services & Research*, 30(4), 382–392.

Smrekar, C. E. (1994, June). *The character and content of family-school interactions in a school-linked integrated services model.* Paper presented at the annual meeting of the American Educational Research Association (AERA), New Orleans.

Smrekar, C. E. & Mawhinney, H. B. (1999). Integrated services: Challenges in linking schools, families and communities. In J. Murphy & K. S. Louis (Eds.), *Handbook of Research on Educational Administration.* San Francisco, CA: Jossey-Bass.

Spillane, J. P., White, K. W., & Stephan, J. L. (2009). School principal expertise: Putting expert-aspiring principal differences in problem-solving processes to the test. *Leadership and Policy in Schools*, 8(2), 128–151.

Stokey, E. & Zeckhauser, R. (1978). *A primer for policy analysis.* New York: W. W. Norton.

Tashman, N., Weist, M., Acosta, O., Bickham, N., Grady, M., Nabors, L., & Waxman, R. (2000, June). Toward the integration of prevention research and expanded school mental health programs. *Children's services: Social policy, research & practice*, 3(2), 97–115.

Waller, W. (1976). *The sociology of teaching.* New York: John Wiley & Sons. (Original work published 1932).

Wang, M. C., Haertel, G. D., & Walberg, H. J. (1997). The effectiveness of collaborative school-linked services. In L. C. Rigsby, M. C. Reynolds, & M. C. Wang (Eds.), *School-community connections: Exploring issues for research and practice* (pp. 283–309). San Francisco, CA: Jossey-Bass.

Weible, C. M. (2006). An advocacy coalition framework approach to stakeholder analysis: understanding the political context of California marine protected area policy. *Journal of Public Administration Research and Theory, 17*, 95–117.

Weick, K. E. (1976). Educational organizations as loosely coupled systems. *Administrative Science Quarterly, 2*(1), 1–19.

Weimer, D. L. & Vining, A. D. (2005). *Policy analysis: Concepts and practice* (4th ed.). Upper Saddle River, NJ: Prentice Hall.

Weist, M., Ambrose, M., & Lewis, C. (2006, January). Expanded school mental health: A collaborative community-school example. *Children & Schools, 28*(1), 45–50.

White House Task Force for Disadvantaged Youth, The (2003, October). *Final Report*. Washington, DC: Author.

Wood, P. W. & Boyd, W. L. (1981). Declining enrollments and surburban [sic] school closings: The problem of neighborhoods and neighborhood schools. *Educational Administration Quarterly, 17*, 98–119.

Youth Risk Behavior Surveillance System (YRBSS). (2011). Retrieved from: www.cdc.gov/HealthyYouth/yrbs/index.htm

Zetlin, A. & Boyd, W. L. (1996). School-community linkages. In M. Wang, M. Reynolds, & H. Walberg (Eds.), *Handbook of special and remedial education: Research and practice* (2nd ed.) (pp. 433–447). Oxford, UK: Elsevier Science.

Zucker, L. G. (1987). Institutional theories of organization. *Annual Review of Sociology, 13*, 443–464.

CHAPTER 7

The Politics of Interest Groups in Education

Sue Winton and Deborah Gonzalez

CHAPTER OVERVIEW

Politics may be characterized as "who gets what, when, and how" (Lasswell, 1965). Politics involve choices about how to distribute power, status, wealth, opportunities, and other social goods (Young, Levin, & Wallin, 2008). Public education is inherently political because it involves making decisions about how to organize schools, what knowledge children study, and which goals are pursued. Understanding politics requires that one understands power: Where is it located? What are its effects? How might it be wielded to achieve desired ends? This chapter introduces theories of power and interest groups that attempt to answer these questions. The theories and research reviewed in the chapter will help aspiring educational leaders meet the expectations of ISLLC's (Council of Chief State School Officers, 2008) Standard 6: "An education leader promotes the success of every student by understanding, responding to, and influencing the political, social, economic, legal, and cultural context" (p. 15).

Specifically, the chapter's review of ways that interest groups exercise power to influence education, and its discussion of the political skills educational leaders can hone and use, will help aspiring leaders understand schools' various contexts and develop their ability to influence them in ways that meet the needs of all children, families, and caregivers (Standards 6.1 and 6.2). The chapter introduces emerging trends and initiatives in education that demand leaders use political acumen and skill to promote the success of every student (Standard 6.3).

The chapter and its accompanying activities enable aspiring educational leaders to:

- describe the goals, strategies, and outcomes of different kinds of interest groups that aim to influence education at local, district, state, national, and international levels;

- identify aspects of a school and/or district's political, social, economic, legal, and cultural contexts that influence policy and practice;
- understand the political nature of educational leaders' work and identify political skills and strategies they can use to influence local, district, state, and national decisions.

The chapter begins with the description of a classic problem facing Claire Xiang, principal of Glen Ravine Elementary School (ES): How to distribute scarce resources among competing groups. While reading the case, identify the different groups who are affected by the problem and what their different goals and concerns (i.e., their interests) may be.

CASE 7.1: WHO GETS SPACE AT GLEN RAVINE ES?

Claire Xiang is the principal of Glen Ravine ES. The school is located in an urban center and, like in many schools in cities across the U.S., there never seems to be enough time, money, or people to realize the vision for the school developed by students, parents, school staff, and community members. An element of the school's vision is to provide students with a well-rounded education. This commitment emerged from some parents' and teachers' concerns that the focus on math, literacy, and science in the curriculum and state tests reduces the amount of time available during the school day for the arts, health and physical education, and other non-tested activities. Not everyone shares this concern, however. Some teachers are worried about the academic performance of some subgroups of students on statewide assessments since there is talk at the state level about linking teacher pay to students' test performance.

In discussions with the school council about how to broaden students' experiences at school, it was proposed that new groups be allowed to use the school gym and classrooms after school. Currently, the gym and one classroom are used daily by a local community-based organization (CBO) that runs the After 4 Club. The After 4 Club is part of the CBO's larger neighborhood improvement strategy. The club's staff is comprised mainly of people from the local community who attended Glen Ravine Elementary themselves and who know many of the students and parents from the neighborhood. When the Club first offered programs a few years ago, many children attended. They received homework help and played a variety of sports and games. Now, only a handful of children participate each day, and they spend a lot of time playing cards and board games. Most of these children's parents use the club as a form of childcare until they finish work.

The school's Parent Teacher Association (PTA) suggested organizations that focus on drama, art, or sports be invited to run activities at the school since so few students attend the After 4 Club. In fact, Claire receives calls on a regular basis from different groups asking to use the facilities. In speaking to her colleagues from neighboring schools, Claire has learned that many groups will pay substantially to use the space, something that the After 4 Club does not currently do (its programs are offered free of charge). Colleagues' schools use this money to purchase computers and other supplies for the classrooms.

Two of these groups, SportFun and Art Smart, are local franchises of national for-profit businesses. Their names are familiar to some parents, especially those on the PTA. Before the last meeting, Claire overheard the PTA president and a few other parents discussing ways to enroll kids in Tomorrow's Stars, a local charter school. Claire is familiar with SportFun and Art Smart: she's been receiving pencils, calendars, and balls from them since she came to the school last year.

Claire wonders how many students will be able to afford classes offered by these businesses. She doesn't like the idea of forcing the After 4 Club to leave the school so for-profit companies can make money. On the other hand, parent involvement in the school is already low, and Claire doesn't want to lose the support of current PTA members. She also thinks all students would benefit from the revenue brought in by rental fees.

The local university, Mount Royal, has approached Claire as well. They would like to develop a partnership with Glen Ravine and other schools in the neighborhood that would like to see the university's teacher candidates provide tutoring services at the schools either as part of the aspiring teachers' practice teaching requirements or as part-time employment during the school year. The university hopes that by working with low-income students, its graduates will develop a commitment to working in urban schools while elementary students will be inspired to go to college. The program also may help the college graduates develop relationships between local schools and the district, which might lead to future employment. In addition to academic instruction, the university's program organizes games and provides mentoring to students at no extra cost. Researchers from the university collect data on the program so its predetermined curriculum (based on state-standards) can eventually be evaluated for effectiveness. The university is having trouble enrolling students, however, since the program currently is held on campus, which is difficult to access by public transit. Glen Ravine ES would receive the tutoring and activities in exchange for the use of the school's space; it would not bring any additional money to the school.

Claire must determine the process to decide which groups should get to use the school space, facilitate and/or participate in this process, and, ultimately, communicate the decision to the various groups in her school, community, and district officials.

COMPLEXITIES IN THE CASE

This case highlights the complexity of school environments and the multiple groups that influence what happens in schools. Claire must consider the needs, concerns and desires of students (which vary considerably); their parents (including the PTA, those who use the After 4 Club); the local community, including the CBO and its neighborhood improvement strategy; teachers; the district; and herself. Of course, there are many other factors affecting this situation. One factor is the increasing cost of educating students in a climate of reduced spending across the district and state. A second factor is the accountability context that demands that schools demonstrate student learning through standardized tests and permits parents to remove their children from traditional public schools and enroll them in charter schools. Claire's state is also considering tying teacher pay to students' test performance. Third, schools and districts are encouraged to work with local businesses as a strategy to enhance students' funds and experiences. Fourth, urban schools typically have difficulty attracting and retaining qualified teachers. Fifth, many individuals, including many parents, are unemployed or working multiple jobs to cover their basic costs. Claire must determine how to choose which group(s) are permitted to use the school's facilities, participate in the decision-making process, and communicate the final decision to students, parents, district officials, and other affected groups.

THEORIES AND RESEARCH ON INTEREST GROUPS

In the case study above, Claire encountered a range of different groups: the PTA, SportFun and Art Smart, the After 4 Club, different groups of parents, and Mount Royal University. This section introduces the wide range of groups that aim to influence education at local, state, national, and even international levels. It then reviews some theories that attempt to explain how interest groups form and act. Finally, it identifies strategies interest groups use in their efforts to influence policy at the state and federal levels.

What is an Interest Group?

Interest groups, also called advocacy groups, are groups of people who try to influence policy decisions. Interest groups act at all levels: from parents and teachers in schools, to national organizations in Washington, DC. Groups vary in many ways. First, some groups advocate for decisions that will benefit their own members; for example, the Autism Society advocates for the needs of individuals with autism and their families (www.autism-society.org). Other groups push for policy changes that will benefit all children and/or society as a whole (e.g., Environmental Defense Fund). Smith (2005) called the first kind of group "special interest groups" and referred to the second as "public interest groups" (p. 11). Smith (2005) differentiated both of these kinds of groups from social movements that involve individuals and groups working to transform political and/or societal values (e.g., the civil rights or women's movements).

Interest groups may be distinguished further from one another based on their membership's interests and goals. Different kinds of groups include businesses (Ball, 2009), teacher unions (Hartney & Flavin, 2011), religious groups (Lugg & Robinson, 2009), public interest organizations (Orr & Rogers, 2011; Young & Everitt, 2004), philanthropists (Scott, 2009), community-based organizations (Newman et al., 2012; Oakes et al., 2008), parents (Intkonen, 2009; Nespor & Hicks, 2010), professional groups (Spring, 2011), and think tanks (Cibulka, 2001; Hess, 2007).

As stated, advocacy groups operate at all levels of education. Groups at the local level may include parent organizations, such as the New York City Parent Union (www.nycparentsunion.org), community-based organizations, and local businesses. Some businesses, like Sylvan and Mathnasium Learning Centers, have franchises across the country. Groups at the state level include professional organizations of school leaders, such as the New York State Council of School Superintendents, and business roundtables. Other groups such as the National Education Association (NEA) act at the federal level. While some groups focus on one level only, many groups operate at multiple levels simultaneously. For example, Stand for Children, a group that aims to ensure policies enable all children to graduate high school ready for and with access to college (stand.org/), has local, state, and federal chapters. So, too, does the PTA. The NEA has state chapters as well as its national organization. Some international organizations, such as the Organization for Economic Co-operation and Development (OECD), influence federal decisions (Moutsios, 2009).

The OECD is an example of a group that aims to influence many areas of public policy in addition to education. Think tanks such as the Heritage Foundation and many community-based organizations similarly work on education as one of multiple policy areas. The United Interfaith Alliance (UIA), for example, is a faith-based organization whose membership includes religious institutions in the cities of Fall River and New Bedford in Massachusetts. UIA focuses on issues related to public safety, immigration, job training, and most recently education. UIA is an example of a community-based organization (CBO).

Theories of Power and Interest Group Activity

Theories of policy processes and the politics of education recognize interest groups as important actors in these arenas. Education borrowed many of these theories from political science, which in turn borrowed some from sociology and linguistics. This section first introduces various theories of interest group formation and/or activity. It then considers the nature of power and implications of different ways of thinking about power for educational leaders. Some theories of power challenge traditional conceptions of how interest groups engage in and influence politics.

Theories of interest group formation. Definitions of *pluralism* focus on the behavior of individuals in groups and posit that groups form "when like-minded individuals join together to pursue their common interests and pressure or lobby government

LEARNING ACTIVITY 7.1

OECD

International and intergovernmental organizations (e.g., the OECD, World Bank, International Monetary Fund) impact education policy in important ways. The OECD is comprised of 30 member states and 70 cooperating states. Its stated purpose is to "promote policies that will improve the economic and social well-being of people around the world" (Organization for Economic Cooperation and Development, n.d.). The OECD coordinates an international testing program: Programme for International Student Achievement (PISA), an example of how international organizations can influence education policy. Globally, students take PISA tests in literacy and numeracy. Their scores are combined to create an overall score for their country; countries' education systems are then ranked based on test results. Test performance is understood to serve as an indication of a country's ability to compete in the global marketplace as the scores and ranking reflect a country's potential human capital (Lingard, 2010). The quest for global market dominance thus has been translated into competition for highest test scores rankings. Worldwide, governments focus education policy on improving student performance. Researchers analyze PISA to understand the factors that affect school performance and investigate countries which rank high. Then OECD encourages other countries to adopt policies similar to the higher-ranking countries'. Education policymaking has now become transnational as "hardly any country today related to the OECD ignores its data and recommendations on education" (Moutsios, 2009, p. 471). Critics of PISA and the OECD contend its testing of literacy and numeracy leads to devaluing of other non-tested subjects, diminished time for critical thinking in classrooms, and negatively affected teachers' professional lives and self-worth (Lingard, 2010; Westheimer, 2008).

- How has international testing affected the policies in your schools?
- What local interest groups cite international tests in their attempts to affect schooling?
- Many real estate agents use school reputations to sell housing. What kinds of marketing about schools can you find among local housing agents near your schools?

LEARNING ACTIVITY 7.2

Community-Based Organizations

CBOs typically involve members of local communities working together to achieve change in their neighborhoods and districts. Community organizing is an important means of creating sustained and strong public engagement in low-income communities (Warren, 2011b). CBOs may or may not be part of larger district, state, or national networks and may be formally organized through institutions (e.g., churches) or more informally and/or temporarily (Warren, 2011b). The UIA, for example, is a faith-based CBO affiliated with the national network of faith-based community organizations People Improving Communities through Organizing (PICO) and a member of the regional Massachusetts Communities Action Network (MCAN).

Historically, CBOs focused on a range of policy issues yet stayed away from schools; they have only recently begun to focus on education (Shirley, 2011). CBOs aim to influence policy primarily at the school and district level. As part of their efforts, CBOs aim to empower members through increasing their knowledge, providing them with mutual support, and enhancing their confidence to engage with school personnel and processes (Evans & Shirley, 2008; Warren, 2011b). CBOs also focus on leadership development and building relationships between community members to enable collective action on shared concerns (Warren, 2011b).

- What are the influential CBOs in your area?
- In what ways are they influential?

for policies that will favour their group" (Smith, 2005, p. 21). Individuals belong to multiple groups (e.g., by gender, religion, class, geography, etc.), and society is characterized by many groups that potentially clash along multiple points. Thus, pluralism argues that no group will dominate for long since there are so many different groups vying for influence: if one group gets too strong another will form to challenge it (Smith, 2005). Pluralism also assumes that democracy depends on active groups and that the best policies for democracy arise out of competition between groups (Mawhinney, 2001). Pluralist theory assumes all groups have equal ability to influence governments. Policies, then, are the outcome of group struggles to influence policymakers. Policies favor the groups who have the most influence. Group conflict is central to politics in this model (policymakers are viewed as responsive to groups and not as independent policy actors).

What pluralist theory does not explain is how groups or individuals' preferences form (e.g., role of social forces or religion on individuals' preferences). It also does not have a theory to predict the group conflicts that are most likely to arise due to political or societal structures (Smith, 2005), and it cannot predict which group will likely win in a given conflict (Manley, 1983 in Smith, 2005). Critics complain that pluralism rests on an assumption that all groups can equally influence policies. In response to critiques of pluralism, neopluralists made some revisions to the original theory. Neopluralism recognizes that not all individuals have the same ability to influence policy due to inequalities in society that may make it more difficult for groups to form and for groups to influence policy. Neopluralism also recognizes governments as policy actors (i.e., they play an active role in policy formation). Governments might work with some interest groups to develop policy.

Alternatively, Sabatier and Jenkins-Smith's (1999) advocacy coalition framework suggests that policy change processes are best explained by recognizing policy subsystems comprised of "actors from a variety of public and private organizations who are actively concerned with a policy problem or issue . . . and regularly seek to influence public policy in that domain" (p. 119). Within each subsystem there are advocacy coalitions (normally 1–4) made up of individuals and groups with shared beliefs who work together to influence policy so that it reflects their beliefs. Members of advocacy coalitions may include interest group leaders, legislators from multiple levels of government agency officials, journalists, and researchers. The advocacy coalitions within a subsystem compete with one another and use various strategies to influence policy decisions. A coalition's ability to influence policy changes over time as its members learn through experience and encountering new information. Events outside the policy subsystem and the parameters of the policy issue (including rules, cultural values and social structures, natural resources, and attributes of the problem) also impact and limit a coalition's ability to change policy.

Theories of power. Pluralism, neopluralism, and the advocacy coalition framework are based on an understanding of power as something that some groups (or individuals) possess and use to get others, such as formal decision makers, to do something they might otherwise not do. Not all theories understand power in this way. As reflected in the theories above and elsewhere in this volume, one way to think about power is to think about it as individuals or groups having *power over* others (Blase & Anderson, 1995; Goehler, 2000). Differences exist in the amount of power individuals and groups possess. If one individual has more power, then another must have less. From this view, those who have power may use it overtly or covertly, consciously or unconsciously, to achieve their goals.

From a *power over* perspective, educational leaders must understand their political context, learn various strategies that can be used to influence individuals and groups, and recognize that others may use these strategies in their attempts to influence school leaders. In addition, this view of power suggests leaders need to understand how much power various individuals and groups possess in education arenas and how they use such power to affect policy. Strategies for gathering this knowledge are introduced later in this chapter.

One alternative to thinking about power as *power over* is to conceptualize it as working through language and the knowledge and truths it creates i.e., through political discourse. People choose words to represent their positions (Chilton, 2004). Discourses exercise power through constructing possibilities and limitations in the social world (Goverde et al., 2000). Discourses construct social identities and relations in addition to creating and limiting possibilities for what to think, do, or say at particular moments. Discourses affect how ideas and behavior are perceived (Wilson, 2001). For example, the word, *choice*, represents one kind of political position and the words, *right-to-life*, differentiate another group on the same politicized issue. Thus, from this perspective, power does not reside in individuals or groups but in discourses that construct reality and truth in ways that advantage some groups while simultaneously disadvantaging others. Numerous discourses exist at any one time, although some dominate. Importantly, discourses are unstable and can be challenged and remade through human agency.

From a power-as-discourse perspective, educational leaders must understand how discourses in policies and everyday practices create and constrain possibilities for thinking, action, and identities. They must be able to identify dominant and subordinate discourses and understand how to take up the opportunities offered by multiple, conflicting discourses in policy and everyday practice.

Finally, a third way to think about power can be characterized as *power to* (Goehler, 2000). Hannah Arendt proposed that power occurs when individuals come together and collectively create the power to make something happen through communicating and acting together (Goehler, 2000). In this perspective, there is an unlimited amount of power possible, rather than a finite amount contested among groups and individuals as assumed in *power over* definitions. This perspective suggests educational leaders should know how to collaborate with other groups to achieve mutual goals.

HOW DO INTEREST GROUPS ATTEMPT TO INFLUENCE POLICY AT THE STATE AND FEDERAL LEVELS?

While the number of groups trying to influence education policy is greater than ever (Scott, Lubienski, & DeBray-Pelot, 2009), research on these groups is limited (McDonnell, 2009; McLaughlin, 2006; Opfer et al., 2008). This section introduces what is known about how interest groups attempt to influence policy. It begins by examining how groups try to directly influence formal decision-making processes (e.g., in government) and then looks at groups' efforts to influence these processes indirectly. The focus then turns to the ways different groups try to influence local policy processes and decisions at the school and district levels.

Most research on advocacy groups examines how groups influence state and federal decision-making processes. This research finds that groups try to influence government decisions by meeting with legislators, testifying at hearings, drafting legislation, responding to drafts, citing research, writing letters, using the media, asking group members to contact elected officials, disseminating information to members, and conducting research (Opfer, 2001; Renée, 2006). Groups may endorse political candidates, campaign on candidates' behalf, and donate money.

Rather than trying to access elected decision makers directly, some groups try to influence voters instead. They may organize protests, host town hall meetings, engage citizens in dialogues about policy issues, collect data, disseminate research, or circulate alternative narratives about policy effects (Winton, 2010; Winton & Evans, 2012). An advocacy group in Ontario, Canada held public artistic performances to protest cuts to education (Winton & Brewer, 2013). Groups may also challenge the dominant meanings of policy and/or participate in efforts to change the meaning of policy. Fulcher's (1999) comparative study of inclusive education policies, for example, examined how advocacy groups deployed different discourses in their efforts to define the meanings of inclusive education and integration. The findings suggest that groups consciously and unconsciously mobilize different discourses as they struggle to make sense of policy and persuade others to adopt the same understandings (Fulcher, 1999).

INTEREST GROUP ACTIVITY AT THE LOCAL LEVEL

At the school and district levels, various interest groups attempt to influence the decision-making and policy processes of educational leaders, and educational leaders try to influence interest groups. The sections below describe the political activities of both leaders and groups.

How Local Interest Groups Attempt to Influence Educational Leaders

This section introduces how various groups, including businesses, unions, parents, CBOs, foundations, and students attempt to influence educational leaders and the motivations behind various groups' actions. In the discussion of each group, potential answers to the following questions are provided where knowledge exists to answer them:

1. How does this group try to influence educational leaders?
2. Why does this group try to influence educational leaders? How do they benefit? How do others lose?
3. How influential is this group?
4. What are outcomes of this group's involvement in education?

Businesses. Businesses engage in education policy processes in many ways and in many sites. The business community has always been interested in educational reforms as it believes business practices and methods will better prepare workers to gain an economic advantage (Koppich & Esch, 2012). In addition, businesses believe that their involvement will equip students with the skills needed to be successful in the global marketplace. For this reason, businesses attempt to influence educational policy leaders in a variety of ways. Molnar (2006) characterizes their activities as selling in schools, selling to schools, and selling of schools.

In terms of selling in schools, businesses offer schools products (e.g., soda, candy), incentives, corporately sponsored programs (e.g., fast food coupons as rewards, scholarship awards, essay contests) and educational materials (e.g., maps, books), and services in exchange for exclusive contracts, naming rights, and opportunities to market to students (Molnar et al., 2013). Some researchers focus on the benefits accrued to schools through businesses' involvement. Timpane and McNeill (1991), for example, highlighted how large companies, such as General Electric and IBM, fostered school improvement by providing millions of dollars in funding toward college scholarships, technological improvements in schools, and local education improvement programs. Other businesses have provided programs in schools that focus on career preparation, mentorship, and professional development for educators (Timpane & McNeill, 1991). Soter (1993) provided an example of this type of involvement in describing American Express' Academy of Finance in New York City. This program provided career training, academic course work, and job opportunities all in a single course of study (Soter, 1993).

Many businesses will create partnerships to support initiatives in their districts and lobby for educational reforms. Timpane and McNeill (1991) suggested that the above examples fall under a strategy of business involvement of the *helping hand* (Timpane & McNeill, 1991). This form of involvement includes businesses providing money, tutors, equipment, public speakers, etc., to aid schools. Many businesses attempt to promote positive public relations by adopting a sense of corporate civic responsibility and a supportive attitude to promote stability and growth in their communities (Orr, 1996).

Businesses also sell to schools. These activities include selling materials, textbooks, tests, pens—almost everything used in schools. This practice has historically been less controversial than selling in schools (Molnar, 2006). Howard and Preisman (2007) highlighted the ways in which public schools contract work such as transportation, security, cafeteria, and custodial to private sector vendors. They argue that some of these duties could be provided by school employees, eliminating the need for outsourcing.

A more controversial practice is the selling of schools, that is, district and charter schools that are managed by for-profit businesses sometimes called educational management organizations (EMOs). Examples include Edison Schools Inc. and National Heritage Academies. Some businesses leaders believe that school administration should adopt business management practices in order to eliminate educational policies that do not support accountability measures.

While business involvement may provide benefits to schools and communities, some critics argue the partnership and collaboration between schools and businesses do not provide benefits other than donations and volunteers (Bennett & Thompson, 2011). Others argue that educational materials produced by businesses contain biased information that promotes corporate interests, while others argue schools should not encourage students to consume foods and drinks known to contribute to poor health, e.g., obesity, osteoporosis (Molnar et al., 2013). Molnar (2006) pointed out that commercialism in schools promotes the idea of consumption as the way to happiness. Critics of selling in schools also argue schools should be the place students critically and independently examine commercialism (Barbaro & Earp, 2008). However, budget constraints and increasing external pressure to improve student success make it difficult for principals to turn down to offers from businesses (Molnar et al., 2013). Indeed, selling in schools has increased markedly since 1990 (Molnar, 2006).

In trying to exert influence over school leaders, some *supplementary education service* providers in New York City offered principals money, gift certificates, and other incentives for principals' help enrolling students in their programs (Koyama, 2010). Orr (1996) suggested that businesses attempt to influence principals for a variety of reasons. From an employer's perspective, educational quality is of interest as businesses' labor pools are derived from public education (Jackson & Cibulka, 1991). Bennett and Thompson (2011) argued that businesses believe that students must be prepared for the economically productive roles that they will be fulfilling in the globalized economy. Businesses benefit from their interactions in schools as they have a hand in shaping their potential future employees. In addition, providing specific programs within schools allows businesses to measure and report their influence.

Businesses can be very influential in school districts that have a limited amount of resources. As mentioned previously, contributions such as funding, materials, and supports are necessary during times of educational reform (Orr, 1996). Some educational leaders welcome the interaction of businesses in their schools as they can often provide greater public legitimacy within the community (Bennett & Thompson, 2011). For example, school district leaders may appreciate the support that local businesses provide them, including funding, goods and services, and human capital (Bennett & Thompson, 2011).

Unions. While business involvement is prevalent in many schools across America, so is the presence of unions. A key function of unions is to negotiate collective bargaining agreements (CBAs) with districts on teachers' behalf. CBAs determine many district policies by providing regulatory mandates on teachers' work, such as compensation, hiring regulations, transfer processes, grievance processes, and evaluation methods (Moe, 2009; Strunk & Grissom, 2010). Moses (2011) highlights that unions are moving beyond the role of protectors-of-teachers to expand their involvement to include educational policy and the administration of schools. Chicago teachers, for example, protested efforts to mandate teachers' lesson plans and, through their strike action in 2012, achieved assurances there would be textbooks and materials available on the first day of school, privacy for clinicians, an anti-bullying clause, paperwork reduction, and the ability to create their own lesson plans (Sokolower, 2012–2013).

Unions also influence local school board elections (Strunk & Grissom, 2010). Orr (1996) argued that teachers are able to vote on their desired candidates, which in turn provides a strong voice in school matters if their candidate is elected. According to Orr (1996), unions accomplish this task by using two strategies: campaign activities supporting the selected candidate and influencing members to vote. A union's ability to rally together behind issues and be heard provides them with a strategic place within the education system (Orr, 1996).

Unions set up the governing mandates that surround teachers' employment. Provisions in CBAs such as class size limits, evaluation procedures, staffing decisions, preparation time, and grievance procedures help promote positive work and learning environments and protect teachers' rights.

With regards to local school board elections, it is reasonable to suggest that the policy preferences of unions will be aligned with their union-endorsed candidates (Moe, 2006). If these prospects are voted in, they most likely will support and negotiate policies that are in tune with union initiatives (Strunk & Grissom, 2010). In this way, unions have influenced the bargaining process by choosing their own bargaining opponent.

As teachers' working conditions are outlined in contracts negotiated between unions and districts, educational leaders must adhere to said agreements. Moses (2011) argued that teachers' unions are very powerful within schools as they are able to organize themselves effectively and secure teachers' work rights. Unions that have more restrictive CBAs have regulations that may limit the options of administration (Strunk & Grissom, 2010). Moe (2006) listed limitations imposed on principals, including the inability to dismiss poor-performing teachers, evaluation monitors, and limits on teacher assignments. In addition, board members whose campaigns were backed by union members can further influence the ability of unions in supporting their initiatives. Moe (2006) argued that election outcomes are more vulnerable to the interests of those who vote, which are the few. These elected officials make decisions on policies, ranging from curriculum to budgets (Moe, 2006). In this way, unions influence schools through their CBAs in a bottom–up strategy (Moe, 2006).

Alternatively, Jacoby (2011) argued that teachers are agents for students and, as such, their interests should be taken into consideration. In negotiating their terms of employment, teachers submit to contracts that limit their authority and autonomy. If contracts are insufficient to compensate teachers, the professional practice of teachers may diminish (Jacoby, 2011).

While CBAs are meant to outline the rights of teachers, these contracts may have negative effects on other stakeholders. The stronger the CBA, the less administrators are able to make changes (Strunk & Grissom, 2010). Even in instances where it would be beneficial to students and teachers to make changes, such as making changes to negative working conditions, union regulations supersede any potential benefits (Strunk & Grissom, 2010). Moe (2006) argued that some union objectives, such as smaller classrooms and increased spending, are beneficial to students, while other mandates that protect incompetent teachers have a negative effect on student outcomes.

On the other hand, Jacoby (2011) argued that without unions, districts would have to represent the interests of both teachers and students. As both groups have conflicting interests, union contracts are necessary to align these goals. Contracts make it possible for teachers' and students' needs to be compatible. As teachers are agents for students, districts must consider teachers as their interests may be the same. For example, smaller class sizes are beneficial to both teachers and students. Additionally, contracts that secure better wages and working conditions will also attract better workers, endorse professional development, and reduce employee turnover (Moe, 2009). District leaders should uphold the labor interests of teachers as they are the professionals who deliver the educational services to students (Jacoby, 2011).

Parents. Parent group influence is becoming more and more prevalent in school systems. Parents are the group most likely to speak on behalf of students and to exercise influence when they are organized (Orr, 1996; Shatkin & Gershberg, 2007). Parents often will try to influence school leaders when they believe their core values are being threatened or that their voices, ideas, and opinions are not being heard (Malen & Cochran, 2008). Parents are able to influence school reform in part because they are not entangled in political negotiations internal to the school system (Moore, 1992). Additionally, parents sometimes look for support from other organizations, like non-profits, who may also be able to help parents influence school policy development (Shatkin & Gershberg, 2007).

Parental influence varies based on class, however (Horvat et al., 2003). Resources that middle-class parents possess through their networks affect aspects of their children's education such as teacher behavior and program placement. Principals and teachers also adjust their behavior in response to anticipated interests of middle- and upper-class parents (Brantlinger, 2003). Middle- and upper-class parents sometimes influence education by participating in public protests and boycotts, and using other confrontational tactics (Malen & Cochran, 2008). Principals are more able to resist parental influence in low-income areas.

Parental influence can often result in the success or failure of school reform (Orr, 1996). Their involvement, or lack thereof, can have a direct impact on principals as failed reforms reflect poorly on leadership. On the other hand, Shatkin and Gershberg (2007) explained that parents can create improved school-community relations under certain conditions. Their involvement can lead to new initiatives in schools that will aid in community participation such as literacy assistance or ESL instruction (Stone et al., 1999). Gawlik (2008) argued that parents who support a school's objectives and programs are an asset in building autonomy and effectiveness. As parents have numerous sources of influence, such as relationships with superintendents and other external authorities, their influence can further enhance the influence of principals as they become a support mechanism.

Participating in education processes also provides parents with opportunities to develop their leadership skills and improve their communities (Shatkin & Gershberg, 2007). Shatkin and Gershberg's (2007) examination of outcomes of parent participation on school site councils found that their participation can lead to curriculum and instruction that meets the needs of communities. Collaboration between parents, community members, principals, teachers, and staff also enhances school-community relationships. This interaction can lead to enhanced performance in schools as parents become more involved in their children's education (Shatkin & Gershberg, 2007).

Community-based organizations (CBOs). Some parents engage with other community members in CBOs. CBOs' efforts in schools and districts focus on achieving equitable education processes, practices, and outcomes for students in low-income communities and fostering respectful and mutual relationships between school officials and community members (Orr & Rogers, 2011). Strategies for influencing leaders include letter writing, circulating petitions, confronting leaders with data, meeting with decision makers, protesting, conducting research, and participating in public meetings (Lopez, 2003; Warren, 2011a).

For example, in 2007, a number of CBOs in Boston coordinated a campaign for the reallocation of district funds in Boston public schools to employ additional family and community outreach coordinators in the district's schools (Evans & Shirley, 2008). Campaign tactics included the circulation of an issues newsletter, email blasts, parents' testimonies at public hearings, and letters and phone calls to Boston School Committee members, city counselors, and Boston's mayor (Evans & Shirley, 2008). Consequently, the Boston School Committee approved a revised budget that allocated funds for six new family and community outreach coordinators and an additional staff member for the Office of Family and Community Engagement (Evans & Shirley, 2008).

Foundations. While foundations' and philanthropic organizations' donations amount to less than 1 percent of total educational funding, these interest groups have become very influential in educational policy and practice (Koppich & Esch, 2012; Kumashiro, 2012; Scott, 2009). Current educational reforms, such as the privatization of schooling (e.g., charter schools), have allowed for individuals with no educational background to make decisions about educational policy (Kumashiro, 2012).

Although some foundations, such as Foundations IT, have made contributions to education by providing grants, health services, access to arts and culture, conservation, and economic support (Orr, 1996), other venture philanthropists have focused on improving school reform through business management strategies such as standardization, competition, and high-stakes accountability systems (Scott, 2009). Many of these venture philanthropies advocate for the privatization of public education through the outsourcing of school management. For-profit companies manage many school districts with high levels of charter school growth (Kumashiro, 2012).

Currently, federal funds seemingly align with philanthropic foundation funds effectively combining to change educational policies relating to evaluation and accountability, alternative credentialing and linking teacher pay to performance (Koppich & Esch, 2012). For example, large philanthropies, such as the Bill and Melinda Gates Foundation, have significant influence on teaching policies, many of which are similar to those of the federal government. In another example, one initiative that aligns school management with market strategies is the ability to have private providers running schools (Scott, 2009). This convergence has a direct impact on current school leaders who are not only qualified and knowledgeable of educational outcomes, but who also might have a different perspective on issues of equity, diversity, and democracy in education. Venture philanthropies aim to increase student achievement in the global arena (Koppich & Esch, 2012), but such goals can conflict and create barriers with other educational initiatives.

HOW EDUCATIONAL LEADERS ATTEMPT TO INFLUENCE LOCAL INTEREST GROUPS

So far this chapter has focused on the ways interest groups try to influence education and educational leaders. This section introduces findings from research that examines how school and district leaders attempt to influence different interest groups. There is limited research available on this topic even though educational leaders are political actors due to the inherently political nature of education. In the discussion of each group, potential answers to the following questions are provided where knowledge exists to answer them:

1. How do educational leaders try to influence this group?
2. Why do educational leaders try to influence this group? How do leaders benefit? How do others lose?
3. How influential are educational leaders on this group?
4. What are outcomes of educational leaders' efforts to influence this group?

Influencing teachers. Studies in the field of school micropolitics (i.e., politics in schools and districts) find that school leaders use both direct and indirect tactics to influence teachers. Direct tactics include using resources, working conditions, opportunities to influence decisions, support, and performance evaluations as sanctions and rewards. Indirect tactics include controlling access to superiors; managing the principal's approachability; emphasizing differences in authority between the principal and teachers; controlling decision-making processes and meeting agendas; co-optation; buffering; listening; humor; diplomacy; avoidance; and strategic use of data (Blase & Anderson, 1995; Crow & Weindling, 2010; Malen & Ogawa, 1988; Marsh, 2012). The political tactics principals use affect those used by teachers. Teachers who work with principals who wield power overtly use protective, reactive, and nonthreatening strategies such as avoidance, ingratiation, and rationality to achieve protective goals (Blase, 1991). Teachers working with principals who use covert tactics are more likely to report using diplomacy, visibility, and extra work as political strategies (Blase & Anderson, 1995).

In a study of inclusive and equity-minded principals, Ryan (2010) determined that the principals use the following strategies to promote democratic goals: persuading others; persisting; experimenting; being honest; keeping others off-balance; playing ignorant; working the system; and quietly advocating. To persuade others to promote equity and inclusion principals circulate information, guide discussions, provoke, ask critical questions, encourage discussion, preach, use language carefully, compliment superiors, and use government language. These strategies enable agenda-setting, the "first step in effective political leadership" (Bolman & Deal, 2008, p. 214). Agenda-setting involves developing a change agenda and a plan for achieving it.

Influencing business. Koyama (2010) examined Supplementary Education Services (SES) in New York City schools and identified strategies principals used to influence SES providers to act in ways that furthered principals' goals.

Some principals offered incentives such as increased student enrolment to providers who would accommodate the schedules of CBOs in their schools, while other principals threatened not to renew contracts with SES providers if they did not adjust their programs to reflect the schools' staff, curriculum, structure, and instruction. One principal demanded the SES provider show evidence of progress through test scores, and the provider recognized that improved test scores would determine whether the provider's contract was renewed.

Influencing parents. School leaders, along with teachers, typically act to protect established interests and contain conflict (Malen & Cochran, 2008). Principals do so in part through public reassurances, selective application and enforcement of policies, and private compacts (Malen & Cochran, 2008). Principals influence site-based governing bodies (comprised of parents and/or teachers) by controlling meeting agendas, meeting times, resources, and decision-making processes (Malen & Ogawa, 1988). School leaders also may reach out to parents to gain support for school-led initiatives, however (Malen & Cochran, 2008). These efforts may enable parents and administrators to identify shared interests and improve their relationships. These interactions create opportunities for both administrators and parents to show good will (Malen & Cochran, 2008).

IMPLICATIONS FOR PRACTICE: INFLUENCING AND WORKING WITH INTEREST GROUPS

It is critical that leaders understand how to act politically because their political behavior affects teaching, learning, change efforts, school governance, relationships, and democracy in education (Blase & Anderson, 1995; Blase & Blase, 2002; Malen & Cochran, 2008; Malen & Ogawa, 1988; Ryan, 2010). This section introduces practical strategies for working with and influencing interest groups. Importantly, the same strategies can be used in efforts to achieve very diverse, even opposing, goals. This section pays particular attention to strategies that reflect commitments to equity, diversity, and social justice for all families and communities.

Developing political acumen is essential for educational leaders. Political acumen is the ability to read one's political environment and determine which political strategies to use, when, and with whom (Ryan, 2010). Understanding one's political environment involves multiple analyses including the following:

(a) identifying channels of informal communication;
(b) knowing about key people in the district;
(c) identifying interest groups in the community and at the state level as well as their relative amounts of influence;
(d) learning, and understanding the district's conventions and priorities;
(e) getting to know the school or district community and staff;
(f) analyzing possibilities for mobilizing individuals and groups, internal and external to the school or district; and

(g) anticipating counterstrategies that others are likely to employ (Pichault 1993, in Bolman and Deal, 2008; Ryan, 2010). Leaders can acquire this knowledge through listening, interacting with a range of people, sitting on district-wide committees, working in different districts, and using focus groups and surveys (Ryan, 2010).

Leaders can use their knowledge of their political environments to develop networks and build alliances. They must identify whose support they need to achieve their goals, and then they need to build relationships with these key groups and individuals (Bolman & Deal, 2008; Ryan, 2010). To do so they should make themselves visible and be in places where they are likely to encounter those they wish to meet (Ryan, in press). Leaders also need to understand who/which groups might resist their initiatives and/or disagree with their goals, why, and how much, and then establish connections with these parties to facilitate communication, negotiation, and education (Kotter, in Bolman and Deal, 2008).

Educational leaders need to know how to negotiate (Bolman & Deal, 2008, Fraatz, 1989). Negotiation is back-and-forth communication designed to reach an agreement when two or more parties have some shared interests and others that conflict (Bolman & Deal, 2008; Fisher & Ury, 2011). Fisher and Ury's (2011) principled approach to negotiation involves separating the people with whom you are negotiating from the issue you are discussing; focusing on interests rather than positions; coming up with mutually beneficial options; and developing and using objective criteria to make choices.

Building relationships, forming networks, and negotiating all depend in part on leaders' ability to communicate effectively. A range of strategies is possible, and leaders should vary their strategies according to their audience. Means of sending information to others include newsletters, podcasts, phone messages, websites, video messages, community bulletin boards, local media, email, and computer screens in school hallways (Hopkins, 2008). Strategies for learning from others include face-to-face meetings, focus groups, and surveys (Hopkins, 2008). A favored communications strategy of administrators committed to inclusive practices is dialogue (Ryan, in press). Dialogue requires leaders listen to others and try to understand them (Ryan, in press). Listening effectively involves establishing eye contact (where culturally appropriate), avoiding interruptions, asking questions, refraining from talking too much, and comparing the speakers' experiences to one's own (Ryan, in press).

An important task of leaders is to appropriate district, state, and federal policies that advantage some groups while disadvantaging others. Appropriation occurs when policy that is created in one place is interpreted and ultimately remade by those who encounter it someplace else (Levinson et al., 2009). This process is inevitable and can be undertaken strategically to support goals of equity and social justice. One strategy involves looking for policy language that has many possible meanings and choosing to define it in ways that further leaders' goals (Anderson, 2009). For example, they can adopt critical understandings of democracy and citizenship that are committed to equity, diversity, and social justice rather than neoliberal definitions that emphasize individual choice. A second strategy involves looking for absences and contradictions in policies that can be used as opportunities to support practices that further their goals. For example, district leaders in Massachusetts grappling with a law mandating structured English immersion programs for ELL, grouped students with the same first language in the same classrooms rather than spreading them across the district and continued to offer bilingual programs where they were not specifically forbidden by law (de Jong et al., 2005). These actions enable the continuance of practices that recognized the value of students' first language. How leaders and their school and district communities appropriate policies can challenge or perpetuate the status quo (Anderson, 2009).

REFERENCES

Anderson, G. L. (2009). *Advocacy leadership: Toward a post-reform agenda in education*. New York: Routledge.

Ball, S. J. (2009). Privatising education, privatising education policy, privatising educational research: Network governance and the "competition state". *Journal of Education Policy*, *24*(1), 83–99.

Barbaro, A. (producer) & Earp, J. (writer). (2008). *Consuming kids: The commercialization of childhood*. Northampton, MA: Media Education Foundation.

Bennett, J. V. & Thompson, H. C. (2011). Changing district priorities for school-business collaboration: Superintendent agency and capacity for institutionalization. *Educational Administration Quarterly*, *47*(5), 826–868.

Blase, J. (1991). The micropolitical orientation of teachers towards closed school principals. *Education and Urban Society*, *23*(4), 356–378.

Blase, J. & Anderson, G. L. (1995). *The micropolitics of educational leadership: From control to empowerment*. New York: Teachers College Press.

Blase, J. & Blase, J. (2002). The micropolitics of instructional supervision: A call for research. *Educational Administration Quarterly*, *38*(1), 6–44.

Bolman, L. G. & Deal, T. E. (2008). *Reframing organizations: Artistry, choice and leadership* (4th ed.). San Francisco, CA: Jossey-Bass.

Brantlinger, E. (2003). *Dividing classes: How the middle class negotiates and rationalizes school advantage*. New York: Taylor & Francis.

Chilton, P. (2004). *Analysing political discourse: Theory and practice*. New York: Routledge.

Cibulka, J. G. (2001). The changing role of interest groups in education: Nationalization and the new politics of education productivity. *Educational Policy*, *15*(1), 12–40.

Council of Chief State School Officers (2008). *Educational leadership policy standards 2008*. Retrieved July 8, 2010, from www.ccsso.org/publications/details.cfm?PublicationID=365

Crow, G. M., & Weindling, D. (2010). Learning to be political: New English headteachers' roles. *Educational Policy*, *24*(1), 137–158.

de Jong, E. J., Gort, M., & Cobb, C. D. (2005). Bilingual education within the context of English-only policies: Three districts' responses to question 2 in Massachusetts. *Educational Policy*, *19*(4), 595–620.

Evans, M. P. & Shirley, D. (2008). The development of collective moral leadership among parents through education organizing. *New Directions for Youth Development*, *117*, 77–91.

Fisher, R., & Ury, W. L. (2011). *Getting to yes: Negotiating agreement without giving in.* New York: Penguin.

Fraatz, J. M. B. (1989). Poltical principals: Efficiency, effectiveness, and the political dynamics of school administration. *International Journal of Qualitative Studies in Education, 2*(1), 3–24.

Fulcher, G. (1999). *Disabling policies? A comparative approach to education policy and disabilty* (2nd ed.). Sheffield, UK: Philip Armstrong Publications.

Gawlik, M. A. (2008). Breaking loose: Principal autonomy in charter and public schools. *Educational Policy, 22*(6), 783–804.

Goehler, G. (2000). Construction and use of power. In H. Goverde, P. G. Cerny, M. Haugaard, & H. Lentner (Eds.), *Power in contemporary politics* (pp. 41–58). London: Sage.

Goverde, H., Cerny, P. G., Haugaard, M., & Lentner, H. (2000). General introduction: Power in contemporary politics. In H. Goverde, P. G. Cerny, M. Haugaard, & H. Lentner (Eds.), *Power in contemporary politics* (pp. 1–33). London: Sage Publications.

Hartney, M. & Flavin, P. (2011). From the schoolhouse to the statehouse: Teacher union political activism and U.S. state education reform policy. *State Politics & Policy Quarterly, 11*(3), 251–268.

Hess, E. (2007). False equivalency: Think tank references on education in the news media. *Peabody Journal of Education, 82*(1), 63–102.

Hopkins, G. (2008, 01/21/2009). *Principals share lessons learned about communicating with parents, others.* Retrieved June 10, 2013, from www.educationworld.com/a_admin/admin/admin 511.shtml

Horvat, E. M., Weininger, E. B., & Lareau, A. (2003). From social ties to social capital: Class differences in the relations between schools and parent networks. *American Educational Research Journal, 40*(2), 319–351.

Howard, R. W. & Preisman, J. (2007). The bankrupt "revolution": Running schools like businesses fails the test. *Education and Urban Society, 39*(2), 244–263.

Intkonen, T. (2009). Stories of hope and decline: interest group effectiveness in national special education policy. *Educational Policy, 23*(1), 43–65.

Jackson, B. L. & Cibulka, J. G. (1991). Leadership turnover and business mobilization: The changing political ecology of urban school systems. *Journal of Education Policy, 6*(5), 71–86.

Jacoby, D. (2011). Teacher unionization in school governance. *Educational Policy, 25*(5), 762–783.

Koppich, J. E. & Esch, C. (2012). Grabbing the brass ring: Who shapes teacher policy? *Educational Policy, 26*(1), 79–95.

Koyama, J. (2010). *Making failure pay: For-profit tutoring, high-stakes testing, and public schools.* Chicago: University of Chicago Press.

Kumashiro, K. K. (2012). When billionaires become educational experts. *Academe, 98*(3), 10–16.

Lasswell, H. D. (1965). *Politics: Who gets what, when, and how* (9th ed.). Cleveland, OH: Meridian Books, The World Publishing Company.

Levinson, B. A. U., Sutton, M., & Winstead, T. (2009). Education policy as a practice of power: Theoretical tools, ethnographic methods, democratic options. *Educational Policy, 23*(6), 767–795.

Lingard, B. (2010). Policy borrowing, policy learning: Testing times in Australian schooling. *Critical Studies in Education, 51*(2), 129–147.

Lopez, M. E. (Producer). (2003, June 9, 2013). *Transforming schools through community organizing: A research review.* Retrieved from www.hfrp.org

Lugg, C. & Robinson, M. (2009). Religion, advocacy coalitions, and the politics of U.S. public schooling. *Educational Policy, 23*(1), 242–266.

Malen, B. & Cochran, M. V. (2008). Beyond pluralistic patterns of power: Research on the micropolitics of schools. In B. S. Cooper, J. G. Cibulka, & L. D. Fusarelli (Eds.), *Handbook of education politics and policy* (pp. 148–178). New York: Routledge.

Malen, B. & Ogawa, R. T. (1988). Professional-patron influence on site-based governance councils: A confounding case study. *Educational Evaluation and Policy Analysis, 10*(4), 251–270.

Marsh, J. (2012). The micropolitics of implementing a school-based bonus policy: The case of New York City's Compensation Committees. *Educational Evaluation and Policy Analysis, 34*(2), 164–184.

Mawhinney, H. (2001). Theoretical approaches to understanding interest groups. *Educational Policy, 15*(1), 187–214.

McDonnell, L. M. (2009). A political science persepctive on education policy analysis. In G. Sykes, B. Schneider, & D. N. Plank (Eds.), *Handbook of education policy research* (pp. 57–70). New York: Routledge.

McLaughlin, M. W. (2006). Implementation research in education: Lessons learned, lingering questions, and new opportunities. In M. I. Honig (Ed.), *New directions in policy implementation: Confronting complexity* (pp. 209–228). Albany, NY: State University of New York.

Moe, T. M. (2006). Union power and the education of children. In J. Hannawya & A. J. Rotherham (Eds.), *Collective bargaining in education: Negotiating change in today's schools* (pp. 229–255). Cambridge, MA: Harvard Education Press.

Moe, T. M. (2009). Collective bargaining and the performance of the public schools. *American Journal of Political Science, 53*(1), 156–174.

Molnar, A. (2006). The commercial transformation of public education. *Journal of Education Policy, 21*(5), 621–640.

Molnar, A., Boninger, F., Harris, M. D., Libby, K. M., & Fogarty, J. (2013). *Promoting consumption at school: Health threats associated with schoolhouse commercialism—The fifteenth annual report on schoolhouse commercializing trends: 2011–2012*. Retrieved from http://nepc. colorado.edu/publication/schoolhousecommercialism-2012

Moore, D. R. (1992). The case for parent and community involvement. In G. A. Hess, Jr. (Ed.), *Empowering teachers and parents*. Westport, CT: Bergin & Garvey.

Moses, E. (2011). *Public education reform: How teachers' unions are using schools as political tools*. Doctoral dissertation, Georgetown University, Washington, DC.

Moutsios, S. (2009). International organisations and transnational education policy. *Compare, 39*(4), 469–481.

Nespor, J. & Hicks, D. (2010). Wizards and witches: Parent advocates and contention in special education in the USA. *Journal of Education Policy, 25*(3), 309–334.

Newman, A., Deschenes, S., & Hopkins, K. (2012). From agitating in the streets to implementing in in the suites: Understanding education policy reforms initiated by local advocates. *Educational Policy, 26*(5), 720–758.

Oakes, J., Renée, M., Rogers, J., & Lipton, M. (2008). Research and community organizing as tools for democratizing educational policymaking. In C. Sugrue (Ed.), *The future of educational change: International perspectives* (pp. 136–154). New York: Routledge.

Opfer, V. D. (2001). Beyond self-interest: Educational interest groups and congressional influence. *Educational Policy, 15*(1), 135–152.

Opfer, V. D., Young, T. V., & Fusarelli, L. D. (2008). Politics of interest: Interest groups and advocacy coalitions in American education. In B. S. Cooper, J. G. Cibulka, & L. D. Fusarelli (Eds.), *Handbook of education politics and policy* (pp. 196–216). New York: Routledge.

Organization for Economic Cooperation and Development (n.d.). About. Retrieved April 5, 2013, from www.oecd.org/about/.

Orr, M. (1996). Urban politics and school reform: The case of Baltimore. *Urban Affairs Review*, *31*(3), 314–345.

Orr, M. & Rogers, J. (2011). Unequal schools, unequal voice: The need for public engagement for public education. In M. Orr & J. Rogers (Eds.), *Public engagement for public education* (pp. 1–24). Stanford, CA: Stanford University Press.

Renée, M. (2006). *Knowledge, power, and education justice: How social movement organizations use research to influence education policy*. Dissertation, UCLA, Los Angeles.

Ryan, J. (2010). Promoting social justice in schools: Principals' political strategies. *International Journal of Leadership in Education: Theory and Practice*, *13*(4), 357–376.

Ryan, J. (in press). Promoting inclusive leadership in diverse schools. In I. Bogotch & C. M. Shields (Eds.), *International handbook of educational leadership and social (in)justice* (Vol. 29). Dordrecht: Springer International Handbooks of Education.

Sabatier, P. A. & Jenkins-Smith, H. C. (1999). The advocacy coalition framework. In P. A. Sabatier (Ed.), *Theories of the policy process* (pp. 117–166). Boulder, CO: Westview Press.

Scott, J. (2009). The politics of venture philanthropy in charter school policy and advocacy. *Educational Policy*, *23*(1), 106–136.

Scott, J., Lubienski, C., & DeBray-Pelot, E. (2009). The politics of advocacy in education. *Educational Policy*, *23*(1), 3–14.

Shatkin, G. & Gershberg, A. I. (2007). Empowering parents and building communities: The role of school-based councils in educational governance and accountability. *Urban Education*, *42*(6), 582–615.

Shirley, D. (2011). A brief history of public engagement in American public education. In M. Orr & J. Rogers (Eds.), *Public engagement for public education* (pp. 27–51). Stanford, CA: Stanford University Press.

Smith, M. (2005). *A civil society? Collective actors in Canadian political life*. Peterborough, ON: Broadview Press.

Sokolower, J. (2012–2013). Lessons in social justice unionism. *Rethinking Schools*, Winter 2012–2013, 11–17.

Soter, T. (1993). A business plan for education. *Management Review*, *82*(9), 10–16.

Spring, J. (2011). *The politics of American education*. New York: Routledge.

Stone, C., Doherty, K., Jones, C., & Ross, T. (1999). Schools and disadvantaged neighborhoods: The community development challenge. In R. Ferguson & W. Dicken (Eds.), *Urban problems and community development* (pp. 339–380). Washington, DC: Brookings Institution.

Strunk, K. O. & Grissom, J. A. (2010). Do strong unions shape district policies? Collective bargaining, teacher contract restrictiveness, and the political power of teachers' unions. *Educational Evaluation and Policy Analysis*, *32*(3), 389–406.

Timpane, P. M. & McNeill, L. M. B. (1991). *Business impact on education and child development reform: A study prepared for the Committee for Economic Development*. New York: Committee for Economic Development.

Warren, M. R. (2011a). Building a political constituency for urban school reform. *Urban Education*, *46*(3), 484–512.

Warren, M. R. (2011b). Community organizing for education reform. In M. Orr & J. Rogers (Eds.), *Public engagement for public education* (pp. 139–172). Stanford, CA: Stanford University Press.

Westheimer, J. (2008). *No child left thinking: Democracy at risk in American schools: Democratic Dialogue Series, No. 17*. Retrieved from: www.democraticdialogue.com/DDpdfs/DD17-Westheimer.pdf

Wilson, J. (2001). Political discourse. In D. Schiffrin, D. Tannen, & H. E. Hamilton (Eds.), (2001). *The handbook of discourse analysis* (pp. 398–145). Malden, MA: Blackwell.

Winton, S. (2010). Democracy in education through community-based policy dialogues. *Canadian Journal of Educational Administration and Policy* (114). Retrieved from: www.umanitoba.ca/publications/cjeap/articles/comm-toc.html

Winton, S. & Brewer, C. (2013). *People for education: A critical policy history*. Paper presented at the annual meeting of the American Educational Research Association.

Winton, S. & Evans, M. P. (2012). *Research by/for the people: The role of research in community-based organizations*. Paper presented at the annual meeting of the American Educational Research Association.

Young, J., Levin, B., & Wallin, D. (2008). *Understanding Canadian schools: An introduction to educational administration*. Toronto, ON: Nelson Education.

Young, L. & Everitt, J. (2004). *Advocacy groups*. Vancouver, BC: University of British Columbia Press.

CHAPTER 8

School Leaders' Professional and Civic Political Voice

Bradley W. Carpenter and Sarah Diem

CHAPTER OVERVIEW

The environment in which many of today's school leaders work has grown increasingly complex. Among the complexities at the school level, a combination of district, state, and federal education accountability provisions aim at turning around persistently low-achieving (PLA) public schools. All principals must calculate the risk of their schools falling into policy-defined categories of low performance. In particular, principals of PLAs often face societal inequities in their schools' communities along with policies (perhaps) inadvertently designed to heighten some of these inequities. For example, a common option in accountability policies since the 1980s is an opt-out, or school choice, provision, where PLAs had to notify parents that they could enroll their children elsewhere (Jennings & Rentner, 2006; Lindle & Cibulka, 2006; McDermott, 2007). The problem with setting up choices that reduce student enrollment at PLAs is that typically these schools are under-resourced, and because funding for schools depends on enrollment, deliberately inviting people to withdraw for another school sets up a rich-get-richer, poor-get-poorer result (Aikens, 2005; Darling-Hammond, 2007; Roza et al., 2004).

This chapter illustrates how principals face dilemmas about carrying out policies that seem destined to hurt their students and their schools. How can principals find the appropriate professional and political voice to improve these kinds of situations for the best interest of their students, families, schools, and communities? The case used for this chapter describes the diverse range of issues often faced by principals serving within large urban school districts. Yet, in smaller districts, these conflicts between what is good for a school in light of what might be useful for the rest of the district can occur as well. Specifically, this case challenges the reader to consider how a newly appointed principal must embrace her job and her roles as a civic and political leader. This case examines the plight of Jessica, a first year principal recently assigned to a PLA campus. The case begins shortly after Jessica's appointment to Young High School, in a district where the political mood falls out from a complicated set of school choice policies intended to aid the district's desegregation efforts. Given three years to turn around the academic standing of Young High School, Jessica must navigate social and political complexities associated with school improvement politics in a district valuing school choice and intra-district competition.

CONTEXTUAL BACKGROUND

Today's school leaders navigate complex and high-stakes accountability policies that are combined from the federal government to the state and then at the district level. All these policies aim at increased student achievement, and most of the associated policy measures are weighted heavily toward test results. Most of these policies increasingly utilize student test scores to evaluate school personnel. Consequently, those tasked with preparing school leaders find themselves on the defensive; as such, these programs are held accountable for the preparation of leaders able to successfully navigate this new era of education policy and politics (Cibulka, 2009; Goldring & Schuermann, 2009). While NCLB effectively launched an era of educational reform shaped by the tenets of high-stakes accountability, the focus on school-level leadership accountability intensified recently through revision of the federal Title I School Improvement Grants (SIG). The latest modifications to the SIG program offered state and local education agencies a choice among four prescriptive turnaround strategies: (a) turnaround, (b) restart, (c) school closure, and (d) transformation. All these strategies call for replacement of the school-level leader, the principal.

The continued promotion of school choice policies in public schools adds yet another layer of complexity for principals. Principals in low-performing schools must face a double-edged, accountability policy sword in that low-performing schools have higher achievement hurdles than their better performing and wealthier schools plus the consequence of persistent low performance is a requirement to notify parents and students that they can choose to attend another school (Aikens, 2005; Balfanz et al., 2007). Since 2007, school choice policies were complicated further by judicial rulings in *Parents Involved in Community Schools v. Seattle (PICS)*. In the majority decision for *PICS*, the U.S. Supreme Court offered a complicated ruling on what kinds of criteria school districts might use in balancing diversity among enrollments across schools. Some achievement statistics suggest that income gaps are more significant than racial or ethnicity gaps (Reardon, 2013). Taken nationally, those statistics may mask regional differences in performance based on race, sex, or ethnicity (Darling-Hammond, 2007; Reardon & Yun, 2003; Roza et al., 2004). Yet another dimension of school choice is the ongoing free-market values undergirding this initiative. These expectations are that competition increases performance for all schools (Chubb & Moe, 1990; Friedman, 1962). Manifestly, these assumptions and provisions for competitive school choices are woven into the four current turnaround models. The policies encourage public, private, and charter operators to participate as alternative providers. Proponents of school choice believe that by establishing a free, market-based competitive environment, student academic achievement and overall school performance will rise (Lubienski, 2005). This policy assumption creates a worrisome conundrum for PLA principals because, as designed, such policies affect PLAs' ability to attract and retain students in light of other school options. Moreover, research repeatedly questions whether parents are truly able to assume their role as savvy consumers of school choices (Cullen et al., 2005; Holme & Wells, 2008). The issues with completely free-market, deregulated choice policies are that they yield greater levels of stratification for already low-performing schools (Aikens, 2005; Balfanz et al., 2007; Blank et al., 1996; Frankenberg & Siegel-Hawley, 2008). On the other hand, regulated policies, with equity-minded goals, can lead to increased diversity and equitable outcomes (Blank et al., 1996; Frankenberg & Siegel-Hawley, 2008).

ISLLC Standard 6 tasks principals with promoting the "success of every student by understanding, responding to, and influencing the political, social, economic, legal, and cultural context" (ISLLC 2008, p.15). Therefore, the purpose of this chapter is to examine the challenges school leaders must face when attempting to realize their civic and political voice within uniquely complex policy environments. This examination is shaped by two guiding questions: (a) how should today's school leaders use their civic and political identity to confront the inequitable consequences associated with school choice, intra-district competition, and the resegregation of public schools? (b) in what ways can today's school leaders constructively push against district and federal policies that contribute to inequitable consequences while maintaining their position of leadership and not causing damage to their careers? To explore each of these questions via a contextually relevant scenario, we highlight a case focused on leadership within a school district that has faced a number of legal and political challenges to its student assignment policies over the last decade. Within this case, we highlight a number of the specific difficulties associated with accepting a role as a new leader in a school publically

LEARNING ACTIVITY 8.1

Before Reading the Case

Visit the state agency's website to download and read how it has chosen to implement federal policy for Title 1.

1. Who was involved in developing the state's plan for federal approval?
2. When was that plan submitted, and what was the U.S. Department of Education's response?
3. What provisions are necessary for school leaders to implement?

identified as persistently low achieving. Several issues arise in this case of a first year principal tasked with meeting the guidelines of the Title I SIG program. First, the dominating task concerns test scores and school improvement. Yet, the complexity of the school's population illustrates why this task is not a straightforward fix. These complexities include an increasing divide among racial and ethnic groups, escalating poverty among students, families and neighborhoods, and the novice status of the school's leadership.

CASE 8.1: CIVIC AND POLITICAL LEADERSHIP AMID SCHOOL TURNAROUND, SCHOOL CHOICE, AND INCREASED COMPETITION

Prior to the school desegregation policy implemented in 1975, both the city of Jacksontown and the county in which it was located—Southern County—experienced extreme stratification among residential areas. Jacksontown itself had experienced growing levels of residential segregation patterns since the early 1920s, as White working-class immigrants established enclaves representative of their ethnicity while Blacks were restricted primarily to central areas within the city. Whereas the central areas within Jacksontown would become permanent features of Black residential life, the ethnic enclaves housing White working-class immigrants served as a transitory stage as immigrants began to assimilate into the dominant culture.

As Jacksontown transitioned through the 1930s and 1940s, residential development increased in northern and southern areas of the city, further increasing residential segregation between Jacksontown and its suburbs. From 1940 to 1970, the dissimilarity index[1] (Grannis, 2002) in Jacksontown underscored very high levels of residential segregation between Blacks and Whites, with the figure ranging from the lowest level of 70 in 1940, to its highest level of 83.6 in 1970. Moreover, the Black population was increasing, particularly in the southern end of the city, resulting in White flight from this area and a decrease in the White population by almost 50 percent during the 1960s and 1970s.

From 1960 to 1990, suburbanization played an integral role in the 31 percent population decline in Jacksontown and the 80 percent population growth in Southern County. Additionally, the suburban development in Southern County led to an increase in the geographical separation of Blacks and Whites. The city of Jacksontown became characterized as the *Black core* while the suburbs in Southern County represented the *White fringe*.

At the time of the 1954 *Brown v. Board of Education* decision, the Jacksontown metropolitan area contained two separate school district systems: a city district (Jacksontown) and a suburban district (Southern County). Two years after the *Brown* decision, in 1956, both school districts implemented policies to address de jure segregation. In Southern County, the new policies allowed Black high school students to attend their neighborhood schools; previously they rode buses to city high schools. Black elementary students in Jacksontown continued to attend all-Black schools located within their neighborhoods.

In Jacksontown, a geography-based student assignment plan was implemented that included provisions for an open transfer policy. Approximately 85 percent of White students assigned to attend previously all-Black schools requested transfers, as did 45 percent of Black students assigned to formerly all-White schools. The open transfer policy was a typical strategy employed throughout the South after *Brown* (Orfield, 2005). The intent of the policy was to block any type of meaningful desegregation from occurring in schools (Orfield, 2005). While the Jacksontown and Southern County plans technically ended de jure segregation in the districts, the open transfer options of both plans permitted persistent residential segregation and resulted in racially segregated schools.

Sixteen years after the geography-based student assignment plan was implemented, the Jacksontown School District continued to remain highly segregated. From 1956 to 1973, the Jacksontown School District transitioned from a student population of 26.2 percent Black and 73.8 percent White, to an equal racial split district-wide, but school enrollments were more unequal. Nineteen of the 46 elementary schools were predominately Black (80 percent to 100 percent), 21 elementary schools were 90 to 100 percent White, and 14 of the 19 non-vocational middle and high schools were either completely Black or White. During this time, the percentage of Black students in the Southern County School District only rose from 3.8 percent in 1956 to 4.6 percent in 1973, while the White student population nearly tripled in size. Additionally, the majority of Black students in Southern County attended racially identifiable schools.

In 1971, a state-level suit was filed, requesting desegregation be achieved through the merger of the Jacksontown and Southern County school systems. By 1974, the state courts ordered both systems to desegregate, with the judge citing the existence of continued segregation internal to both school systems despite *Brown*'s mandate. The judge also required merger of Jacksontown and Southern County school systems into one unified school district. When the two school systems merged in 1975, the Southern County schools enrolled approximately 90,000 students, only 4 percent were Black. The Jacksontown schools' population included 45,000 students, of which 54 percent were Black. The new unified school district represented approximately 135,000 students; 20 percent were Black.

During the 1975–1976 school year the new unified, countywide system implemented its desegregation plan. The plan established clusters of schools that were either predominately White or Black. Buses moved students within these clusters in order to achieve a more racially balanced mix of students in schools. Students who lived in school attendance areas in which they were a minority stayed in their local schools. The plan indirectly provided an incentive for both Black and White families to consider residential changes that might lead to housing desegregation. In elementary schools, the plan projected between 12 percent and 40 percent Black enrollments, and in secondary schools, a range of 12.5 percent and 35 percent Black. Under the initial cluster plan, White students were only bused two of their 12 years in school while Black students felt the largest burden in the desegregation plans riding buses away from their neighborhoods for 10 of their 12 years in school. The district reassigned administrators, teachers, and staff throughout the district to reflect the system-wide racial composition of the staff. The student assignment criteria took into consideration school size and neighborhood locations so that residential areas could be paired to achieve integration.

The merger of the Jacksontown and Southern County school districts into the Southern County Public Schools (SCPS) led to a rapid increase in enrollment in Jacksontown's parochial schools as well as White flight to districts in counties surrounding the city. As a common reaction during school desegregation, upper-class White families literally purchased an exemption from desegregation efforts by either moving to districts not affected by the policy, or by sending their children to private schools (Edgar, 1998; LeLoudis, 1996). The new countywide desegregation plan also resulted in increased levels of violence throughout the county. However, despite protests and incidents of targeted violence, busing continued, even after the court's active supervision of the desegregation plan ended in 1978.

In 1998, after implementing several iterations of student assignment and school choice plans, SCPS found itself facing its first lawsuit against the plan. Six African American parents argued against a district policy capping the number of African American students permitted to enroll in a historically Black high school magnet academy. The parents argued that the enrollment limit on Black students was unconstitutional and requested elimination of the racially based policy. Eventually, the District Court ruled that racial guidelines established by the school board were an appropriate effort to comply with the 1975 continuing desegregation order. Further, the judge ruled that no party could challenge racial guidelines in the SCPS school choice plan until the vacating of the 1975 desegregation decree.

Two years later, in 2000, the same 1998 plaintiffs appeared in the District Court, claiming they were denied entry to the high school magnet academy, and argued for the desegregation decree to be lifted and won, ending 25 years of court-ordered desegregation. Along with that decision, the judge ordered the SCPS school board to redesign its admission procedures at its other magnet schools. As much as a year after the judge disbanded the SCPS desegregation decree, the school board voluntarily continued implementing its race-conscious student assignment plan modified to a degree to reflect the court's ruling regarding magnet school assignment.

In 2007 in *Parents Involved v. Seattle District No. 1 (PICS)*, the U.S. Supreme Court ruled against use of race as a single enrollment criterion. SCPS, since, received a number of challenges to the latest iteration of its desegregation plan. The district had been using race as a factor in its student assignment process for decades, and thus worked through numerous iterations of its plan to achieve diversity guidelines set forth by the court.

In 2010, the school board reviewed the student assignment plan, paying particular attention to choices available to parents, length of time for buses to transport students to schools, and how to accomplish diversity. Currently, the SCPS policy has 13 uniquely defined clusters (groups of schools that exchange students to ensure each school has a diverse student population). The plan incorporates race, income, and education to maintain parental choice. SCPS uses geographic territories defined by U.S. Census block groups (statistical divisions of census tracts that contain between 600 and 3000 people) and categorized as 1, 2, or 3. Category 1 block groups are those with lower concentrations of White residents with lower income and education levels while Category 3 has the highest education and income levels and percentage of White residents; Category 2 falls in between. SCPS brought in consultants to analyze the plan, and they recommended modernizing the district's transportation system along with installing an online system for parents to make school choices. In 2012, the school board adopted a revised student assignment plan, which also included kindergarten students and ESL students in the school's diversity index. This plan was implemented in August 2012.

Turnaround Comes to Town

During the summer of 2012, six SCPS campuses were identified as residing within the state's bottom 5 percent of public schools. As a result, and in accordance with the SIG program, the State Department of Education (SDOE) tasked SCPS to choose one of the four prescribed Title I SIG school improvement models—turnaround, restart, transformation, and closure—for each of the six identified campuses. Due to the fact that each of the six schools was the first school chosen to participate in the revised Title I SIG program, they were labeled as SCPS Cohort #1. Of the six schools identified within Cohort #1, four were high schools with a 2010 average graduation rate of 55.2 percent; the other two were middle schools, both of which had failed to make Adequately Yearly Progress (AYP) for three consecutive years. Although the majority of the schools were located within the South End of Jacksontown, there was no specific relationship among any of the six schools, as the two middle schools were not considered to be designated feeder schools for any of the low-performing high schools, and none of the six schools was located within the same district-defined cluster.

After lengthy deliberation by each of the campuses' site-based decision making (SBDM) committees, each of the six schools chose to implement the SIG turnaround option. Under the revised SIG guidelines, turnaround mandates that schools do the following: (a) replace the principal; (b) re-hire no more than 50 percent of the school staff; (c) implement a research-based instructional program; (d) provide extended learning time; and (e) implement a new governance structure. In other words, each of the six SCPS campuses faced a hiring spree. They had to hire a new principal and re-interview all current teaching staff. Then they also had to decide which teachers had the capacity necessary to facilitate the turnaround of student success rates. They could re-hire 50 percent. Then, to bring the instructional staff to 100 percent, these schools had to recruit and hire more teachers. Complicating this intensive summer activity to staff a school by fall, the school governance committee had to be disbanded, which provided new principals with ultimate decision-making authority. Thus, the hiring decisions fell on the shoulders of new principals. While any one of the aforementioned tasks is rife with a number of complexities, SCPS district officials further complicated the situation. SCPS chose to replace all of the six outgoing principals with assistant principals. That is, none of the six had any previous experience as a building principal. In addition, none of these new principals was familiar with any of the six schools as they had been selected from other higher performing campuses within the district.

From Books, Buses, and Discipline into the Turnaround Fire

Jessica dreaded the upcoming meeting with her instructional leadership team (ILT), as she fully understood the news she was about to deliver would not be well received. As principal for only two weeks, Jessica discovered a drastic drop in predicted freshman enrollment numbers at Young High School (YHS). Although Jessica had a great deal of confidence in her leadership abilities, she had never served as a leader on a low-performing campus before. In fact, while Jessica had earned a reputation as a highly effective assistant principal over the last eight years, she had spent her 13 years' experience as an educator at one of SCPS's highest performing campuses. Jessica was entering new territory, as her previous experiences as a teacher and assistant principal were all nested within a finely refined academic system much different from the seemingly dysfunctional system in place at YHS.

Once highly regarded by the parents and stakeholders of SCPS, YHS had fallen upon challenging times. Over the course of the last decade, YHS devolved from a school with a population of over 1000 students to a school housing less than 500 students. Also, YHS suffered from factors associated with historically low-performing schools, including: (a) lack of leadership; (b) teacher turnover; (c) declining test scores; (d) burgeoning dropout rates; (e) increased suspensions; (f) the deficit mindset of many YHS personnel and East End community members, which viewed the significant influx of students of color as a problem; and (g) lack of parental involvement.

Individually, each of these factors pose a unique challenge for a school leader, but Jessica's plight heightened with layers of issues from the district's desegregation efforts, the district's school choice policies, intra-district competition, alongside state and federal turnaround policies. At the local level, the SCPS student assignment plan offers parents a number of school choice options, allowing them to select from schools serving their home address, magnet schools, magnet programs, optional programs, and/or any other schools within their elementary or high school network within their cluster of schools. At the state and federal levels, policies associated with NCLB and the Race to The Top (R2T) allow parents with children attending persistently low-performing schools to choose other schools deemed successful as defined by AYP. Although YHS is located within a higher socioeconomic northern enclave of the community, YHS's neighbors now overwhelmingly refuse to send their children to the school. Subsequently, during the time when student scores began to falter at YHS, parents in the North End community began sending their children to the private and traditionally high-achieving public schools located nearby. Four high-achieving private schools and three high-achieving public schools geographically surround YHS. Presumably the lowered freshman enrollment number signaled an even larger exodus of neighborhood students to surrounding schools.

Along with other schools, YHS had selected a career theme: mechanical engineering. Jessica's predecessors had designated a substantial amount of resources building the mechanical engineering program at YHS; however, the program and its marketing failed to entice the upper middle-class parents living within the North End of the Jacksontown community. Therefore, YHS was competing against nearby schools that had tailored their offerings to meet the interests of the surrounding community. For example, YHS was located close to Benton High School (BHS), which had developed a successful international studies program allowing both students and parents to travel abroad during the school year.

Ultimately, the evacuation of the neighborhood students when combined with YHS's inability to lure potential students to its campus left YHS with just over 400 students on a campus designed for 800 students. In addition, while the demographic make-up of Jessica's staff was largely homogeneous (over 95 percent White), more than 95 percent of YHS's current student population was composed of low-income students of color. These facts further complicated YHS's turnaround efforts, as Jessica–while allowed by the SIG guidelines to downsize the staff up to 50 percent of the teachers considered to be ineffective—also considered most of her middle-class teachers to be culturally incompetent; that is, they were largely unable to reach students from diverse backgrounds. The failure to attract and retain culturally competent teachers contributed to the negative cycle at YHS where teachers failed to reach students and parents, therefore students and parents chose not to engage in the student improvement process. These factors contributed to students failing to meet expectations on standardized examinations, and thus YHS was labeled as a PLA. The publically announced PLA moniker contributed to the enrollment drop as nearby parents chose to send their children to other campuses, which subsequently reduced the amount of funding YHS would receive from the district, thus, forcing the YHS administration to let go some of its more qualified teachers and administrators.

Dire Straits

Jessica opened the ILT meeting by presenting the district's predicted enrollment numbers and telling her team, "Folks, we are in dire straits." Begrudgingly, Jessica informed the ILT that the district's data team was projecting over 50 percent of YHS's incoming freshmen would be granted a district-approved petition to attend a different high school campus outside of YHS's cluster. This was particularly troubling news, as it meant instead of receiving 200 incoming freshman, YHS would only see approximately 100 of the students slotted by the district's student assignment plan to attend YHS.

Members of the ILT team sat quietly with their heads down, realizing the potential implications of the district's decision to allow students to enroll at other schools. Decreasing enrollment meant yet another reduction in resources and staff. After a few moments of silence, a few members of the ILT began to complain, specifically citing the district's unequal enforcement of the student assignment plan. This line of reasoning struck a chord with many of the ILT members.

Suddenly, Derek, one of Jessica's assistant principals, shouted, "How in the heck are we supposed to compete with the schools surrounding us if people in central office continue to succumb to political pressure?" Derek's comment referenced the fact that SCPS district officials permitted many of the East End community schools to continue accepting YHS neighborhood students despite upsetting the district's student assignment plan percentage guidelines.

Other ILT members greeted Derek's comment with instant affirmation. They vented about the negative cycle in which YHS seemed caught and which, at the moment, seemed inescapable. Shawna, another one of Jessica's assistant principals, followed up on Derek's comments outlining YHS's predicament:

> Look, everyone, to stay in compliance with the district's desegregation policies, we bus in over 70 percent of our entire population. While I personally love these kids, we still have too many teachers who are culturally incompetent, and thus create academic and discipline-related nightmares for us on a daily basis. Even I have to admit that most of them are not choosing to attend YHS because of our magnet programs. They are coming to us because either they were not accepted at the higher performing schools that surround us, or because they were not accepted to those schools closer to their residential neighborhood due to district desegregation quotas. Therefore, while we've been able to engage and win over many of these students, we still have a large number of students who have yet to buy into our mission and vision at YHS. The same can be said for parents. How many people attended our family literacy night? That's right, three. Guys, we have a largely apathetic student and parent population, yet we have only two more years to turn around this school. If we don't figure out how to better navigate this situation all of us will soon be out of jobs!

Jessica reeled at this sudden outburst of anger from the ILT. These sentiments put Jessica in a tenuous position. On the one hand, she agreed that the currently assignment policy benefited some schools while hurting others. On the other, as an assistant principal at one of the schools benefitting from the inequitable enforcement of the student assignment policy, Jessica recalled the ways in which that school's administrators had coached parents to better navigate the district's formal policies for their own benefit. In short, Jessica had insider knowledge of the inequities in the district's administration of its student assignment plan, plus she recognized how risky her position was if she acknowledged this view while still tasked with the turnaround requirements for YHS.

Jessica called for a 10-minute recess, thinking that a few minutes away from the table would allow tempers to cool. As Jessica sat alone, she began to question whether she was the person for this job. Overwhelmed, Jessica mentally considered her next steps: How as a first year principal could she use her voice to challenge and potentially reshape district-level policies? How quickly could she equip her struggling, culturally incompetent teachers with culturally competent mindsets and pedagogical skill sets? How was she going to use her public voice to engage a group of parents who had disinvested in the school itself? How could she use her civic connections to educate the community about her efforts, her struggles, her successes, and her needs?

LEARNING ACTIVITY 8.2

What's Your Advice for Jessica?

1. Think about the opt-out provision of accountability policies, and explain both the advantages and disadvantages to whom?
2. If you were Jessica, would you explain to the ILT how much you know about the inequities in the district student assignment plan? Why? Or why not?
3. What would you advise Jessica to do when she reconvenes the ILT in a few more minutes?
4. Given the other political analyses in this volume, what political strategies are available to Jessica and the ILT? Are there other stakeholders they need to involve?

ISSUES MOVING FORWARD

School leaders daily confront tensions between local needs and larger community issues along with mandates and regulations that seemingly impede forward motion. Several research-based strategies are available for school leaders to act strategically in their political milieu. The next sections examine the following: (1) the role of the school leader amid school turnaround policies; (2) the role of the school leader in an increasingly segregated, competitive, choice-oriented public school system; (3) the political navigation of organizational change via various frameworks of leadership; and (4) the civic and political role of the school leader responsible for garnering community and parental involvement.

REALIZING CIVIC AND POLITICAL IDENTITY AMID SCHOOL TURNAROUND

School Leaders as Political Agents

In an era defined by an increasingly complicated federal policy environment (DeBray & McGuinn, 2009), the field of educational leadership must revisit and re-examine the political role of the school leader within the school setting. While the political and micropolitical roles of school leaders have been of interest to educational leadership scholars (Ball, 1991; Blase, 1991; Iannaccone, 1975; Marshall & Scribner, 1991), school leaders continue to grapple with the incompatible policies, which also may be inequitably enforced. Fortunately, the somewhat recent re-authoring of the Interstate School Leaders Licensure (ISLLC) Standards has challenged educational scholars and practitioners to reconsider the political identity of educational leaders. Specifically, in 2008, ISLLC Standard 6 was restated to include an explicit focus on the expectations of school leaders as influencers within the political environment stating, "An education leader promotes the success of every student by understanding, responding to, and influencing the political, social, economic, legal, and cultural context" (CCSSO, 2008, p. 15). Seemingly, principals have now been given the standards-based approval to establish their identities as professional and civic advocates, leaders able to ensure their school communities are provided with the resources necessary to survive and thrive in resource stringent policy environments.

While scholars such as Bolman and Deal (1984, 1991), Sergiovanni (1994), and many others have addressed organizational leadership via a political framework, a relatively new body of literature provides more critically oriented insight for today's and tomorrow's leaders. Particularly, a growing number of educational leadership scholars have begun to focus on politically oriented leadership from a social justice perspective (Blackmore, 2009; Jean-Marie, 2010; Jean-Marie et al., 2009; Marshall & Oliva, 2006; McKenzie et al., 2008; Theoharis, 2007, 2009, 2010). This critically oriented shift within educational leadership scholarship is due partly to demographic changes occurring within our public schools. The need for educational leaders to develop the skill sets necessary to support our increasingly diverse student body is critical, especially in light of the fact that our modern teaching force is predominately White and relatively inexperienced with students from different demographic groups (Evans, 2007). Subsequently, educational practitioners must purposefully focus on procuring the skill sets necessary to "advocate, lead, and keep at the center of their practice and vision issues of race, class, gender, disability, sexual orientation, and other historically marginalizing conditions in the United States" (Theoharis, 2010, p. 93).

A Shifting Policy Landscape: Leadership amid School Turnaround Reform Efforts

Over the course of the past three decades, shifting policy contexts of Western democracies have altered professional expectations of public school leaders (Carpenter & Brewer, 2012). This evolution of expectations for school leaders can be attributed largely to a neoliberal policy response to a faltering economy. Specifically, due to the poor status of the global economy, public policies, such as those that shape education, have been tailored largely to the values of market-based liberalism. Therefore, today's educational leaders must navigate a set of policies shaped to heighten standardized measures of success including ranking of teacher and principal performance to assign pay, along with redistribution of school governance and authority, and establishment of competitive funding.

The most current iteration of the federal Title I SIG program serves as a primary example of how market-based values impinge on the traditional role of school leader. Revised in 2009, the current Title I SIG program explicitly endorses greater accountability measures for school leaders, including the removal of administrators deemed to be incapable of facilitating the turnaround of a chronically low-performing campus. Additionally, the revised Title I SIG program pushes school districts toward seeking market-based solutions via its restart option, which requires unsuccessful schools be converted to an effective charter operator, charter management organization, or education management organization (U.S. Department of Education, 2009, p. 31). Under these conditions, school leader positions represent heightened risk and even less job security than ever experienced in public schooling. School leaders must realize their political identity in a way that allows them to navigate the constraints of a high-stakes accountability policy environment while meeting the needs of the communities they are called to serve.

Viewing Race and Race-related Issues via School Choice

School desegregation plans have long included parental choice options. Today, new models of student assignment give parents more options for their children's education, typically allowing parents to send their children to schools outside of their neighborhoods. The successful enactment of school choice policies provides parents and students with a number of quality choices, both in regards to schools and specific academic or extracurricular programs. Yet, there is still a concern among critics of school choice policies that an increase in choice will lead to an increase in isolation of the most disadvantaged students in the worst schools, whose parents may lack the necessary information and/or resources to make the best choices for their children (Gill, 2005). Several studies that have examined intra-district choice policies in urban contexts find that they tend to lead to greater between-school segregation: White families choose to send their children to Whiter schools, and non-White families choose schools where they are more well-represented (see Glazerman, 1998; Henig, 1996; Lankford & Wyckoff, 1997; Saporito & Lareau, 1999). Choice plans may result in only some families (those of higher incomes) being able to choose which schools their children will attend (Frankenberg & Siegel-Hawley, 2008; Holme, 2002), which may result in de facto segregation.

Understanding how intra-district school choice affects schools is particularly important for principals as school districts often enact this model in their attempts to equalize educational opportunities (Ryan & Heise, 2002). Thus, it is crucial for school leaders to ensure that families are not only well informed about the options available to them in their district's choice policies, but these leaders also need to ensure that school choice policies are designed and implemented to benefit the most disadvantaged students. These policies must then be executed in an equity-minded fashion (i.e., adopting race- and class-conscious choice policies that encourage diversity) (Holme et al., 2013).

Engaging Others and Leveraging Community Resources

As public trust in the K-12 educational system continues to erode, school leaders must critically reflect on the ways in which they involve the educational stakeholders associated with their school community. Leaders attempting to engage the greater community can ill afford to endorse traditional models of community/parent engagement. Such models conceptualize schools as rigid, hierarchical organizations, which tend to marginalize opportunities for authentic parent involvement (Epstein et al., 2002). Additionally, traditional models fail to account for the values determining how parents from historically marginalized populations choose to interact with their children's education (Cooper, 2009). Leaders must aspire to enact transformative models of involvement, which encourage outreach efforts built upon the presence of an inclusive and respectful atmosphere; continual, reciprocal, and transformative learning; and the significant alteration of traditional participation roles (Young & Carpenter, 2008).

As for the principal's role, leaders operating within districts that honor school choice while serving diverse and geographically fragmented communities should not expect for stakeholders to prioritize the list of needs as defined by the school. Instead, as Khalifa (2012) suggested, principals realize their role as political advocates for community-based goals by leaving the school building, visiting communities, and thus placing community-defined issues at the "center of school-community partnership goals" (p. 461). Advocacy from this perspective has an explicit social justice orientation, thus further supporting many scholars in the field of educational leadership who have begun to espouse the importance of leading from a socially just position (Blackmore, 2009; Jean-Marie, 2010; Jean-Marie et al., 2009; Marshall & Oliva, 2006; McKenzie et al., 2008; Theoharis, 2007, 2009, 2010).

Preparing Leaders

The demographic changes occurring within our public schools present a number of challenges for education leaders. Moreover, as the federal government becomes more assertive in its efforts to turn around the nation's persistently lowest achieving schools, the importance of preparing leaders to serve in diverse communities has become even more important. The majority of PLAs are located in areas with high levels of concentrated poverty and students of color (Noguera & Wells, 2011).

The demands for an emphasis on addressing issues of social justice (Blackmore, 2009; Jean-Marie et al., 2009; McKenzie et al., 2008) are accompanied by criticisms about preparatory programs failing to adequately address issues of diversity and race (Dantley, 2002; López, 2003; Parker & Shapiro, 1992; Tillman, 2004; Young & Laible, 2000). These combined demands and criticisms reveal the degree to which future leaders seem ill-prepared to deal with the complexities of serving diverse schools and communities. "Ultimately, the lack of a programmatic and coherent plan as to how leaders should be prepared to address issues of race and diversity has serious ramifications for those called to serve diverse student populations" (Diem & Carpenter, 2013, p. 59).

When professors, preparation instructors, and mentors expect aspiring leaders to engage in conversations surrounding race and race relations, these aspirants must think in new and different ways (Carpenter & Diem, forthcoming). Preparation programs must weave issues of race and diversity throughout the offered curriculum so they are better able to address the continued inequities present within our public schools, develop a range of potential solutions allowing us to help those students most in need, and ensure leaders are prepared to serve in diverse contexts.

LEARNING ACTIVITY 8.3

Talking About Race and Cultural Competency

Jessica has reflected on the problems with her staff's lack of culturally responsive strategies for addressing YHS students' needs. Assistant Principal Shawna has openly raised this issue in the ILT meeting.

Role play how Jessica might use Shawna's points to generate a constructive conversation of what should happen next.

1. Does it matter who starts the conversation?
2. Does it matter how the conversation is introduced?
3. Does this school need some ground rules for this discussion?
4. Are there some ideas from other chapters in this book that might work in this situation?

NOTE

1   One way to measure neighborhood segregation is by using a dissimilarity index, which measures the relative separation or integration of groups across neighborhoods in a metropolitan area. The dissimilarity index ranges from 0–100, with 0 meaning no segregation or separation between groups and 100 meaning complete segregation between groups (Grannis, 2002).

REFERENCES

Aikens, A. (2005). Being choosy: An analysis of public school choice under No Child Left Behind. *West Virginia Law Review, 108*, 233–266.

Balfanz, R., Legters, N., West, T. C., & Weber, L. M. (2007). Are NCLB's measures, incentives, and improvement strategies the right ones for the nation's low-performing high schools? *American Educational Research Journal, 44*(3), 559–593.

Ball, S. J. (1991). Power, conflict, micropolitics and all that! In G. Walford (Ed.), *Doing educational research* (pp. 166–192). London: Routledge.

Blase, J. J. (1991). The micropolitical orientation of teachers toward closed school principals. *Education and Urban Society, 23*(4), 356–378.

Blackmore, J. (2009). Leadership for social justice: A transnational dialogue. *Journal of Research on Leadership Education, 4*(1), 1–10.

Blank, R. K., Levine, R. E., & Steel, L. (1996). After 15 years: Magnet schools in urban education. In B. Fuller, R. F. Elmore, & G. Orfield (Eds.), *Who chooses? Who loses? Culture, institutions, and the unequal effects of school choice* (pp. 154–172). New York: Teachers College Press.

Bolman, L. G. & Deal, T. E. (1984). *Modern approaches to understanding and managing organizations.* San Francisco, CA: Jossey-Bass.

Bolman, L. G. & Deal, T. E. (1991). *Reframing organizations: Artistry, choice, and leadership.* San Francisco, CA: Jossey-Bass.

Brown v. Board of Education of Topeka, 347 U.S. 483 (1954).

Carpenter, B. W. & Brewer, C. (2012). The implicated advocate: The discursive construction of the democratic practices of school principals in the USA. *Discourse: Studies in the Cultural Politics of Education.* DOI: 10.1080/01596306.2012.745737.

Carpenter, B. W. & Diem, S. (forthcoming). Talking race: Facilitating critical conversations in educational leadership preparation programs. *Journal of School Leadership.*

Chubb, J. E. & Moe, T. M. (1990). *Politics, markets & America's schools.* Washington, DC: The Brookings Institution.

Cibulka, J. G. (2009). Declining support for higher-education leadership preparation programs: An analysis. *Peabody Journal of Education, 84*(3), 453–466.

Cooper, C. W. (2009). Parent involvement, African American mothers, and the politics of educational care. *Equity & Excellence in Education, 42*, 379–394.

Council of Chief State School Officers. (2008). *Educational leadership policy standards: ISLLC 2008.* Retrieved from www.ccsso.org/

Cullen, J. B., Jacob, B. A., & Levitt, S. D. (2005). The impact of school choice on student outcomes: An analysis of the Chicago public schools. *Journal of Public Economics, 89*(5/6), 729–760.

Dantley, M. E. (2002). Uprooting and replacing positivism, the melting pot, multiculturalism, and other important notions in educational leadership through an African American perspective. *Education and Urban Society, 34*(3), 334–352.

Darling_Hammond, L. (2007). Race, inequality and educational accountability: The irony of 'No Child Left Behind'. *Race Ethnicity and Education, 10*(3), 245–260.

DeBray-Pelot, E. & McGuinn, P. (2009). The new politics of education: Analyzing the federal education policy landscape in the post-NCLB era. *Educational Policy, 23*(1), 15–42.

Diem, S. & Carpenter, B. W. (2013). Examining race-related silences: Interrogating the education of tomorrow's educational leaders. *Journal of Research in Leadership Education, 8*(1), 56–76.

Edgar, W. B. (1998). *South Carolina: A history*. Columbia, SC: University of South Carolina Press.

Epstein, J. L., Sanders, M., Simon, B., Salinas, K. C., Jansorn, N. R., & Van Voorhis, F. L. (2002). *School, family, and community partnerships: Your handbook for action* (2nd ed.). Thousand Oaks, CA: Corwin.

Evans, A. E. (2007). School leaders and their sensemaking about race and demographic change. *Educational Administration Quarterly, 43*(2), 159–188.

Frankenberg, E. & Siegel-Hawley, G. (2008). *The forgotten choice? Rethinking magnet schools in a changing landscape*. Los Angeles: University of California, The Civil Rights Project.

Friedman, M. (1962). *Capitalism and freedom*. Chicago: University of Chicago Press.

Gill, B. (2005). School choice and integration. In J. R. Betts & T. Loveless (Eds.), *Getting choice right: Ensuring equity and efficiency in education policy* (pp. 130–145). Washington, DC: Brookings Institution Press.

Glazerman, S. (1998, April). *School quality and social stratification: The determinants and consequences of parental school choice*. Paper presented at the annual meeting of the American Educational Research Association, San Diego, CA.

Goldring, E. & Schuermann, P. (2009). The changing context of K-12 Education administration: Consequences for Ed.D. program design. *Peabody Journal of Education, 81*(1), 10–43.

Grannis, R. (2002). Discussion: Segregation indices and their functional inputs. *Sociological methodology, 32*(1), 69–84.

Henig, J. R. (1996). The local dynamics of choice: Ethnic preferences and institutional responses. In B. Fuller, R. F. Elmore, & G. Orfield (Eds.), *Who chooses? Who loses? Culture, institutions, and the unequal effects of school choice* (pp. 95–117). New York: Teachers College Press.

Holme, J. J. (2002). Buying homes, buying schools: School choice and the social construction of school quality. *Harvard Educational Review, 72*, 177–205.

Holme, J. J., Frankenberg, E., Diem, S., & Welton, A. D. (2013). School choice in suburbia: The impact of choice policies on the potential for suburban integration. *Journal of School Choice: International Research and Reform, 7*(2), 113–141.

Holme, J. J. & Wells, A. S. (2008). School choice beyond district borders: Lessons for the reauthorization of NCLB from interdistrict desegregation and open enrollment plans. In R. Kahlenberg (Ed.), *Improving on No Child Left Behind: Getting education reform back on track* (pp. 139–215). New York: Century Foundation Press.

Iannaccone, L. (1975). *Education policy systems: A study guide for educational administrators*. National Ed.D. Program for Educational Leaders, Nova University.

Jean-Marie, G. (2010). "Fire in the belly": Igniting a social justice discourse in learning environments of leadership preparation. In A. K. Tooms & C. Boske (Eds.), *Bridge leadership: Connecting educational leadership and social justice to improve schools* (pp. 97–124). Charlotte, NC: Information Age Publishing.

Jean-Marie, G., Normore, A., & Brooks, J. S. (2009). Leadership for social justice: Preparing 21st Century school leaders for a new social order. *Journal of Research on Leadership in Education, 4*(1), 1–31.

Jennings, J. & Rentner, D. S. (2006). Ten big effects of the No Child Left Behind Act on public schools. *Phi Delta Kappan, 88*(2), 110–113.

Khalifa, M. (2012). A new paradigm in urban school leadership: Principal as community leader. *Educational Administration Quarterly, 48*(3).

Lankford, H. & Wyckoff, J. (1997, June). *The effect of school choice and residential location on the racial segregation of K-12 students.* Unpublished manuscript, State University of New York, Albany, NY.

LeLoudis, J. L. (1996). *Schooling the new South: Pedagogy, self, and society in North Carolina, 1880–1920.* Chapel Hill, NC: The University of North Carolina Press.

Lindle, J. C. & Cibulka, J. G. (2006). Accountability. In F. W. English (Ed.), *Sage encyclopedia of educational leadership Vol. 1* (pp. 2–12). Thousand Oaks, CA: Sage.

López, G. R. (2003). The (racially neutral) politics of education: A critical race theory perspective. *Educational Administration Quarterly, 39*, 68–94.

Lubienski, C. (2005). Public schools in marketized environments: Shifting incentives and unintended consequences of competition-based educational reforms. *American Journal of Education, 111*(4), 464–486.

Marshall, C. & Oliva, M. (2006). *Leadership for social justice: Making revolutions in education.* Boston: Pearson.

Marshall, C. & Scribner, J. (1991). "It's all political": Inquiry into the micropolitics of education. *Education and Urban Society, 23*(4), 347–355.

McDermott, K. A. (2007). "Expanding moral communities" or "blaming the victim"? The politics of state education accountability policy. *American Education Research Journal, 44*(1), 77–11.

McKenzie, K., Christman, D., Hernandez, F., Fierro, E., Capper, C., Dantley, M., Gonzalez, M., Cambron-McCabe, N., & Scheurich, J. (2008). Educating leaders for social justice: A design for a comprehensive, social justice leadership preparation program. *Educational Administration Quarterly, 44*(1), 111–138.

Noguera, P. A. & Wells, L. (2011). The politics of school reform: A broader and bolder approach to Newark. *Berkeley Review of Education, 2*(1), 5–25.

Orfield, G. (2005). The Southern dilemma: Losing Brown, fearing Plessy. In J. C. Boger & G. Orfield (Eds.), *School resegregation: Must the South turn back?* (pp. 1–25). Chapel Hill, NC: The University of North Carolina Press.

Parents Involved in Community Schools v. Seattle School District No. 1, et al., 551 U.S. 05–908 (2007). 127 S. Ct. 2738.

Parker, L. & Shapiro, J. (1992). Where is the discussion in educational administration programs? Graduate student voices addressing an omission in their preparation. *Journal of School Leadership, 2*(1), 7–33.

Reardon, S. F. (2013). The widening income gap. *Educational Leadership, 70*(8), 10–6.

Reardon, S. F. & Yun, J. T. (2003). Integrating neighborhoods, segregating schools: The retreat from school desegregation in the South, 1990–2000. *North Carolina Law Review, 81*(4), 1563–1596.

Roza, M., Hill, P. T., Sclafani, S., & Speakman, S. (2004). How within-district spending inequities help some schools to fail. *Brookings Papers on Education Policy, 7*, 201–227.

Ryan, J. E. & Heise, M. (2002). The political economy of school choice. *Yale Law Journal*, *111*(8), 2043–2136.

Saporito, S. & Lareau, A. (1999). School selection as a process: The multiple dimensions of race in framing educational choice. *Social Problems*, *46*, 418–435.

Sergiovanni, T. (1994). *The principalship: A reflective practice perspective*. Boston: Allyn & Bacon.

Theoharis, G. (2007). Social justice educational leaders and resistance: Toward a theory of social justice leadership. *Educational Administration Quarterly*, *43*(2), 221.

Theoharis, G. (2009). *The school leaders our children deserve: Seven keys to equity, social justice, and school reform*. New York: Teachers College Press.

Theoharis, G. (2010). Sustaining social justice: Strategies urban principals develop to advance justice and equity while facing resistance. *International Journal of Urban Educational Leadership*, *4*(1), 92–110.

Tillman, L. C. (2004). (Un)intended consequences? The impact of the Brown v. Board of Education decision on the employment status of black educators. *Education and Urban Society*, *36*(3), 280–303.

U.S. Department of Education (2009). *Title I: Improving the academic achievement of the disadvantaged*. Retrieved from www2.ed.gov/policy/elsec/leg/esea02/pg1.html

U.S. Department of Education. (2010). *A blueprint for reform: The reauthorization of the Elementary and Secondary Education Act*. Arlington, VA: Author.

Young, M. D. & Carpenter, B. (2008). Preparing educational leaders to build transformative communities of involvement: The importance of trust. *Journal of School Public Relations*, *29*, 276–311.

Young, M. D. & Laible, J. (2000). White racism, antiracism, and school leader preparation. *Journal of School Leadership*, *10*, 374–415.

CHAPTER 9

Forecasting Future Directions for Political Activism in School Leadership

Kenyae L. Reese and Jane Clark Lindle

Throughout this volume, we have explored the social and political complexities associated with school leadership in the early 21st century. This volume is a response to the repeated demands for school leaders to understand and enact their roles as political actors. As a reply, these chapters examined the challenges and opportunities faced by school leaders who must realize their civic and political voice within unique and complex policy environments. This chapter attempts a projection of how current trends continue to spell out roles for school leaders' political advocacy on behalf of students.

Over the course of the past three decades shifting policy contexts have altered the professional expectations of public school leaders (Carpenter & Brewer, 2012). As early scholars in the field of politics in education noted in their time, yesteryear's stance on purifying the educational profession through avoidance of politics was fruitless (Layton & Scribner, 1989; McCarty & Ramsey, 1971). Avoidance will never meet student needs, promote success for families and communities nor accommodate the complicated ecologies of schooling or learning (Fusarelli & Williams, Chapter 6 in this volume). The nature of schooling, its conditions, its governance, and burgeoning prescriptions from educational policies point toward a horizon of continued micro- and macro-political moments in and around schools. School leaders must develop political acumen or they, students, and staff, truly will suffer the consequences, emotionally and professionally (Beatty, Chapter 2 in this volume; Ryan 2010).

Today, school leaders and those aspiring to lead schools must navigate social and political complexities. This volume's chapters reveal a consistent theme about future school leaders' need for political acumen.

Twenty-first century leaders are called upon to be politically perceptive professionals able to accomplish several professional services such as the following: (a) negotiate scarce resources despite declining budgets; (b) collaborate with a variety of stakeholders despite opposing interests, and (c) champion the cause of the underserved and marginalized in their school communities. They must accomplish these feats without succumbing to either performativity (Ball, 2000) or emotional labor (Hochschild, 1983). School leaders must achieve these ideals, while acknowledging emotions in their work and accepting their own vulnerabilities (Bridges, 2012). It is up to school leaders to expose their vulnerabilities to provide a basis for growing trust and developing mutual understanding between them and educational stakeholders.

Yet, trust is a balancing act and while tensions loom between how scholars and practitioners view these matters, the public's mistrust in public schools has swung the pendulum nearly off track. The lack of trust in public schools has increased the role of parents as advocates, not just mere volunteers or simply involved individuals (Chandler, 2009). Diminishing confidence and trust in public schools has spawned a burgeoning array of charter schools, voucher and school choice programs, alternative routes to school teacher and leader preparation programs, and online schools (see the following chapters in this volume: López, Chapter 5; Fusarelli & Williams, Chapter 6; Carpenter & Diem, Chapter 8). In order to balance the pendulum, they need to use the best traditions of political analysis (Lasswell, 1965; Stout et al., 1995). School leaders must engage in continual cycles of asking themselves why? who? what? and how to take the next steps.

Ultimately, what is meant by the study of politics or school leaders' use of political savviness? As Winton and Gonzalez reassured us in Chapter 7, all things political rest in the questions of "who gets what, where, and how" (Lasswell, 1965) with all the intricacies those answers entail. However, those answers are not without waves of political influences tied to the work of 21st century school leaders. Such work remains undergirded continually with political influences vacillating among trust, confidence, emotions, conflict and power. The appropriateness of the title of this volume as political contexts of educational leadership highlights a slight division of meaning between scholars and practitioners. While scholars tend to view school leaders' work as political plights deriving from struggles between conflict and power, practitioners experience these dilemmas as battles between professionalism and emotions.

FORECASTING THE INTERSECTIONS OF POWER, CONFLICT, TRUST, AND EMOTIONS

In this text, Beatty's Chapter 2 most explicitly connects practitioners' experiences of micropolitical incidents and macro policy-induced tensions to inextricably linked issues of professional identity and emotional efficacy. Preparation programs may have gone awry by not acknowledging these deeply overlapping issues sooner (Bridges, 2012). Certainly, work by Hargreaves and others have alerted us to the connections of emotions and learning and in the environments surrounding teaching (Hargreaves, 1998, 2000; Leithwood & Beatty, 2008; Nias, 1996). Emotional trauma also visits school leaders, and the literature has been scant, but powerful (Ackermann & Maslin-Ostrowski, 2002; Lindle, 2004). One natural conclusion forecasts that the policy environment pressures on schools will not lessen, and thus, understanding how politics and emotions intertwine in professional work is even more critical for future leaders and for developing better preparation for them (Bridges, 2012).

Drake and Goldring provided a thorough backdrop depicting the complex entanglements of community stakeholders' power in Chapter 3. They noted that school-level decisions are indelibly etched with various dimensions of power. Their reminders of these dimensions including relational power—acknowledging the dependency and interdependencies of power in relationships, and sanctioning realities among school personnel—offer continuing insights about the power issues between parents and school personnel (Auerbach, 2012). Thus, successful principals both sense and address the informal and formal aspects of power in their schools. Forecasting ahead depicts a greater need for school leaders and aspirants to under-stand the aspects and functions of power to a greater degree. School leaders must have the know-how to manage professional and civic agendas while building alliances, strengthening networks, and proactively forming authentic partnerships (Auerbach, 2012; Ryan, 2010). To do so requires leaders to diagnose the external environment of their schools and be savvier about understanding power relationships (Goldring & Sullivan, 1996).

The intersections of conflict, power, and trust also require an insightful and reflective leader who is willing to face her or his fears of critique and reflect on the content of that criticism. In Chapter 4, Fusarelli and Petersen clearly illustrated that issues of territory, autonomy, responsibility, and participation in school decision making can alter political power and escalate conflicts and feelings of mistrust. Their case captures the need for district-level leadership to conduct political analyses for understanding competing power factions in a community as well as recognizing how shifts in demographics and social conditions shape those factions. Power in and of itself can be politically damaging, but as Beatty reminded us in Chapter 2, it is the convergence of these matters that shape and reshape the emotional terrain of schools and that of its leaders. School leaders need to remain sensitive to how economic and social conditions literally shape the political domains of school districts.

The investigation of emotions and its effects on leaders and school improvement initiatives is understudied in educational leadership (Leithwood & Beatty, 2008; Lindle, 2004), but its place in the work of 21st century leaders and aspirants is apparent. The political terrain and influence of policies now and of the future will require aspiring and current school leaders to have a greater understanding of the inner workings of micropolitics and the related phenomenon of emotions. Rather than capitulate under pressure, proactive leaders, who use political knowledge and skills, can initiate and influence policy for the benefit of all students. This is no small feat, however. Leaders of the future will have to engage in emotional meaning making: learning to access their own inner processes and creating the psychological safety for others to do the same. This takes a level of discipline, self-reflection, and a willingness to model the way for others. As Beatty further points out in Chapter 2, school leaders should lead from a place of "active emotional understanding." That is, a place of vulnerability, sensitivity, and emotional awareness of themselves and others that offers opportunities for collaboration that are otherwise difficult to achieve.

FORECASTING EMOTIONAL MEANING MAKING AS SOCIAL JUSTICE LEADERSHIP

One could argue that leading with emotions in mind (Leithwood & Beatty, 2008) is also an impetus for being culturally responsive and socially just. Often the world of home and the world of school are inseparable for students, teachers, and leaders (Beatty, Chapter 2 this volume; Drake & Goldring, Chapter 3 this volume). Neither students, teachers, parent, nor leaders leave their feelings at schoolhouse gates. Emotions encased in biases and prejudices against others enter the school doors along with the individual as López describes (Chapter 5, this volume). Sometimes these deeply held assumptions impede teaching and learning because of lack of cultural awareness and consequent absence of cultural responsiveness (Carpenter & Diem, Chapter 8 this volume). Cultural conflicts and misunderstandings i.e., lack of trust between and among racial-ethnic groups, between teachers and students, and between schools and communities highlight the need for school leaders to address ensuing issues in ways that respect and honor individual cultures. López notes that school leaders' awareness of self-identification and how it may conflict with forced ethnic or racial labeling is particularly important. These conflicts arise due to the impact of socioeconomic and cultural mobility, notably immigration (Suarez-Orozco & Paez, 2008; Suarez-Orozco, Suarez-Orozco, & Todorova, 2008). School leaders must be alert to the manner in which larger events, even natural disasters, instigate localized tensions among groups in their schools and communities.

In the future, it will be imperative for school leaders to be culturally sensitive and demonstrate inter-and intra-cultural awareness in increasingly diverse schools, especially given that the majority of the teaching force is predominately White and largely inexperienced with cultural norms of racially ethnic diverse students (Evans, 2007). Furthermore, 21st century leaders must be proactively disciplined to find effective and comprehensive responses to meet the service, support, and learning needs of all learners, particularly those with language and learning difficulties. Moreover, school leaders of the future should be conscious of and quick to adopt race- and class-conscious choice policies that encourage diversity (Holme, Franken-berg, Diem, & Welton, 2013) and socially just approaches (Theoharis, 2007).

Engaging in social justice leadership is not solely about recognizing needs at the student level; rather it requires school leaders to address issues of trust between parents and school faculty (Tschannen-Moran, 2004; Van Maele & Van Houtte, 2011). Effective and mutually beneficial school-family-community partnership work requires school leaders to uphold an "ethic of care" (Johnson, 2007) and exemplify a social justice mindset irrespective of the racial-ethnic and socioeconomic composition of those inside or outside of the building. Reminiscent of what authors Carpenter and Diem (Chapter 8, this volume) promote, implementing culturally responsive practices necessitates school leaders to move beyond simply establishing a welcoming environment for stakeholders, rather a call toward an action-oriented stance of providing parents, community members, and other partners avenues for structured, regular involvement and decision making within schools. This chapter clearly illustrates the emotional and professional risks of confronting the assumptions and biases found in any school community.

This century's school leaders face deeply divided communities, which simultaneously connect to globalized and factional influences. School leaders will continue to encounter localized biases exacerbated by globalized media feeding nonsense to bolster ill-informed assumptions. Students and staff bring these poorly evidenced but strongly held convictions into schools, and school leaders must have the knowledge and skills to calm the conflicts, and manage the environment for optimum teaching and learning.

FORECASTING AN ENTREPRENEURIAL SPIRIT TO COLLABORATIVE UNDERTAKINGS

The dispersion of decision making and partnerships across schools and stakeholders often shakes the boundaries between stability and change, and adds to the political dynamics of schools' governing structures. Yet, decades of research in favor of partnerships as a means to support student achievement are conclusive. "When schools, families, and community groups work together to support learning, children tend to do better in school, stay in school longer, and like school more" (Henderson & Mapp, 2002, p. 6). In an age of increased accountability, schools—particularly failing schools in disenfranchised communities—need to show increased student achievement and political savviness that can come from effective partnering with parents, communities, businesses, interest groups, and other stakeholders.

Furthering this notion in Chapter 6, Fusarelli and Williams contend that today's and tomorrow's schools are those that offer coordinated services and partnerships among a number of agencies across educational, social, and health fields. Commonly known as full-service or community schools, these types of schools aim to bring the community to the school by addressing many of the factors that disrupt student achievement and healthy, connected communities through on-site services offered during and beyond the normal school day (Dryfoos & Maguire, 2002). The success of community schools can only go as far as the policies that are in place to support them. Students and their communities can thrive based on school administrators' and stakeholders' efforts to use school campuses as the optimal location to address healthcare and an influx of social services. These sentiments will continue to be debated in the future as social and religious organizations try to assert their political influence.

Nevertheless, as the demand for more effective and diverse strategies increases in schools, community schools provide a creative strategy with proven success. Rightfully so, school leaders must have the skills and aptitude to build sustainable partnerships, and frankly, to operate entrepreneurially: "An educational entrepreneur is someone who changes the school system in significant and fundamental ways and may disrupt the status quo and transform the system itself" (Teske & Williamson, 2006, p. 45). This forward view of leadership parallels what authors Fusarelli and Williams call boundary spanners. Boundary-spanning leadership creates cradle-to-career solutions that bolster a sense of community in schools and collaborative school cultures. Boundary spanners view parents and community agencies as partners with a valid voice and stake in school decision making. School leaders as boundary spanners in the future can also help to transform the system by mobilizing school members to engage in community service and give rise to place-based education that capitalizes on sustainable relationships built between schools and the communities they serve. To make way, leaders of the future need to be attuned to how much power various individuals and groups possess and how such power may affect policy and leaders' ability to negotiate political tensions, particularly in the case of interest groups such as unions, CBOs, and foundations.

FORECASTING SOCIAL MEDIA AS POLITICAL TERRAIN

An often forgotten political and social influence is that of the media and social media, perhaps with the exception of cyber bullying that plagues many schools today (Campbell, 2005; Mckenna, 2007). While school leaders of the past were inundated with media presence that was of the local variety, the globalization of social media such as Facebook, Twitter, and Instagram potentially expose today's and tomorrow's leaders to ramifications from every word and decision as the spark to a national or international viral catastrophe at the click of a button. Increased media presence has also changed the way parents interact and influence school matters and likely how they will do so in the future. Web-savvy parents have become a form of grassroots activists (Chandler, 2009). These parents use the internet and related technology to spread the word among themselves about possible changes to policy and then pressure school leaders into making political decisions to support their cause. Traditional media outlets such as newspapers and television stations will continue to put school leaders at risk as they respond to the nimble sensationalism of new media competitors. Discussed in detail in Chapter 4 by authors Fusarelli and Petersen, the media can politicize school and school board matters by identifying decisions by party affiliation. School leaders of the future will need to be more mindful of the potential dangers associated with social media and work collaboratively with others to make it work to their benefit.

The underlying issue for the future of school leaders as it relates to social media is reminiscent of the question Professor Michael Kirst asked in the title of his classic text *Who Controls Our Schools?* (1984). Knowledgeworks Foundation (2012) out of Ohio is an example of an interest group that forecasts trends in schools, pointing out opportunities and challenges for educational systems that link back to Dr. Kirst's original question. One such trend is that of disruption theory. Disruptions are social trends that shift society's understanding of how things work, and in effect, force new practices as a matter of surviving the new normal (Christensen, 2006). According to Knowledgeworks (2012), a critical piece of the rise of social media is the degree to which local schools will lose the ability to have direct impact on what students learn because of students' connections to social media and other ways of learning. With that said, school leaders in the 21st century will have to garner their political acumen to find creative ways to navigate the intricacies of social media and corral the political drama that promises to ensnare them.

FORECASTING THE FUTURE: PUTTING IT ALL TOGETHER

How, who, what, and where will the trends on school leaders' political advocacy for students lead? The complexity of schools and the increasingly complicated federal policy environment coupled with the scarcity of resources requires school leaders in the 21st century to be politically adept, able to navigate the political contour. Throughout this volume, authors have argued that school leaders must realize their political identity and find their civic and political voice as part of a collective enterprise. While none of these chapters promotes political behavior as an end in itself, school leaders and their aspirants must anticipate how policies, trends, issues, and social incidents affect students and learning. This volume advances the notion that school leaders must raise the level of consciousness toward practices and policies that are in the best interest of students, and be relentless in their efforts to be political advocates to the benefit of both students and society.

THE SIGNIFICANCE OF ISLLC STANDARD 6

Mounting demands between state and federal accountability structures "are rewriting administrators' job descriptions every year, making them more complex than ever. Today, education leaders must not only manage school finances, keep buses running on time, and make hiring decisions, but they must also be instructional leaders, data analysts, community relations officers, and change agents. They have to be able to mobilize staff and employ all the tools in an expanded toolbox" (Council of Chief State School Officers, 2008, p. 3). To that end, education leadership is more important than ever. Ringing through these chapters are the sentiments that improving student achievement depends on the effective and simultaneous orchestration of individual and collective initiatives among school leaders and education stakeholders (Fusarelli & Lindle, 2011).

Principals and candidates for school leadership, then, need a firm understanding of the intersections of local, state, and federal policy, laws, and the work of districts and schools. The fact that principals bare this knowledge was a foundational principle defining the role of school leader (Cooper et al., 2004; Murphy et al., 2007; Lupini

& Zirkel, 2003; Zirkel, 1997). Concurrent with an understanding of policy and laws comes the emerging expectation that all students should succeed in school irrespective of background, ability, or language barriers. Educational leaders are held accountable for student achievement and are critically important in efforts to improve social opportunities for students, particularly in disenfranchised communities (Theoharis, 2007). When students are not succeeding, society now expects schools—and by society, we mean its leaders—to find resources and strategies to create success. These types of challenges add stipulations on leaders to be well-versed in holistic approaches to solving the most complex of problems.

The Interstate School Leaders Licensure Consortium (ISLLC) Standards for School Leaders (2008) reflect decades of lessons learned from policy and practice about the imperative work that school leaders and aspirants must put forth in order to meet demanding requirements for improving schools and raising achievement (Council of Chief State School Officers, 2008; National Policy Board for Educational Administration, 2011). As mentioned throughout the chapters, a constellation of social, economic, and demographic factors are creating unusual demands as well as exceptional opportunities for school leaders. While the seven Standards of ISLLC are interrelated variables that cannot function in isolation, Standard 6, perhaps more than the others, speaks to the leadership of the future that is able to understand, influence, and effectively respond to these demands within the standards-based and accountability clad new normal of schools.

REFERENCES

Ackerman, R. & Maslin-Ostrowski, P. (2002). *The wounded leader: How real leadership emerges in times of crisis*. San Francisco CA: Jossey-Bass.

Auerbach, S. (Ed.). (2012). *School leadership for authentic family and community partnerships: Research perspectives for transforming practice*. New York: Routledge.

Ball, S. (2000). Performativities and fabrications in the education economy: Towards the performative society. *Australian Educational Researcher, 27*(2), 1–25.

Bridges, E. (2012). Administrator preparation: Looking backwards and forwards. *Journal of Educational Administration, 50*(4), 402–419.

Campbell, M. A (2005). Cyber bullying: An old problem in a new guise? *Australian Journal of Guidance and Counselling, 15*(1), 68–76.

Carpenter, B. W. & Brewer, C. (2012). The implicated advocate: The discursive construction of the democratic practices of school principals in the USA. *Discourse: Studies in the Cultural Politics of Education, 33*.

Chandler, M. A. (2009, January 30). Well-connected parents take on school boards. *The Washington Post*, p. A01.

Christensen, C. M. (2006). The ongoing process of building a theory of disruption. *Journal of Product Innovation Management, 23*, 39–55.

Cooper, B. S., Fusarelli, L. D., & Randall, E. V. (2004). *Better policies, better schools: Theories and applications*. Boston: Allyn & Bacon.

Council of Chief State School Officers (2008). *Educational leadership policy standards: ISLLC 2008*. Washington, DC: Author. Retrieved from: www.ccsso.org/Documents/2008/Educational_Leadership_Policy_Standards_2008.pdf

Dryfoos, J. & Maguire, S. (2002). *Inside full service community schools*. Thousand Oaks, CA: Corwin Press.

Evans, A. E. (2007). School leaders and their sensemaking about race and demographic change. *Educational Administration Quarterly*, *43*(2), 159–188.

Fusarelli, B. C. & Lindle, J. C. (2011). The politics, problems, and potential promise of school-linked social services: Insights and new directions from the work of William Lowe Boyd. *Peabody Journal of Education*, *86*(4), 402–415.

Goldring, E. & Sullivan, A. (1996). Beyond the boundaries: Principals, parents and communities shaping the school environment. In K. Leithwood, J. Chapman, D. Corson, P. Hallinger, & A. Hart (Eds.), *International handbook of educational leadership and administration*, Volume 1 (pp. 195–222). Norwell, MA: Kluwer Academic.

Hargreaves, A. (1998). The emotional politics of teaching and teacher development: with implications for educational leadership. *International Journal of Leadership in Education: Theory and Practice*, *1*(4), 315–336.

Hargreaves, A. (2000, April). *Emotional geographies: Teaching in a box*. Paper presented at the annual meeting of the American Educational Research Association, New Orleans, Louisiana.

Henderson, A. T., Mapp, K. L., & Southwest Educational Development Lab., A. X. (2002). A new wave of evidence: The impact of school, family, and community connections on student achievement. *Annual Synthesis*, 2002.

Holme, J. J., Frankenberg, E., Diem, S., & Welton, A. D. (2013). School choice in suburbia: The impact of choice policies on the potential for suburban integration. *Journal of School Choice: International Research and Reform*, 7(2), 113–141.

Hochschild, A. R. (1983). *The managed heart: The commercialization of human feeling*. Berkeley, CA: University of California Press.

The Interstate School Leaders Licensure Consortium (ISLLC) *Standards for school leaders* (Council of Chief State School Officers, 2008).

Johnson, L. (2007). Rethinking successful school leadership in challenging U.S. schools: Culturally responsive practices in school-community relationships. *International Studies in Educational Administration*, *35*(3), 49–57.

Kirst, M. W. (1984). *Who controls our schools? American values in conflict*. Stanford, CA: Stanford Alumni Association.

KnowledgeWorks. (2012, November). *Recombinant education*. Cincinnati, OH: Author. Retrieved from: http://knowledgeworks.org/sites/default/files/Print-Friendly%20Forecast%203_0.pdf

Lasswell, H. D. (1965). *Politics: Who gets what, when, and how* (9th ed.). Cleveland, OH: Meridian Books, The World Publishing Company.

Layton, D. & Scribner, J. D. (Eds.), (1989). *Teaching educational politics and policy*. Tempe, AZ: University Council for Educational Administration.

Leithwood, K. & Beatty, B. (2008). *Leading with teacher emotions in mind*. Thousand Oaks, CA: Corwin Press.

Lindle, J. (2004). Trauma and stress in the principal's office: Systematic inquiry as coping. *Journal of School Leadership*, *14*(4), 378–410.

Lupini, W. & Zirkel, P. (2003). An outcomes analysis of education litigation. *Educational Policy*, *17*(2), 257–279.

McCarty, D. J. & Ramsey, C. E. (1971). *The school managers: Power and conflict in American public education*. Westport, CT: Greenwood.

Mckenna, P. (2007). The rise of cyberbullying. *New Scientist*, *195*(2613), 26–27.

Murphy, J., Elliott, S., Goldring, E., & Porter, A. C. (2007). Leadership for learning: A taxonomy and model of leadership behaviors. *School Leadership and Management*, *27*(2).

National Policy Board for Educational Administration (2011). *Educational leadership program standards: 2011 ELCC building level*. Washington, DC: Author. Retrieved from: www. ncate.org/LinkClick.aspx?fileticket=zRZl73R0nOQ%3d&tabid=676

Nias, J. (1996). Thinking about feeling: The emotions in teaching. *Cambridge Journal of Education, 26*(3), 293–306.

Ryan, J. (2010). Promoting social justice in schools: Principals' political strategies. *International Journal of Leadership in Education: Theory and Practice, 13*(4), 357–376.

Stout, R. T., Tallerico, M., & Scribner, K. P. (1995). Values: The "what?" of the politics of education. In J. D. Scribner & D. Layton (Eds.), *The study of educational politics: The 1995 commemorative yearbook of the Politics of Education Association (1969–1994)* (pp. 5–20). Washington, DC: Falmer.

Suarez-Orozco, M. M. & Paez, M. M. (Eds.), (2008). *Latinos: Remaking America*. Berkeley, CA: University of California Press.

Suarez-Orozco, C., Suarez-Orozco, M., & Todorova, I. (2008). *Learning a new land: Immigrant students in American society*. Cambridge, MA: Belknap Press.

Teske, P. & Williamson, A. (2006). Entrepreneur at work. In F. M. Hess (Ed.), *Educational entrepreneurship: Realities, challenges, and possibilities*. Cambridge, MA: Harvard Education Press.

Theoharis, G. (2007). Social justice educational leaders and resistance: Towards a theory of social justice leadership. *Educational Administration Quarterly, 43*(2), 221–258.

Tschannen-Moran, M. (2004). *Trust matters*. San Francisco, CA: Jossey-Bass.

Van Maele, D. & Van Houtte, M. (2011). Collegial trust and the organizational context of the teacher workplace: The role of a homogeneous teachability culture. *American Journal of Education, 117*(4), 437–464.

Zirkel, P. (1997). The "explosion" in education litigation: An update. *West's Education Law Reporter, 114*(2), 341–351.

Contributors

Brenda R. Beatty, University of Melbourne, has served as Deputy Director of the Melbourne Graduate School of Education's Master's in School Leadership, and as the designer and Director of the Monash Master's in School Leadership. She has designed, directed, and delivered various professional development initiatives for the Victoria Department of Education (DEECD). Dr. Beatty recently authored the content for DEECD's Bastow Institute modules: *Leading Instructional Practice*, *Leading Communities*, and *Leading Curriculum and Assessment*. Her research, writing, and presentations about the emotions of school leadership, leading with teacher emotions in mind, collaborative culture building, and leadership development have been recognized around the world. Her doctoral thesis, *Emotion Matters in Educational Leadership* won the *Thomas B. Greenfield Award* for best doctoral dissertation in Educational Leadership in Canada. With Professor Ken Leithwood, Dr. Beatty co-authored *Leading with Teacher Emotions in Mind*. In a longitudinal study she is currently exploring the evidence of impact from her programmatic approaches to leadership development. Dr. Beatty is a Fellow of the national Australian Council for Educational Leaders.

Bradley W. Carpenter is an Assistant Professor of Leadership, Foundations, and Human Resource Education (ELFH) at the University of Louisville, Kentucky. He is a former public school teacher, assistant principal, and principal. Dr. Carpenter's research agenda focuses on various issues and aspects of the politics of schools and communities. He studies the following: (a) politics of school improvement reform policies; (b) the ways in which school building leaders, parents, and communities participate in collaborative decision making; and (c) the possibilities that exist for education leaders asked to advocate for their children and their school communities at the state and federal levels of policy making. Dr. Carpenter's work also investigates how professors within the field of educational administration facilitate conversations surrounding social justice, race, racism, and race relations. His work has appeared among such publications as *Journal of Education for Students Placed At-Risk*, *International Journal of Leadership in Education*, and *Journal of School Leadership*.

Sarah Diem is an Assistant Professor in the Department of Educational Leadership and Policy Analysis at the University of Missouri. Her research focuses on the social and cultural contexts of education, paying particular attention to how the politics and implementation of educational policy affect diversity outcomes. She is also interested in how conversations surrounding race and race relations are facilitated in the classroom and whether these discussions are preparing future school leaders to address critical issues that may impact the students and communities they will oversee. She received her Ph.D. in Educational Policy and Planning from The University of Texas at Austin, M.P.A. from the University of Oregon, and B.A. from The University of Texas at Austin. Dr. Diem's work has been published in *Educational Administration Quarterly*, *The Urban Review*, *Education Policy Analysis Archives*, and *Journal of Research in Leadership Education*. Dr. Diem is also co-editor of *Global Leadership for Social Justice: Taking it from the Field to Practice*.

Timothy A. Drake is a Ph.D. student in K-12 Education Leadership and Policy at Peabody College, Vanderbilt University. His research interests include education leadership, data-driven decision making, and data visualization. Tim has recently worked with an aspiring principals program in Metropolitan Nashville Public Schools to help participants use data to develop school improvement interventions. Tim is currently working on projects sponsored by the Gates Foundation and the Tennessee Department of Education examining principal data use for human capital decision making and data use for the formation of teacher performance excellence groups, respectively. Tim received a Master's degree in International Education and Management from Vanderbilt University and a B.A. in History Teaching from Brigham Young University.

Bonnie C. Fusarelli is Associate Professor of Educational Leadership at North Carolina State University, a Faculty Research Fellow at The Friday Institute for Educational Innovation, and a NC State University Faculty Scholar. Her research focuses on educational leadership and policy, the politics of school improvement, educational equity, and organizational change, with a particular focus on state-level education reform and leadership development. She has received funding from the U.S. Department of Education, the National Science Foundation, the Bill and Melinda Gates Foundation, and the NC Department of Public Instruction. Dr. Fusarelli is the recipient of numerous teaching awards at both the K-12 and university level, including being an inductee into NC State's Academy of Outstanding Teachers. Currently Dr. Fusarelli is Principal Investigator and Director of the Northeast Leadership Academy, a Race to the Top funded initiative to prepare innovative school leaders for rural schools (http://go.ncsu.edu/nela).

Lance D. Fusarelli is Professor, Director of Graduate Programs, and Program Coordinator of Educational Leadership in the Department of Leadership, Policy, and Adult and Higher Education at North Carolina State University. His research interests include the politics of education, federal education policy, demographic change, social policy, educational reform, and school superintendents. Recent publications include the *Handbook of Education Politics and Policy* (Routledge, 2008) and "School reform in a vacuum: Demographic change, social policy, and the future of children" in the *Peabody Journal of Education* (2011). He received his B.A. in History and American Studies from Case Western Reserve University, an M.A. in Government from the University of Texas at Austin and a Ph.D. in Educational Administration from the University of Texas at Austin.

Ellen B. Goldring is Patricia and Rodes Hart Professor of Education Policy and Leadership, and Chair, Department of Leadership, Policy and Organizations, Peabody College at Vanderbilt University. She is a fellow of the American Educational Research Association, and is Vice-President of AERA's Division L-Policy and Politics. Dr. Goldring's research interests focus on the intersection of education policy and school improvement with particular emphases on school organization, school choice, and education leadership. She was principal investigator of the Institute of Education Sciences' supported National Center on School Choice and co-edited the Center's book, *School Choice and School Improvement: Research in State, District, and Community Contexts* (Harvard Education Press, 2011). Her current projects include *Supporting Principals to Use Teacher Effectiveness Measures for Human Capital Decisions*, funded by the Bill and Malinda Gates Foundation.

Deborah Gonzalez is currently a Master of Education student at York University in Toronto, Ontario, Canada. In 2008 she received her B.A.S. with specialized honors in Marketing from York University. Following her undergraduate career she attended James Cook University in Queensland, Australia and earned a Graduate Diploma of Education. Her current area of interest and research focus is on educational policy and its impact on educational stakeholders at the micropolitical level. Under the guidance of her supervisor, Professor Sue Winton, she hopes to explore how businesses influence policies and the decision-making processes of school leaders at the local level. Deborah currently teaches secondary school business and mathematics in York Region, Ontario, Canada.

Jane Clark Lindle is Eugene T. Moore Distinguished Professor of Educational Leadership at Clemson University. Her research program explores the micropolitical influences of educational policy on the practices of school leaders, teachers and their relationships with students, families, and communities. Recently, her work has focused on how academic policy and school–home relationships affect students' safety at school. She has served as Principal Investigator or co-investigator on 24 funded grants or contracts, written three and co-authored two books, 14 book chapters and monographs, and more than 50 research reports and policy briefs. Lindle is an experienced elementary/secondary principal and special education teacher licensed/certified in three states: Kentucky, North Carolina, and Wisconsin. She is a past Editor of *Educational Administration Quarterly*, past President of the Politics of Education Association, and recipient of awards for outstanding research, publications, and service from scholarly and professional organizations as well as institutions of higher education.

Gerardo R. López is Professor of Political Science at Loyola University New Orleans. His research focuses on parental involvement, migrant education, and critical race theory. His recent work addresses the politics of Latino immigration and the experiences of undocumented students in the U.S. educational system. His work has been published in *Educational Administration Quarterly*, *American Educational Research Journal*, *Harvard Educational Review*, *Journal of School Leadership*, *Journal of School Public Relations*, and *International Journal of Qualitative Studies in Education*, among other scholarly outlets. His recent co-authored book, *Persistent Inequality: Contemporary Realities in the Education of Undocumented Latina/o Students* (Routledge, 2010), utilizes LatCrit and Critical Race Theory to examine the educational challenges faced by this particular population.

George J. Petersen has been a public school teacher, administrator, and university faculty member. Currently, he is Dean and Professor in the Graduate School of Education at California Lutheran University. Dr. Petersen is the author or co-author of three books and over 100 book chapters, professional articles, research papers, monographs, and commissioned reports. Much of Dr. Petersen's scholarly work has focused on the executive leadership of district superintendents, their beliefs, roles, and work in the area of instructional leadership and policy. Dr. Petersen's work is recognized for its quality and impact with numerous awards including the University of California Santa Barbara's Gevirtz School of Education *Distinguished Alumni Award*, the University of Missouri-Columbia's *Excellence in Teaching Award* every year from 1998 to 2004. As a public school teacher, Dr. Peterson received the *Sallie Mae Outstanding Teaching Award*, a national award given to the top 100 teachers in the U.S.

Kenyae L. Reese is doctoral candidate in Educational Leadership and Eugene T. Moore Graduate Assistant at Clemson University. Her research agenda explores the doctoral student experiences of mid-career and seasoned professionals. She is particularly interested in micropolitical relationships between advisors and advisees, and identity struggles of practitioners in Ph.D. programs. Kenyae's preferred methodologies interweave additional lines of inquiry including visual methodologies, reflective practices, and sustainable leadership for disenfranchised school communities. She has won numerous awards across business and educational sectors, and served as a professional school counselor for one of the largest school districts in the country. Kenyae earned a Master's degree in College Student Affairs and an Education Specialist degree in School Counseling from the University of Georgia. She also holds a Master's degree in School Leadership from the Harvard Graduate School of Education.

Cathy Chada Williams has a background in Marketing Education and has taught in North Carolina high schools. Her involvement in education policy includes experience as the School-to-Career Coordinator for the Wake County (NC) Public School System. She earned her Master of School Administration degree from North Carolina State University and served at Ligon Magnet Middle School and Enloe High School as an assistant principal before accepting the position of principal of East Garner Magnet Middle School. She has a Ph.D. from NC State University.

Sue Winton is an Assistant Professor at York University in Toronto, Ontario, Canada. Her research examines implications of education policy and policy processes for critical democracy. Previous studies include comparative critical policy analyses of U.S. and Canadian safe schools and character education policies; examination of new media's impact on the theory of political spectacle and education policy; and a rhetorical analysis of a school district's character education policy. Her current research examines influences on policy processes at local and provincial levels. She is a former elementary school teacher and has taught in Mexico, Canada, and the USA.

Glossary

Advocacy Coalition Framework is theory that suggests that policy change processes are best explained by recognizing policy subsystems comprised of "actors from a variety of public and private organizations who are actively concerned with a policy problem of issue . . . and regularly seek to influence public policy in that domain" (Sabatier & Jenkins-Smith, 1999, p. 121).

Agency refers to the ability of individuals to act; and in politics, it particularly implicates that individual's autonomy and social capital (or power) to align and cooperate with others (Shipps, 2008).

Agenda-setting is a leadership process described as developing a vision and a plan for achieving it (Bolman & Deal, 2008).

Appropriation is the process in which a policy that is created in one place is interpreted and remade by those who encounter it someplace else (Levinson et al., 2009).

Behavioral Approach to Decision Making recognizes information asymmetries and subjectivity in the decision making process. This approach often leads to the use of procedures or rules of thumb, acknowledging suboptimization, or accepting the less than best possible outcome. The behavioral approach to decision making includes the notion of satisficing, wherein individuals or groups examine alternatives only until a solution that meets minimal requirements, or satisfactory outcomes or decisions, is found (Moorhead & Griffin, 1998).

Civic Capacity is a term about the degree to which a cross-sector coalition comes together in support of a task of community wide importance (Stone, 1998, p. 234). Civic capacity emphasizes the collective role of community stakeholders, going beyond the view that any one single institution, such as a school, can address the needs of its constituency.

Coalition Building is focused on working with parents or community members or stakeholders with common goals (Goldring & Rallis, 1993) leading toward a group decision.

Collaborative School-Linked Service Programs—designed to help children and families beset by problems of poverty, teenage pregnancy, single parenthood, substance abuse, limited healthcare, and/or inadequate and unaffordable housing by incorporating the provision of health and human services into the function of the school (Wang et al., 1995).

Cooptation tends to view parents as "external elements to placate" rather than as "true, equal partners." (Goldring & Rallis, 1993, pp. 84–85) and this view can deter effective group decisions.

Coordinated Services, as a term, describes a model of inter-agency collaboration to provide students and families services for education and health. The location of social services at schools is intended to reach students where they already spend a significant portion of time and to ensure academic success by meeting non-academic needs (Crowson & Boyd, 1993; Dryfoos, 1998). Many inter-professional tensions and micropolitical issues arise in the coordinated environment (Fusarelli & Lindle, 2011).

Decision Making is the process of choosing among alternatives (Moorhead & Griffin, 1998). Most decisions involve multiple people and can have effects on other people. All decisions have the potential to generate conflict because of lack of involvement of the stakeholders or over-involvement of a few whose decisions have effect on many others who were not consulted. The potential for conflict often politicizes decisions.

Dependent Power is a dimension of power where the power of an actor or group is derived from the function of the other person's dependence on the actor (Bacharach & Lawler, 1980).

Dissatisfaction Theory is a conclusion drawn from research by Lawrence Iannaccone and Fred Lutz about school board elections. They found that uncontested school board elections and sustained tenure on a school board indicated general community satisfaction with schools. In contrast, a contested election tended to signal changes in the community ranging from economic declines or increases, increase or decrease in population, changes in ethnicity, and other social conditions. These changes often produced changes in board membership and that change often threatened the tenure of the school superintendent (Lutz & Iannaccone, 1978, 2008).

Ecological Systems Theory, created by Urie Bronfenbrenner (1979), is a schema focused on the context (and to a lesser degree, the quality of that context) of a child's environment. The key question being: How does a child's world help or hinder continued development? While the family environment is the center of that ecology, schools and communities form a nested connection.

The implications are for a shared responsibility in providing a variety of services to ensure any individual's success as well as the health and wellbeing of the system.

Emotional Labor is a term that describes the turmoil a person feels when suppressing authentic emotions and simultaneously acting out completely different feelings (Hochschild, 1983).

Emotional Meaning Making, a term coined by Brenda R. Beatty (2002), refers to school leaders' awareness of their own emotions, how they deal with those emotions, and also, how they handle the emotions of others. Emotional situations are tied to learning and to work in schools. Other authors who have written about emotions in school leadership include Ackerman and Maslin-Ostrowski (2002) and Bridges (2012).

English as a Second Language (ESL): The study of English by speakers whose primary language is not English. English as a Second Language programs in public schools are governed by specific rules and/or guidelines, which describe the type of training needed by ESL teachers, the type of curriculum and learning goals for the program, pedagogical approaches for instruction, and methods for evaluating student needs and progress.

Environmental Leadership is a type of school leadership that focuses on integrating the external with internal school-based processes and procedures and linking implicitly with the school's community, broadly defined (Goldring & Sullivan, 1996).

Group Polarization describes the situation where a group's average post-discussion attitudes tend to be more extreme than pre-discussion attitudes (Moorhead & Griffin, 1998).

Groupthink refers to groups that are unified and cohesive and tend toward unanimity in thought, often at the expense of appraising alternative courses of action (Moorhead & Griffin, 1998).

Interest Group, as a term, commonly is understood to be a group of people who try to influence decisions toward a particular cause.

Internalized Racism refers to ethnic and racial self-hatred that emerges from a history of White supremacy and oppression. Hatred and racial animus toward other minority groups is a manifestation of this form of racism, as it emerges from (and reproduces) the same ideological mindset of White supremacy and oppression (Fanon, 1952).

Leadership for Authentic Partnerships describes principals whom families and community organizers see as full partners and participants in setting the goals and direction of the school. These partnerships include transformative, inclusive, and social justice models of school leadership, where groups pro-actively seek equity and cultural responsiveness, reaching out to marginalized students and families (Auerbach, 2012).

Leadership for Nominal Partnerships describes times when principals are compelled to communicate more with stakeholders through norms and policies, and is characterized by a desire to maintain power. This often means that the school leaders view families and community organizers as liabilities rather than assets, and the desire to continue to exercise a unilateral "power over" others (Auerbach, 2012).

Leadership for Preventative Partnerships describes tactics and attitudes of principals who seek to maintain control over goals, buffering outsiders like parents and community organizations from the school, and exercising a unilateral "power over" other groups (Auerbach, 2012).

Leadership for Traditional Partnerships is a term used to describe principals who create "family-friendly schools" (Henderson et al., 2007) by cooperating with parents and communities through joint planning and implementation (Auerbach, 2012).

Media refers to both traditional news sources such as network television and hardcopy or—more and more—website newspapers. In addition, new media influences the political environment of schools as community members and parents often resort to blogs and social media to convey their views, valid critiques, and also, invalid rumors about school governance or other activities (Chandler, 2009).

Micropolitics is the description and study of daily interactions between individuals and groups who are trying to negotiate for scarce resources, for personal—or other—advantage. Some of the authors who have defined and described micropolitics include Ball (1987), Lindle (1994), Malen (1995), Blase and Anderson (1995), and more recently, Marsh (2012).

Miranda Rights are invoked in the prescriptive warning that arresting law enforcement must use to alert criminal suspects against self-incrimination when being placed under arrest. Arresting officers usually provide criminal suspects in custody this verbal warning before official interrogation to prevent the admissibility of any statements being used against them during criminal proceedings. This warning emerges from the U.S. Supreme Court case, *Miranda v Arizona* (1966).

Performativity is a concept developed in the context of education by Ball (2003). The political pressure to seem to be playing the proper policy-mandated role takes precedence over authentically doing the job. Teaching-to-the-test can be considered a type of performativity.

Pluralism is a theory that explains that interest groups form "when like-minded individuals join together to pursue their common interests and pressure or lobby government for policies that will favor their group" (Smith, 2005, p. 21).

Policy Transfer refers to the phenomenon of policies whose features migrate and immigrate in to other states and nations worldwide (Ball, 2001, 2003; Levi-Faur & Vigoda-Gadot, 2006).

Political Acumen refers to the ability to read one's political environment and determine which political strategies to use when, and with whom (Ryan, 2010).

Political Discourse is a form of power analysis, which borrows from linguists to analyze discussions and rhetoric about issues, problems, movements, or policies (Shiffrin et al., 2001). In particular, interest groups and individuals choose specific words to represent a particular political perspective (Wilson, 2001).

Power is the potential ability of a person or group to exercise control over another person or group (Moorhead & Griffin, 1998, p. 385).

Problem Finding is a little-recognized term with a long history in leadership preparation and micropolitics (Immegart & Boyd, 1979). Problem finding is a combination of monitoring data and events while asking good questions about how and why these conditions exist (Copland, 2003).

Problem Framing generally describes the definitional phase of perceiving a problem. The framing of a problem is a matter of interpreting the problem (Spillane et al., 2009). Problem framing requires acknowledgment of the multiple perceptions and perspectives that might both mask and unmask the fundamental issues, assumptions and underlying causes. Without careful problem framing, the range of solutions may be limited and certainly unsuccessful (Copland et al., 2009).

Rational Approach to Decision Making describes individuals or groups, who attempt to follow a logical pattern of steps to arrive at a conclusion, including (a) stating the goal; (b) identifying the problem; (c) determining the decision type (programmed or unprogrammed); (d) collecting data and information, generating, evaluating, and choosing among alternatives; (e) then implementing the plan (Moorhead & Griffin, 1998).

Relational Power describes a dimension of power that analyzes the interactional dynamics of power relationships (Bacharach & Lawler, 1980).

Sanctioning Power is a dimension of power that accounts for the actual changes actors can and do make to shape each other's outcomes (Bacharach & Lawler, 1980).

Sazón refers to seasoning or spices used in Latin American cuisine. This term can be used to connote an overall zest or feeling reminiscent of Latino culture, tastes, preferences, etc.

School Board Elections are the most overtly competitive opportunity for citizens to vote for the specialized jurisdictional boards that govern public schools. Most school board elections are deemed non-partisan, but the reality is that these elections inherently are political (Hess, 2008). Many of these seats are not contested and voter turnout tends to be light except in jurisdictions where conflict has arisen due to economic or social changes in the community (Lutz & Iannaccone, 1978).

Sheltered English Instruction is an approach to teaching English language learners (ELL) that provides for both language and content instruction. Regardless of subject or discipline, all teachers can use this approach. In sheltered English classes, teachers use basic, clear, and simple language to communicate content, while utilizing a host of instructional scaffolding techniques to build on student's prior knowledge

Social capital refers to the set of resources that inhere in relationships of trust and cooperation between and among people (Warren, 2005, p. 136), or the features of social organization, such as networks, norms, and social trust, that facilitate coordination and cooperation for mutual benefit (Putnam & Leonardi, 1993).

Special Districts is a legal definition of the jurisdictions governed by school boards. These jurisdictions, for more than 10,000 U.S. public school districts, are deliberately differentiated from, and independent of, local municipalities such as counties, cities, towns, or townships (Berkman & Plutzer, 2005; Bowman & Kearney, 1986).

Structured English Immersion is an approach to teaching ELL that provides for significant exposure to the English language. Typically, under Structured English Immersion, English will be the primary language of instruction as the primary focus is to learn the language and not academic content per se.

Undocumented is the preferred term to describe a non-citizen who lives in a country without proper documentation. The term is preferred over more contentious terms such as "illegal" and/or "illegal alien" as these latter terms connote criminality. In the U.S., being an undocumented person is a civil offense rather than a criminal one.

White flight is a term used to describe large scale migration of White individuals from racially-mixed areas to racially-homogenous ones. The term is often associated with suburbanization, and the out-migration of White individuals from urban cities.

REFERENCES

Ackerman, R. & Maslin-Ostrowski, P. (2002). *The wounded leader: How real leadership emerges in times of crisis*. San Francisco, CA: Jossey-Bass.

Auerbach, S. (Ed.). (2012). *School leadership for authentic family and community partnerships: Research perspectives for transforming practice*. New York: Routledge.

Bacharach, S. B. & Lawler, E. J. (1980). *Power and politics in organizations*. San Francisco, CA: Jossey-Bass.

Ball, S. J. (1987). *The micro-politics of the school: Towards a theory of school organization*. London: Methuen.

Ball, S. J. (2001, December). Global policies and vernacular politics in education. *Curriculo sem Fronteiras, 1*(2), xxvii–xliii. Retrieved from: www.curriculosemfronteiras.org/vol1iss2 articles/balleng.pdf

Ball, S. J. (2003). The teacher's soul and the terrors of performativity. *Journal of Education Policy*, *18*(2), 215–228.

Beatty, B. (2002). *Emotion matters in educational leadership: Examining the unexamined*. Unpublished doctoral dissertation, Ontario Institute for Studies in Education, University of Toronto.

Berkman, M. B. & Plutzer, E. (2005). *Ten thousand democracies: Politics and public opinion in America's school districts*. Washington, DC: Georgetown University Press.

Blase, J. & Anderson, G. (1995). *The micropolitics of educational leadership*. New York: Cassell.

Bolman, L. G. & Deal, T. E. (2008). *Reframing organizations: Artistry, choice and leadership* (4th ed.). San Francisco, CA: Jossey-Bass.

Bowman, A. O. & Kearney, R. C. (1986). *The resurgence of the states*. Upper Saddle River, NJ: Prentice Hall.

Bridges, E. (2012). Administrator preparation: Looking backwards and forwards. *Journal of Educational Administration*, *50*(4), 402–419.

Bronfenbrenner, U. (1979). *The ecology of human development*. Cambridge, MA: Harvard University Press.

Chandler, M. A. (2009, January 30). Well-connected parents take on school boards. *The Washington Post*, p. A01.

Copland, M. A. (2003). Leadership of inquiry: Building and sustaining capacity for school improvement. *Educational Evaluation and Policy Analysis*, *25*(4), 375–395.

Copland, M. A., Knapp, M. S., & Swinnerton, J. A. (2009). Principal leadership, data, and school improvement. In T. J. Kowalski & T. J. Lasley II (Eds.), *Handbook of data-based decision making in education* (pp. 153–172). New York: Routledge.

Crowson, R. L. & Boyd, W. L. (1993). Structures and strategies: Toward an understanding of alternative models for coordinated children's services. In K. L. Alves-Zervos & J. R. Shafer (Eds.), *Synthesis of research and practice: Implications for achieving schooling success for children at-risk* (pp. 61–94). Publication Series #93–5. Philadelphia: Temple University, National Education Center on Education in the Inner Cities. (ERIC Document Reproduction Services No. 364 652).

Dryfoos, J. G. (1998). *Safe passages: Making it through adolescence in a risky society, what parents, schools, and communities can do*. New York: Oxford University Press.

Fanon, F. (1952/2008). *Black skin, white masks*. New York: Grove Press.

Fusarelli, B. C. & Lindle, J. C. (2011). The politics, problems, and potential promise of school-linked social services: Insights and new directions from the work of William Lowe Boyd. *Peabody Journal of Education*, *86*(4), 402–415.

Goldring, E. & Sullivan, A. (1996). Beyond the boundaries: Principals, parents and communities shaping the school environment. In K. Leithwood, J. Chapman, D. Corson, P. Hallinger, & A. Hart (Eds.), *International handbook of educational leadership and administration*, Volume 1 (pp. 195–222). Norwell, MA: Kluwer Academic.

Goldring, E. B. & Rallis, S. F. (1993). *Principals of dynamic schools: Taking charge of change*. Newbury Park, CA: Corwin Press

Henderson, A. T., Mapp, K. L. Johnson, V. L., & Davies, D. (2007). *Beyond the bake sale: The essential guide to family-school partnerships*. New York: The New Press.

Hess, F. M. (2008). Money, interest groups, and school board elections. In T. L. Alsbury (Ed.), *The future of school board governance: Relevancy and revelation* (pp. 137–154). Lanham, MD: Rowman & Littlefield Education.

Hochschild, A. R. (1983). *The managed heart: The commercialization of human feeling*. Berkeley, CA: University of California Press.

Immegart, G. L. & Boyd, W. L. (1979). *Problem-finding in educational administration: Trends in research and theory*. Lexington, MA: Free Press.

Levi-Faur, D. & Vigoda-Gadot, E. (2006). New public policy, new policy transfers: Some characteristics of a new order in the making. *International Journal of Public Administration, 29,* 247–262.

Levinson, B. A. U., Sutton, M., & Winstead, T. (2009). Education policy as a practice of power: Theoretical tools, ethnographic methods, democratic options. *Educational Policy, 23*(6), 767–795.

Lindle, J. C. (1994). *Surviving school micropolitics: Strategies for administrators.* Lancaster, PA: Technomic Publishing.

Lutz, F. W. & Iannaccone, L. (Eds.), (1978). *Public participation in local school districts.* Lexington, MA: Lexington Books.

Lutz, F. W. & Iannaccone, L. (2008). The dissatisfaction theory of American democracy. In T. L. Alsbury (Ed.), *The future of school board governance: Relevancy and revelation* (pp. 3–24). Lanham, MD: Rowman & Littlefield Education.

Malen, B. (1995). The micropolitics of education: Mapping the multiple dimensions of power relations in school politics. In J. D. Scribner & D. H. Layton (Eds.), *The 1994 commemorative yearbook of the politics of educational association (1969–1994)* (pp. 147–167). Washington, DC: Falmer.

Marsh, J. (2012). The micropolitics of implementing a school-based bonus policy: The case of New York City's compensation committees. *Educational Evaluation and Policy Analysis, 34*(2), 164–184.

Miranda v. Arizona, 384 U.S. 436 (1966).

Moorhead, G. & Griffin, R. W. (1998). *Organizational behavior: Managing people and organizations.* Boston: Houghton Mifflin Company.

Putnam, R. D. & Leonardi, R. (1993). *Making democracy work: Civic traditions in modern Italy.* Princeton, NJ: Princeton University Press.

Ryan, J. (2010). Promoting social justice in schools: Principals' political strategies. *International Journal of Leadership in Education: Theory and Practice, 13*(4), 357–376.

Sabatier, P. A. & Jenkins-Smith, H. C. (1999). The advocacy coalition framework. In P. A. Sabatier (Ed.), *Theories of the policy process* (pp. 117–166). Boulder, CO: Westview Press.

Schiffrin, D., Tannen, D., & Hamilton, H. E. (Eds.), (2001). *The handbook of discourse analysis.* Malden, MA: Blackwell.

Shipps, D. (2008). Urban regime theory and the reform of public schools: Governance, power and leadership. In B. S. Cooper, J. G. Cibulka, & L. D. Fusarelli (Eds.), *Handbook of education politics and policy* (pp. 89–108). New York: Routledge.

Smith, M. (2005). *A civil society? Collective actors in Canadian political life.* Peterborough, ON: Broadview Press.

Spillane, J. P., White, K. W., & Stephan, J. L. (2009). School principal expertise: Putting expert-aspiring principal differences in problem solving processes to the test. *Leadership and Policy in Schools, 8*(2), 128–151.

Stone, C. N., (1998). Civic capacity and urban school reform. In C. N. Stone (Ed.), *Changing urban education* (pp. 250–274). Lawrence, KA: University of Kansas Press.

Wang, M. C., Haertel, G. D., & Walberg, H. J. (1995). *Effective features of collaborative school-linked services for children in elementary school: What do we know from research and practice?* San Francisco, CA: Jossey-Bass.

Warren, M. R. (2005). Communities and schools: A new view of urban education reform. *Harvard Educational Review, 75*(2), 133–74.

Wilson, J. (2001). Political discourse. In D. Schiffrin, D., Tannen, & H. E. Hamilton (Eds.), (2001). *The handbook of discourse analysis* (pp. 398–145). Malden, MA: Blackwell.

Index